The Annotated
Ultimate Alphabet

The Annotated Ultimate Alphabet

Mike Wilks

HENRY HOLT AND COMPANY

NEW YORK

Published in the United States by
Henry Holt and Company, Inc., 115 West 18th Street,
New York, New York 10011.

Library of Congress Catalog Card Number: 88-81517
ISBN 0-8050-0918-3

First American Edition
Designed by Bernard Higton
Printed in Italy by Arnoldo Mondadori
1 3 5 7 9 10 8 6 4 2

ISBN 0-8050-0918-3

INTRODUCTION

It has been said before but it bears saying again: looking is not the same as seeing. Seeing is understanding what you are looking at. Sight is by far our most developed sense and we gather the vast majority of information about the world around us by looking at things. It is precisely because this faculty is so highly developed that we tend to take it for granted and fail to use it to its full capacity. This is in part due to an innate limiting factor. If we were to try to comprehend all of the information that enters the brain via our eyes we would be overwhelmed with sensory overload, such is the sheer volume of visual stimuli that we are all exposed to. Our brain naturally filters out much of what we see, allowing us to concentrate only on those things which enable us to conduct our lives efficiently. If you add to this our over-familiarity with the visual sense compared with the others, the problem of seeing, as opposed to looking, begins to become apparent. To see rather than merely look we must make a huge effort.

Children are credited with having sharper eyes than adults. This is partly true as they are looking more intently and seeing the world around them — perhaps for the first time — but also they have not yet 'learnt' what to ignore or what to relegate to the background. Over the years, this process of cutting out what we feel to be unnecessary becomes a habit. Artists must break this habit and re-acquire a child-like vision and see things once more as they are in order to formulate their own new priorities of the world and thus make the world anew in their work.

The images in this book were first published in 1986 as *The Ultimate Alphabet*. They formed the basis for an international competition to identify as many of the items depicted as possible. Now that the competition is over it frees me to publish the book in its complete form — and in the form in which it was originally conceived. In *The Annotated Ultimate Alphabet* each picture is accompanied by an outline drawing which is keyed with numbers. These numbers relate to the definitions of the items depicted which are listed in alphabetical order.

In the first book I stated that I had *consciously* included a certain number of words in each picture — 7,777 in total. Later I realized that I had inadvertently included some additional things and these items were added to the answer list when preparing *The Annotated Ultimate Alphabet* so that the total number of words recorded here is now 7,825. Since then I have received hundreds of fascinating congratulatory letters (too many to answer personally), which chronicled the trials and tribulations, joys of discovery and moments of frustration during the Ultimate Alphabet journey. Some of these letters pointed out *yet more* words that I had not realized were included in the paintings, but it was too late to include these in the 'definitive' list. Anyone with expert knowledge in any particular field might spot *still more* things than I, taking a more general view, have included in this book. In fact, I suspect that the list will never be complete; the sharp-eyed will be discovering new words in the paintings for years to come.

Plainly this book is neither a dictionary nor an encyclopedia: it is not even principally about words. What dictionaries fail to do, and what even the very best encyclopedias only partially succeed in doing, is to convey what things look like. This book is primarily concerned with just that — the appearance of things. It does, of course, include definitions of the items I have depicted but they are very simple, bald statements. I am sure you will want to consult other reference books for more information about the item than the space available permitted me to include.

I hope that this book will inspire you, as it did me, to look beyond the boundaries of the twenty-six small worlds depicted here and into the wider worlds of knowledge that are to be found within the pages of encyclopedias and dictionaries, and to explore these realms for yourself.

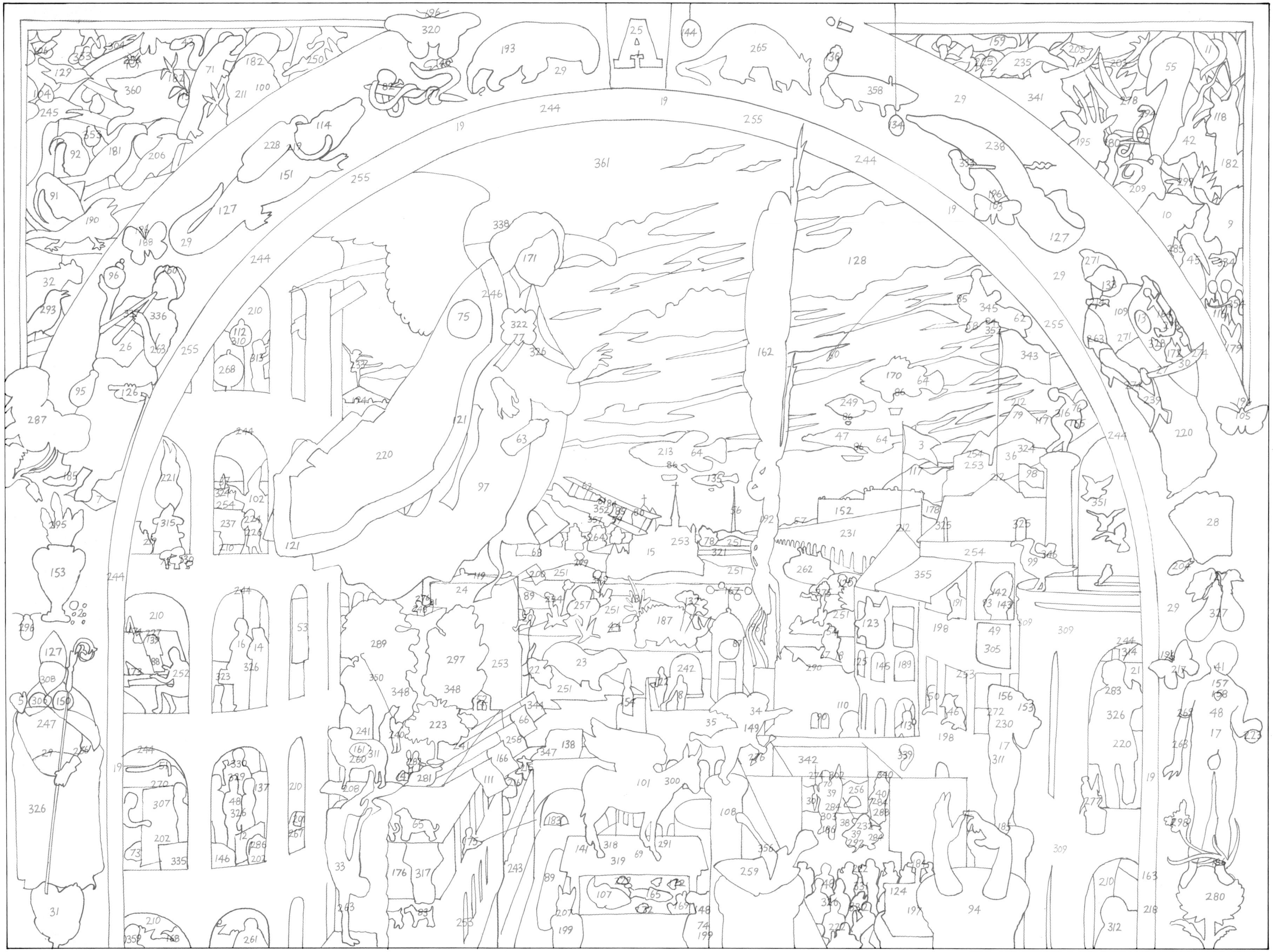

1 A First letter of the alphabet
2 A Braille alphabet
3 A International signal flag
4 A Manual alphabet – Anglo/Australian system
5 A Manual alphabet – American system
6 A Morse code alphabet
7 A Musical notation
8 A Semaphore alphabet
9 AARDVARK Variety of animal
10 AARDWOLF Variety of animal
11 ABACA Variety of palm
12 ABACUS Framed calculating beads
13 ABALONE Edible mollusc
14 ABBESS Superior of a nunnery
15 ABBEY Church or community of monks
16 ABBOT Superior of an abbey
17 ABDOMEN The belly
18 ABLAZE On fire
19 ABREUVOIR Space between bricks or masonry
20 ABSEIL Descending by sliding down a rope
21 ABSTRACT Non-representative art
22 ABUTILON Variety of plant
23 ACANTHOPHOLIS Variety of dinosaur
24 ACACIA Variety of tree or shrub
25 ACANTHUS Variety of plant or design based on this
26 ACCORDION Musical instrument
27 ACCOUTREMENTS Equipment
28 ACE Playing card with single pip
29 ACHROMATIC Colourless/grey
30 ACINACES Short sword or scimitar
31 ACORN Fruit of oak tree
32 ACOUCHY Variety of animal
33 ACROBAT Gymnastic entertainer
34 ACROLITH A statue of marble and wood
35 ACRONYM Word formed from initials of name (TUAB – THE ULTIMATE ALPHABET BOOK)
36 ACROPOLIS Upper part of ancient city
37 ACROTERIA Ornaments on pediment of temple
38 ACTING Performing of plays
39 ACTOR Male performer of plays
40 ACTRESS Female performer of plays
41 ADAM Biblical first man
42 ADDAX Variety of antelope
43 ADDER Variety of venomous snake
44 ADIT Horizontal mine tunnel
45 ADJUTANT BIRD Variety of bird
46 ADMIRAL Highest ranking naval officer
47 ADRIANICHTHYID Variety of fish
48 ADULT Mature or full grown
49 ADVERTISEMENT Public notice
50 ADVOCATE Barrister

51 ADZE Cutting tool
52 AEDICULA Niche
53 AEOLIAN HARP Wind activated string instrument
54 AEOLIPILE Ancient steam turbine
55 AEPYORNIS Variety of extinct bird
56 AERIAL Radio transmitter or receiver mast
57 AERIAL PERSPECTIVE Artistic illusion portraying distance
58 AEROBATICS Stunt flying
59 AERODYNE Aircraft
60 AEROLITE Meteorite
61 AERONAUT Pilot or airman
62 AEROPLANE Flying machine
63 AEROSOL Pressurized spray
64 AEROSTAT Balloon or airship
65 AFGHAN Breed of dog
66 AFGHANISTAN Flag of Central Asian republic
67 AFLAME On fire
68 AFLOAT Floating on water
69 AFRICA Second largest continent
70 AFRICAN Native of Africa
71 AGAMA Variety of lizard
72 AGARIC Variety of fungus
73 AGATE Semi-precious stone
74 AGNIFICATION Person represented as sheep
75 AGNUS DEI Christian motif
76 AGONISTIC Athletic
77 AGRAFFE Clasp or buckle
78 AGROUND Stranded
79 AIGUILLE Pointed mountain peak
80 AILERON Flap on aircraft wing
81 AIM To point or direct
82 AIRBRUSH Artist's fine spray-gun
83 AIRDALE Breed of dog
84 AIRMAN Pilot or flyer
85 AIRSCREW Propeller
86 AIRSHIP Dirigible balloon
87 AIRT Quarter of compass
88 AISLE Area within church

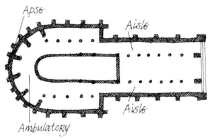

89 AIT Small island
90 AJIMEZ Coupled arched window
91 AKIALOA Variety of bird
92 AKIAPOLAAU Variety of bird
93 AKIMBO Hands on hips, elbows outwards
94 ALABASTER Marble-like stone
95 ALABASTRON Type of flask
96 ALARM CLOCK Clock with pre-setable bell
97 ALB White linen vestment
98 ALBANIA Flag of Balkan republic
99 ALBATROSS Variety of large sea-bird
100 ALBINO Lacking in pigment to skin and hair

101 ALBORAK Mohammed's legendary winged ass
102 ALCHEMIST Medieval magician and philosopher
103 ALCHYMIST Variety of moth
104 ALDER Variety of tree
105 ALDER MOTH Variety of moth
106 ALDER FLY Variety of insect
107 ALEWIFE Variety of fish
108 ALEPH First letter of Hebrew alphabet
109 ALERION Eagle without beak or feet
110 ALFIZ Islamic architectural door moulding
111 ALGERIA Flag of North African republic
112 ALIDADE Movable arm of astrolabe

113 ALIEN Native of another country or world
114 ALLIGATOR Variety of large reptile
115 ALMOND Variety of edible nut
116 ALOE Variety of plant
117 ALP Mountain peak
118 ALPACA Variety of animal
119 ALPENHORN Large Swiss wooden trumpet
120 ALPENROSE Variety of alpine plant
121 ALPHABET Set of letters
122 ALPINIST Mountain climber
123 ALSATIAN Breed of dog (German Shepherd)
124 ALTAR Religious table
125 ALTERNATING CURRENT Electrical symbol for alternating current
126 ALTHORN Brass wind instrument
127 ALTO-RELIEVO High-relief sculpture
128 ALTOCUMULUS Type of cloud formation
129 AMAKIHI Variety of bird
130 AMANITA Variety of fungus
131 AMARANTHUS Variety of plant
132 AMARYLLIS Variety of plant
133 AMAZON Ancient female warrior
134 AMBER Fossilized resin
135 AMBLYOPSIS Variety of fish
136 AMBROSIA BEETLE Variety of insect
137 AMBRY Locker or cupboard
138 AMBULANCE Vehicle for carrying the sick or injured
139 AMBULATORY Area within church
140 AMBUSH BUG Variety of insect

141 AMERICA Large continent between Atlantic and Pacific oceans
142 AMERICAN Native of America
143 AMERIND Original native of America
144 AMETHYST Semi-precious gemstone
145 AMMETER Electrical symbol for ammeter
146 AMMONITE Fossil of extinct mollusc
147 AMMUNITION Projectile fired from gun
148 AMON Ancient Egyptian ram-headed god
149 AMORINO Cupid
150 AMPERSAND Symbol for 'and' (&)
151 AMPHIBIAN Creature able to live both on land and in water
152 AMPHITHEATRE Tiered circular building surrounding arena
153 AMPHORA Style of earthenware vessel
154 AMPOULE Small glass vial
155 AMPUTEE Person with limb removed
156 AMPYX Metal headband
157 AMULET Charm
158 ANACARD Heart-shaped ornament
159 ANACONDA Variety of snake
160 ANADEM Wreath for the head
161 ANAGRAM Word or phrase made from jumbling another word or phrase (ARIES)
162 ANAMORPHOSIS Distorted image that looks normal when viewed from a certain angle
163 ANANYM Name written backwards
164 ANCHOR Device for mooring ship to sea-bottom
165 ANCHOVY Variety of fish
166 ANDORRA Flag of small European principality
167 ANEMOMETER Instrument for measuring wind velocity
168 ANEMONE Variety of plant
169 ANEMONE Variety of marine polyp
170 ANEMONE FISH Variety of fish
171 ANGEL Winged spiritual being
172 ANGELFISH Variety of fish
173 ANGLE Corner or space between two intersecting lines
174 ANGLEPOISE Type of adjustable work-lamp
175 ANGLER Fisherman
176 ANGLERFISH Varety of fish
177 ANGLEWORM Earthworm
178 ANGOLA Flag of South-west African republic
179 ANGORA Variety of rabbit
180 ANHINGA Variety of bird
181 ANI Variety of bird
182 ANIMAL Non-human creature
183 ANKER Type of cask or keg
184 ANKH Looped cross
185 ANKLE Part of leg between foot and calf
186 ANKLET Ornament for ankle
187 ANKYLOSAURUS Variety of extinct dinosaur
188 ANNULET Variety of moth
189 ANODE Electrical symbol for anode
190 ANOLE Variety of lizard
191 ANORAK Hooded Eskimo jacket
192 ANT Variety of insect
193 ANT-EATER Type of insect-eating mammal
194 ANTEFIX Classical architectural ornament
195 ANTELOPE Deer-like animal
196 ANTENNA Feelers on insect's head
197 ANTEPENDIUM Altar covering
198 ANTHEMION Type of architectural ornament

199 ANTHROPOMORPHOSIS Whole or partial transformation into human form
200 ANTIGUA Flag of Caribbean island
201 ANTIMACASSAR Ornamental covering for chair back
202 ANTIQUE Object from former times
203 ANTLER Horn or male deer
204 ANTLION Variety of larval insect
205 ANTPITTA Variety of bird
206 ANTSHRIKE Variety of bird
207 ANUBIS Ancient Egyptian jackal-headed god
208 ANVIL Heavy iron block for shaping metal
209 AOUDAD Variety of animal
210 APARTMENT Room or set of rooms in a building
211 APE Tailless primate
212 APEX Summit or tip
213 APHANIUS Variety of fish
214 APHID Variety of insect
215 APIARIST Bee-keeper
216 APIARY Place where bees are kept
217 APOLLO Variety of butterfly
218 APOSTROPHE A grammatical sign (')
219 APPARATUS Instruments or equipment
220 APPAREL Clothing
221 APPARITION Ghost or unexpected appearance
222 APPLAUSE Approval expressed by clapping hands
223 APPLE Variety of edible fruit
224 APPRENTICE Learner of trade or craft
225 APRICOT Variety of edible fruit
226 APRON Type of protective garment
227 APSE Area within church
228 AQUALUNG Underwater breathing apparatus
229 AQUARIUM Transparent tank containing fish
230 AQUARIUS Eleventh sign of zodiac; the water carrier
231 AQUEDUCT Elevated structure for conveying water
232 ARAB Native of Arabia
233 ARABESQUE Ballet position
234 ARABIS Variety of plant
235 ARACARI Variety of bird
236 ARACHNID Spider and scorpion family
237 ARAEOSYSTYLE Classical style of paired column arrangement
238 ARAPAIMA Variety of fish
239 ARBALEST Crossbow
240 ARBORICULTURIST Cultivator of trees
241 ARBORETUM Tree garden
242 ARBOUR Bower
243 ARCADE Arched covered passageway
244 ARCH Curved structure spanning opening
245 ARCHAEOPTERYX Earliest known bird
246 ARCHANGEL Highest ranking angel
247 ARCHBISHOP Highest ranking bishop
248 ARCHER Bowman
249 ARCHERFISH Variety of fish
250 ARCHERIA Variety of extinct amphibian
251 ARCHIPELAGO Group of islands
252 ARCHITECT Designer of buildings
253 ARCHITECTURE Buildings and their design
254 ARCHITRAVE Part of entabliture
255 ARCHIVOLT Inner curve of arch
256 ARCTIC Region around North Pole

Arches

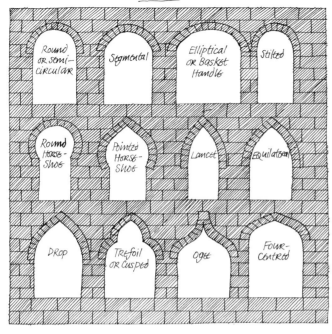

Round or semi-circular · Segmental · Elliptical or Basket Handle · Stilted

Round Horse-Shoe · Pointed Horse-Shoe · Lancet · Equilateral

Drop · Trefoil or Cusped · Ogee · Four-Centred

257 ARCTOTIS Variety of plant
258 ARGENTINA Flag of South American republic
259 ARGUS Variety of fish
260 ARIES First sign of zodiac; the ram
261 ARISTOCRAT Person of noble birth
262 ARK Boat
263 ARM Bodily extremity
264 ARMADA Fleet of warships
265 ARMADILLO Armoured South American animal
266 ARMATURE Internal framework used in sculpture
267 ARMCHAIR Chair with supports for arms
268 ARMILLA Astronomical instrument
269 ARMLET Ornament worn around arm
270 ARMOIRE Large cupboard
271 ARMOUR Defensive body covering
272 ARMPIT Hollow under arm
273 ARMS Heraldic device
274 ARMS Weapons
275 ARNICA Variety of plant
276 ARROW Projectile fired from bow
277 ARROWHEAD Variety of plant
278 ARSINOITHERIUM Extinct rhinoceros-like creature
279 ARTESIAN WELL Man-made spring
280 ARTICHOKE Variety of vegetable
281 ARTILLERY Large guns or cannons
282 ARTILLERYMAN Soldier assigned to artillery
283 ARTIST Practitioner of creative art
284 ARTISTE Performer
285 ARUM LILY Variety of plant
286 ARYBALLOS Style of vase
287 ASARABACCA Variety of plant
288 ASCEND To climb or mount
289 ASH Variety of tree
290 ASH-TRAY Receptacle for tobacco ash

291 ASIA Largest continent contiguous with Europe
292 ASIAN Native of Asia
293 ASITY Variety of bird
294 ASP Variety of venomous snake
295 ASPARAGUS Variety of vegetable
296 ASPARAGUS BEETLE Variety of insect
297 ASPEN Variety of tree
298 ASPHODEL Variety of plant
299 ASPIDISTRA Variety of plant
300 ASS Variety of animal
301 ASSAGAI South African throwing spear
302 ASSAILANT Attacker
303 ASSASSIN Murderer
304 ASSASSIN BUG Variety of insect
305 ASTER Variety of flowering plant
306 ASTERISK Star-like typographical symbol (*)
307 ASTERISM Asterisks arranged in triangular form (⁂)
308 ASTOMOUS Without mouth
309 ASTRAGAL Raised band encircling column
310 ASTROLABE Astrological instrument
311 ASTROLOGY Study of the stars of the zodiac
312 ASTRONAUT Space traveller
313 ASTRONOMER One who studies the stars
314 ATELIER Artist's studio
315 ATHANOR Alchemist's furnace
316 ATHLETE One skilled in physical exercise
317 ATLANTES Architectural columns shaped like men
318 ATLANTIC Ocean between America and Europe and Africa
319 ATLAS Book of maps
320 ATLAS Variety of moth
321 ATOLL Ring-shaped coral island
322 ATOM Symbol of fundamental particle
323 ATTACHE CASE Small case

324 ATTIC Wall above cornice
325 ATTIC Room just below roof
326 ATTIRE Dress or clothing
327 AUBERGINE Variety of vegetable
328 AUCELLA Variety of extinct clam
329 AUCTION Public sale
330 AUCTIONEER Conductor of public sale
331 AUDIENCE Assembly of people witnessing play, concert etc
332 AUDITORIUM Space where audience sits in a theatre or hall
333 AUGER Corkscrew-shaped drilling tool
334 AUK Variety of sea-bird
335 AUKLET Variety of small sea-bird
336 AULETE Flute player
337 AULOS Double-barrelled flute or pipe
338 AURA Halo
339 AURICLE External part of ear
340 AURICOMOUS Golden-haired
341 AUROCHS Extinct European wild ox
342 AURORA Northern lights
343 AUSTRALIA Flag of South-western Pacific country
344 AUSTRIA Flag of European republic
345 AUTOGYRO Rotary-winged aircraft
346 AUTOMATON Mechanical toy
347 AUTOMOBILE Motor car
348 AUTUMN Third season of year
349 AVENS Variety of plant
350 AVERRUNCATOR Long-handled pruning tool
351 AVIARY Large bird-cage
352 AVIATOR Pilot
353 AVOCADO Type of vegetable
354 AVOCET Variety of bird
355 AWNING Canvas shelter or sunshade
356 AXE Cutting tool
357 AXLE Spindle upon which wheel revolves
358 AXOLOTL Variety of amphibian
359 AYATOLLAH Muslim holy man
360 AYE-AYE Variety of animal
361 AZURE Sky-blue

1 B Second letter of the alphabet
2 B Braille alphabet
3 B International signal flag
4 B Morse code alphabet
5 B Musical notation
6 BABBLER BIRD Variety of bird
7 BABERY Grotesque architectural ornamentation
8 BABIRUSA East Indian pig
9 BABOON Large African monkey
10 BABY Infant
11 BACCHUS Ancient Greek god of wine
12 BACK Rear part of upper body
13 BACKGAMMON Type of board game
14 BACKGROUND Part of painting representing distance
15 BACKPACK Pack carried on the back
16 BACKWARD In reverse order
17 BACKWOODSMAN Pioneer of the American backwoods
18 BADGE Emblem of rank or membership of group
19 BADGER Variety of burrowing mammal
20 BAG Flexible container with handles
21 BAGATELLE Table-top game similar to billiards
22 BAGEL Traditional Jewish shaped bread roll
23 BAGPIPE Variety of wind instrument

Bagpipes

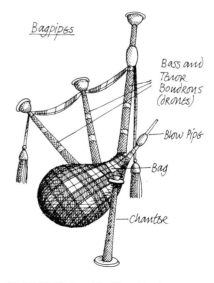

Bass and Tenor Bourdons (drones)
Blow Pipe
Bag
Chanter

24 BAHAMAS Flag of Caribbean island group
25 BAHRAIN Flag of independent Arab emirate

26 BAILEY Outer wall around castle keep
27 BAKER Maker of bread
28 BALACLAVA Woollen covering for the face and head
29 BALALAIKA Russian guitar-like musical instrument
30 BALANCE Scales
31 BALANCING Maintaining a state of equilibrium
32 BALANOID Acorn-shaped
33 BALD Without hair
34 BALDRIC Diagonal sword belt
35 BALI-PONY Breed of horse
36 BALISTER Crossbowman
37 BALISTRARIA Cross-shaped defensive window
38 BALIZE Beacon made from barrel
39 BALK Area of billiard table
40 BALL Spherical object
41 BALLERINA Female ballet dancer
42 BALLET Art of theatrical dancing
43 BALLOON Inflated spherical toy
44 BALUSTER Upright support for handrail
45 BALUSTRADE Row of balusters and handrail
46 BAMBOO Variety of East Indian reed
47 BAMBOO PAGE Variety of butterfly
48 BANANA Variety of tropical fruit
49 BAND Circular strip of metal
50 BAND Group of musicians
51 BANDMASTER Conductor
52 BANDSTAND Platform for musical performances
53 BANDAGE Cloth dressing for wound
54 BANDANA Large handkerchief or neckerchief
55 BANDBOX Cylindrical box
56 BANDERILLA Barbed dart used in bullfighting
57 BANDEROLE Streamer
58 BANDICOOT Variety of Australian marsupial
59 BANDOLEER Cartridge belt
60 BANDSMAN Member of a band
61 BANDURRIA Small lute-like instrument
62 BANGLADESH Flag of Asian republic
63 BANGLE Bracelet
64 BANISTER Staircase handrail
65 BANJO Variety of stringed musical instrument
66 BANJULELE Cross between banjo and ukelele
67 BANNER Flag or standard
68 BANNERMAN Flag or standard bearer
69 BAOBAB Variety of tree
70 BAP Small soft roll of bread
71 BAR Rod
72 BAR Addition to a medal
73 BAR Counter for serving drinks
74 BAR Small section of musical notation
75 BARASINGHA Variety of Indian deer
76 BARB Sharp backward projection
77 BARBADOS Flag of independent Caribbean island
78 BARBEL Variety of fish
79 BARBER Hairdresser (indicated by striped pole)
80 BARBET Variety of bird
81 BARBICAN Fortifications guarding gate or bridge
82 BARCAROLE Gondolier
83 BARD Minstrel
84 BARE Naked
85 BARE-EYE Variety of bird

86 BAREBACK Without a saddle
87 BAREFOOT Without shoes
88 BAREHEADED Without a hat or cap
89 BARGE Freight boat
90 BARGHEST Fabulous dog
91 BARK Outer covering of tree trunk
92 BARK BEETLE Variety of insect
93 BARLEY Variety of cereal
94 BARMAID Female bartender
95 BARMKIN Turret or watchtower
96 BARN-OWL Variety of bird of prey
97 BAROMETER Instrument predicting weather changes
98 BARQUE Type of sailing vessel
99 BARQUENTINE Type of sailing vessel
100 BARRACUDA Variety of large fish
101 BARREL Cask
102 BARREL Tubular part of gun
103 BARREL CACTUS Variety of cactus
104 BARRENWORT Variety of plant
105 BARRISTER Lawyer or advocate
106 BARROW Wheeled handcart
107 BARRY Heraldic design
108 BARTMANNKRUG Type of antique German jug
109 BARYTON Variety of stringed musical instrument
110 BAS-RELIEF Sculpture in low relief
111 BASCULE BRIDGE Hinged bridge

Bridges.

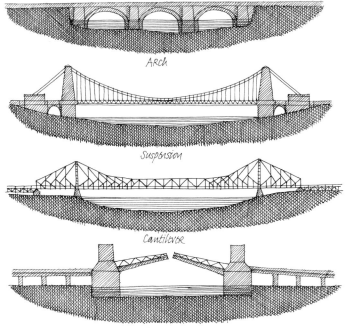

Arch

Suspension

Cantilever

Bascule

112 BASE Support or foundation
113 BASEBALL Ball used in a game of baseball
114 BASEMENT Underground part of building
115 BASKET Wickerwork container
116 BASKET WORK Wickerwork
117 BASKING SHARK Variety of large fish

118 BASS Large stringed musical instrument
119 BASS Variety of fish
120 BASS CLEF Musical notation symbol
121 BASS DRUM Large percussion musical instrument
122 BASSET HORN Clarinet-like musical instrument
123 BASSET HOUND Breed of dog
124 BASSOON Variety of woodwind musical instrument
125 BAST Ancient Egyptian cat-headed goddess
126 BASTION Projecting fortification
127 BAT Nocturnal flying mammal
128 BAT Hitting implement used in sport
129 BACHELOR'S BUTTONS Variety of plant
130 BATFISH Variety of fish
131 BATH-BUN Spiced fruit bun
132 BATH CHAIR Invalid's wheelchair
133 BATH-ROBE Absorbent wrap-around garment
134 BATHER One who bathes or swims
135 BATHING COSTUME Swimsuit
136 BATHYSCAPE Underwater exploration vehicle
137 BATON Conductor's wand
138 BATON Heraldic design
139 BATON BLUE Variety of moth
140 BATTEMENT Ballet position
141 BATTERY Portable electrical power source
142 BATTLE AXE Ancient weapon of war
143 BATTLEMENTS Parapet with crenellations

144 BATTLESHIP Large warship
145 BAY Type of coloration in horses
146 BAY Variety of laurel tree
147 BAYONET Blade attached to rifle barrel
148 BAZOUKI Type of stringed musical instrument
149 BEACON A signal-fire

150 BEADS Small balls threaded on string
151 BEAGLE Breed of dog
152 BEAK Bill of a bird
153 BEAK IRON Pike of an anvil
154 BEAKER Drinking cup
155 BEAN Seed of leguminous plant
156 BEAR Variety of large furry animal
157 BEARD Male facial hair
158 BEAR'S EAR Variety of plant
159 BEARSKIN Style of military headgear
160 BEAST Animal
161 BEAVER Variety of amphibious rodent
162 BED Piece of furniture for sleeping on
163 BED Cultivated plot for plants
164 BEDBUG Variety of insect
165 BEDCLOTHES Sheets and blankets for a bed
166 BEDDING Bedclothes
167 BEDHEAD Upper end of bed
168 BEDLINGTON TERRIER Breed of dog
169 BEDROOM Sleeping chamber
170 BEDSPREAD Coverlet
171 BEDSTEAD Base or framework of bed
172 BEE Variety of winged insect
173 BEE-EATER Variety of insectivorous bird
174 BEECH Variety of tree
175 BEEFEATER Yeoman of the Guard
176 BEEHIVE House for community of bees
177 BEELZEBUB The devil
178 BEER Type of alcoholic beverage
179 BEET Variety of edible root vegetable
180 BEETLE Variety of insect
181 BEGONIA Variety of flowering plant
182 BEIGE Yellowish grey colour
183 BELGIUM Flag of Western European country
184 BELISHA BEACON Beacon indicating pedestrian crossing
185 BELIZE Flag of Central American country
186 BELL Hollow metallic ringing device
187 BELL BIRD Variety of bird
188 BELLFLOWER Variety of flowering plant
189 BELL GLASS Bell-shaped glass vessel
190 BELLADONNA LILY Variety of flowering plant
191 BELLIS Variety of plant
192 BELLOWS Device for blowing air
193 BELLY Stomach or abdomen
194 BELLY DANCER Arab-style dancer
195 BELT Band of material worn around waist
196 BELTANE Ancient Celtic holiday
197 BELTED BEAUTY Variety of moth
198 BELVEDERE High turret commanding view
199 BENCH Long seat
200 BENCH MARK Surveyor's mark
201 BEND Heraldic device
202 BENDING Act of inclining body
203 BENIN Flag of West African country
204 BERET Round flat peakless cap
205 BERGENIA Variety of plant
206 BERMUDA Flag of North Atlantic island
207 BERRY Small stoneless fruit
208 BERYL Variety of precious gemstone (includes emerald)
209 BESOM Type of broom
210 BEST MAN Principal groomsman at wedding
211 BETH Second letter of Hebrew alphabet
212 BEVERAGE A drink
213 BHUTAN Flag of Asian kingdom
214 BHUTAN GLORY Variety of butterfly

215 BIB Article of children's protective clothing
216 BIB Variety of fish
217 BIBLE Judao-Christian sacred scriptures
218 BICEPS Muscles of the upper arm
219 BICOLOURED Two-coloured
220 BICORN Two-horned
221 BICORN Type of cocked hat
222 BICYCLE Two-wheeled self-propelled vehicle
223 BIFOCAL Spectacles with dual-function lenses
224 BIG TOP Large circus marquee
225 BIGHORN Variety of wild sheep
226 BIGHT Loop of a rope
227 BIKINI Ladies' two-piece swimming garment
228 BILL Bird's beak
229 BILL Poster
230 BILL-HOOK Curved cutting tool
231 BILLET Heraldic device
232 BILLIARDS Table-top game played with balls and cue
233 BILLION One thousand million (US numerical system)
234 BINDWEED Variety of plant
235 BINOCULARS Field glasses
236 BIPED Creature with two feet
237 BIPLANE Aircraft with two wings
238 BIRD Flying creature covered with feathers

Parts of a bird

Crest

Ear Feathers

Bill

Lesser Coverts

Breast

Greater Coverts

Abdomen

Secondaries

Under Tail Coverts

Primaries

Rectrices

239 BIRDBATH Ornamental basin for birds to bathe in
240 BIRDWING BUTTERFLY Variety of large-winged butterfly
241 BIRTHDAY CAKE Celebratory cake for birthday
242 BIRTHSTONE Gemstone associated with month of one's birth (shown here bloodstone – March)
243 BISCUIT Thin, flat, crisp cake
244 BISHOP High-ranking Christian clergyman
245 BISHOP'S HAT CACTUS Variety of mitre-shaped cacti
246 BISHOP'S HAT Variety of plant
247 BISON North American buffalo
248 BIT Mouthpiece of horse's bridle
249 BIT Cutting part of drill

250 BITCH Female of canine species
251 BITTERN Variety of bird
252 BLACK The very darkest colour
253 BLACK BEAR Large black-coloured furry mammal
254 BLACK BREAD Type of dark-coloured bread
255 BLACK LETTER Germanic style of lettering
256 BLACK PUDDING Blood sausage
257 BLACKBERRY Fruit of the bramble
258 BLACKBIRD Dark-coloured European bird
259 BLACKBUCK Variety of Asian antelope
260 BLACKCAP Variety of bird
261 BLACKCURRANT Variety of small edible fruit
262 BLACK EYE Bruise around eye
263 BLACKEYE Variety of bird
264 BLACKJACK A card game (also called 21's)
265 BLADE Cutting part of axe, knife or sword
266 BLANCMANGE Opaque jelly formed in a mould
267 BLANK Unmarked or bare
268 BLANKET Woven woollen bed-covering
269 BLAZE A fire
270 BLAZE White marking on horse's face
271 BLAZER Style of sports jacket
272 BLAZING STAR Variety of plant
273 BLAZON Coat of arms or heraldic banner
274 BLEA Wood of tree beneath bark
275 BLEEDING HEART Variety of plant
276 BLEMISH Flaw, stain or disfigurement
277 BLENNY Variety of fish
278 BLESSING Benediction
279 BLIMP Non-rigid dirigible airship
280 BLIND Sightless
281 BLIND Window shade
282 BLINDFOLD Covering for the eyes
283 BLINK Momentary closing of the eyes
284 BLINKERS Side-pieces on horse's bridle to shield eyes
285 BLISTER BEETLE Variety of insect
286 BLOCK Pulley container of lifting tackle
287 BLOCK CAPITAL Plain capital letter
288 BLOCKHEAD Wooden block for hats or wigs
289 BLOND Light-coloured hair
290 BLOOD Red body fluid
291 BLOOD-RED BUTTERFLY Variety of butterfly
292 BLOODHOUND Breed of dog
293 BLOODROOT Variety of plant
294 BLOODSTAIN Discoloration caused by blood
295 BLOODSTONE Type of semi-precious stone
296 BLOODWORT BURNET-MOTH Variety of insect
297 BLOOM Flowering part of a plant
298 BLOSSOM Bloom
299 BLOUSE Light outer garment for upper body
300 BLOUSON Light waist-length tunic
301 BLOW Force air through the mouth
302 BLOW LAMP Flame-producing utensil
303 BLOWFLY Variety of insect
304 BLUE A primary colour
305 BLUE ENSIGN British nautical flag
306 BLUE PETER Nautical signal flag
307 BLUE TIT Variety of bird
308 BLUE WHALE Largest oceanic mammal
309 BLUEBELL Variety of wildflower
310 BLUEBIRD Variety of bird
311 BLUEBOTTLE Variety of flying insect
312 BLUEFIN Variety of tuna fish

313 BLUEFISH Variety of fish
314 BLUETHROAT Variety of bird
315 BLUNDERBUSS Antique large-bore gun
316 BOA Variety of large South American snake
317 BOAR Male pig
318 BOAR FISH Variety of fish
319 BOAT Floating vessel
320 BOATER Style of straw hat
321 BOBCAT North American lynx
322 BOBOLINK Variety of bird
323 BOBUCK Variety of Australian marsupial
324 BODICE Tight-fitting women's upper garment
325 BODKIN Dagger
326 BODY Physical frame of living creature
327 BOGUE Variety of fish
328 BOLE Tree trunk
329 BOLERO Style of short jacket
330 BOLIVIA Flag of South American republic
331 BOLLARD Post
332 BOLSTER Long pillow
333 BOLT Metal fastening pin
334 BOLT Crossbow projectile
335 BOLT Lightning stroke
336 BOMB Explosive device
337 BOMBARDE Type of musical wind instrument
338 BOMBARDON Tuba
339 BOMBAY DUCK Variety of fish
340 BOMBER Aircraft for dropping bombs
341 BOND Style of bricklaying
342 BONES Individual parts of skeleton
343 BONGO Variety of African antelope
344 BONGO-DRUMS Set of small drums
345 BONNET Style of women's hat
346 BONNET-MONKEY Indian macaque monkey
347 BONSAI-TREE Cultivated dwarf plant
348 BOOK Printed volume
349 BOOKBINDING Binding of a book
350 BOOKMARK Place marker
351 BOOM Spar at foot of sail
352 BOOMERANG Australian curved wooden throwing missile
353 BOOT Style of tall footwear
354 BOOZE Alcoholic liquor
355 BORDER Margin
356 BORDURE Heraldic device
357 BORZOI Breed of dog
358 BOSOM Breast
359 BOSS Knob in the centre of a shield
360 BOTANY Study of plants
361 BOTSWANA Flag of Southern African republic
362 BOTTLE Glass container
363 BOTTLENOSE Variety of dolphin
364 BOUGAINVILLAEA Variety of flowering plant
365 BOUGH Large branch of tree
366 BOUND Tied up
367 BOUT Round in boxing match
368 BOUTONNIERE Flower worn in the lapel
369 BOW Weapon for shooting arrows
370 BOW Implement for playing stringed instrument
371 BOW Decorative knot
372 BOW Front end of ship
373 BOWER-BIRD Variety of bird
374 BOWIE KNIFE Large hunting knife
375 BOWING Playing an instrument with a bow
376 BOWL Semi-rounded vessel
377 BOWLER One who bowls

378 BOWLER HAT Style of hat
379 BOWLINE Type of knot
380 BOWLING Playing at skittles
381 BOWMAN Archer
382 BOWSPRIT Spar at bow of ship
383 BOWSTRING String of a bow
384 BOX Angular container

385 BOX Variety of tree
386 BOX To fight with the fists
387 BOX KITE Type of kite
388 BOXER Fist-fighter
389 BOXER Breed of dog
390 BOY Immature human male
391 BRACE A boring tool
392 BRACE A pair
393 BRACELET Wrist ornament
394 BRACER Archer's wrist guard
395 BRACES Trouser suspenders
396 BRACHYCOME Variety of plant
397 BRACKET Wall support for lamp or burner
398 BRACKETS Marks for enclosing words or figures ( )
399 BRAID Plait
400 BRAILLE Tactile alphabet for the blind
401 BRAIN Organ of thought and neural co-ordination
402 BRAKE Device for stopping vehicle

Brass Instruments

Trumpet

Cornet

Bass Tuba

Bugle

French Horn

Trombone

403 BRAKE A thicket
404 BRANCH Small limb of a tree
405 BRAND Burning piece of wood
406 BRAND Mark made with hot iron
407 BRANDING IRON Implement for making brands
408 BRASS Type of musical wind instrument

409 BRASSIERE Women's undergarment for supporting the breasts
410 BRAZIL Flag of South American republic
411 BREACH Forced gap in a wall
412 BREAD Foodstuff baked from flour
413 BREAST Bosom or chest
414 BREASTPLATE Armour protecting breast
415 BREECHES Style of trousers
416 BREVE Musical note
417 BRIC-À-BRAC Curios
418 BRICK-MOTH Variety of moth
419 BRICKS Baked clay building blocks
420 BRICKWORK Structure built from bricks
421 BRIDE Woman getting married
422 BRIDEGROOM Man getting married
423 BRIDESMAID Bride's female attendant
424 BRIDGE Structure spanning gap
425 BRIDGE Structure supporting strings on musical instrument
426 BRIDLE Horse's head-gear

427 BRIEF Summary of legal facts
428 BRIEFS Scanty lower undergarment
429 BRIG Type of sailing vessel
430 BRIGANTINE Type of sailing vessel
431 BRIGHT Style of paint brush
432 BRIM Rim of vessel
433 BRIMSTONE Variety of butterfly
434 BRISKET Breast of an animal
435 BRISTLE Short coarse brush hair
436 BRISTLETAIL Variety of insect
437 BRITAIN United Kingdom
438 BRITANNIA Poetic personification of Great Britain
439 BRITISH Belonging to Great Britain
440 BROADLEAF Tree with broad leaves
441 BROADBILL Variety of bird
442 BROADSWORD Broad-bladed sword
443 BROCADE-MOTH Variety of moth
444 BROCCOLI Variety of vegetable
445 BRODIAEA Variety of plant
446 BROKEN In pieces
447 BROMPTON STOCK Variety of plant
448 BRONTOTHERIUM Variety of extinct rhinoceros
449 BRONTOSAURUS Variety of huge prehistoric reptile
450 BRONZE Metal alloy of copper and tin
451 BRONZE ANNIVERSARY Eight years
452 BROOCH Ornamental pin
453 BROOM Long-handled brush
454 BROUETTE Wheeled sedan chair
455 BROW Forehead above the eyes
456 BROWN A tertiary colour
457 BROWN BAT Variety of bat
458 BROWN BREAD Bread baked with wholemeal flour
459 BRUISE Skin discoloration caused by blow
460 BRUNEI Flag of South-east Asian sultanate
461 BRUNETTE Dark-coloured hair
462 BRUNNERA Variety of plant
463 BRUSH Implement for applying paint
464 BRUSHWORK Marks made by a brush
465 BUBBLE Sphere of air-filled film
466 BUCCANEER Pirate (indicated by flag)
467 BUCK Adult male deer
468 BUCKET Vessel for carrying liquids
469 BUCKLE Fastening for belt
470 BUCKLER Small round shield
471 BUCKSKINS Traditional soft suede garments
472 BUD Undeveloped flower or leaf
473 BUDDHA Eastern religious teacher
474 BUDGERIGAR Variety of Australian bird
475 BUFF Pale yellow colour
476 BUFF-TIP Variety of moth
477 BUFFALO Wild ox
478 BUFFALO WEAVER Variety of bird
479 BUG Insect
480 BUGBANE Variety of plant
481 BUGGER'S GRIPS Style of male whiskers
482 BUGLE Type of military trumpet
483 BUGLER Bugle player
484 BUILDING An edifice
485 BUISINE Long straight medieval trumpet
486 BULB Electric light source
487 BULBUL Variety of bird
488 BULGARIA Flag of South-east European socialist republic

489 BULL male of bovine species
490 BULLFIGHT Public fighting of bull
491 BULLTERRIER Breed of dog
492 BULLFIGHTER Matador
493 BULLRING Arena where bulls are fought
494 BULLDOG Breed of dog
495 BULLET Projectile fired from gun
496 BULLFINCH Variety of bird
497 BULLFROG Variety of frog
498 BULLRUSH Variety of plant
499 BULL'S-EYE Centre of target
500 BULL'S-EYE MOTH Variety of moth
501 BULWARK Side of ship above deck
502 BUMMALO Variety of fish
503 BUMP Swelling
504 BUN Small, round, sweet cake
505 BUN Knot of hair
506 BUNG Stopper
507 BUNTING Decorative flags
508 BUNTING Variety of bird
509 BUOY Floating marker
510 BUPHTHALMUM Variety of plant
511 BURBOT Variety of fish
512 BURDOCK Variety of plant
513 BURGEON To blossom
514 BURGLAR ALARM Intruder warning-bell
515 BURIN Engraver's tool
516 BURMA Flag of South-east Asian socialist republic
517 BURMESE Breed of cat
518 BURNING On fire
519 BURNISHED BRASS Variety of moth
520 BURNOUS Hooded Arab cloak
521 BURUNDI Flag of Central African republic
522 BUSBY Style of military hat
523 BUSH Shrub
524 BUSH-BABY Variety of small nocturnal animal
525 BUSHBUCK Variety of African antelope
526 BUSHSHRIKE Variety of bird
527 BUST Sculpture of head and shoulders
528 BUTCHER Meat trader
529 BUTCHERBIRD Variety of bird
530 BUTT Archery target
531 BUTTER Fat made from churned milk
532 BUTTER BEAN Large haricot bean
533 BUTTERCUP Variety of plant
534 BUTTERFISH Variety of fish
535 BUTTERFLY Variety of flying insect
536 BUTTERFLY FISH Variety of fish
537 BUTTOCKS Posterior or rump
538 BUTTON Fastener for clothing
539 BUTTON-HOLE Hole for button
540 BUTTRESS Wall support
541 BUZZ-SAW Circular saw
542 BYNAME Nickname (Mike for Michael)

1 C Third letter of the alphabet
2 C Braille alphabet
3 C C clef in musical notation
4 C International signal flag
5 C Manual alphabet – American system
6 C Morse code alphabet
7 C Musical notation
8 C Semaphore alphabet
9 C Vitamin C ($C_6H_8O_6$)
10 CABALLINE Equine
11 CABLE Rope
12 CABLE-CAR Transportation on overhead cable
13 CACTUS Variety of prickly plant
14 CADAVER Corpse
15 CADENCY Heraldic mark indicating position within family
16 CADUCEUS Herald's symbolic staff
17 CAGE Barred imprisoning structure
18 CAIRN Raised mound of stones
19 CAKE Baked confection
20 CALAMARY Squid
21 CALDERA Volcanic crater
22 CALEDONIA Heraldic flag of Scotland
23 CALF Young cow or bull
24 CALF Lower leg
25 CALIPASH Upper shell of turtle
26 CALIPEE Lower shell of turtle
27 CALLICHTHYS Variety of fish
28 CALLIGRAPHY Elegant handwriting
29 CALLIPER Adjustable measuring instrument
30 CALTROP Implement for impeding cavalry horses
31 CALVARY Place of the crucifixion
32 CALVARY CROSS Heraldic device
33 CALVITY Baldness
34 CAMBODIA Flag of South-east Asian republic
35 CAMEL Large humped animal
36 CAMEO Style of jewellery
37 CAMERA Photographic apparatus
38 CAMEROON Flag of West African republic
39 CAMOUFLAGE Concealment by means of disguise
40 CAMP Place where tents are pitched
41 CANADA Flag of North American country
42 CANADA GOOSE Variety of bird
43 CANARY Variety of bird
44 CANCER Fourth sign of the zodiac; the crab
45 CANDELABRA Branched candlestick
46 CANDLE Wax stick used for illumination
47 CANDLE-END The stub of a candle
48 CANDLELIGHT The light from a burning candle
49 CANDLESTICK Candle holder
50 CANDLEWICK Wick of a candle
51 CANE Walking-stick

52 CANINE Like a dog
53 CANINE-TOOTH Long pointed tooth
54 CANOE Light self-propelled boat
55 CANTHUS Corner of eye
56 CANTLE A segment
57 CANTON Heraldic division of shield or flag
58 CAP Type of headgear
59 CAPACITOR Electrical symbol for capacitor
60 CAPE VERDE ISLANDS Flag of North Atlantic island group
61 CAPELIN Variety of fish
62 CAPERCAILYE Variety of bird
63 CAPITAL Decorated top of column

Capitals

Doric Ionic Corinthian Composite Venetian

64 CAPITAL Upper case letter
65 CAPRICORN Tenth sign of the zodiac; the goat
66 CAPTIVE Prisoner
67 CAPUCHIN MONKEY Variety of monkey
68 CAPYBARA Variety of large South American rodent
69 CARACOL Spiral shell
70 CARAPACE Upper shell of turtle
71 CARD Playing card
72 CARD Face of compass
73 CARDBOARD Stiffened paper or pasteboard
74 CARDINAL High-ranking Roman Catholic clergyman
75 CARDINAL Variety of bird
76 CARDIOID Heart-shaped
77 CARGO Goods carried by boat
78 CARIBOU North American reindeer
79 CARNELIAN Variety of red gemstone
80 CARNIVORE Flesh-eating animal
81 CARPENTRY Work made in wood
82 CARPUS Wrist
83 CARRIAGE Horse-drawn vehicle
84 CARRICK BEND Type of knot
85 CARROT Variety of vegetable
86 CARRY To bear
87 CARTOUCHE Scroll-shaped ornament or border
88 CARUNCLE Wattle
89 CARVING Piece of carved work
90 CARYATID Column sculptured in the form of a woman
91 CASCADE Waterfall
92 CASE LETTER Outline letter

93 CASH Ready money
94 CASK Barrel
95 CASLON Style of letterform
96 CASQUE Bony headpiece on bird
97 CASSONE Type of large chest
98 CASSOWARY Variety of large bird
99 CASTLE Chess piece
100 CASTOR Small wheel on furniture
101 CAT Variety of animal
102 CAT-FISH Variety of fish
103 CAT-O'-NINE TAILS Nine-thonged whip
104 CATAMOUNT Variety of animal; cougar
105 CATAPULT Slingshot
106 CATARACT Waterfall

107 CATBOAT Cat rigged boat
108 CATENARY Curve formed by hanging rope
109 CATHOLIC Member of Christian sect
110 CATTLE Bovine farm animals
111 CAUCASIAN Member of the white race
112 CAUDATE With a tail
113 CAVE Underground chamber
114 CAVERN Cave
115 CAVICORN Animal with hollow horns
116 CAVITY Hole or hollow
117 CEDAR Variety of tree
118 CEDILLA Type of diacritical mark
119 CEILING Upper limit to chamber
120 CELIBATE Person vowed to unmarried life
121 CELL Electrical symbol for cell
122 CELLO Type of musical instrument
123 CELTIC CROSS Style of cross
124 CEMETERY Graveyard
125 CENSE To burn incense
126 CENSER Incense burner
127 CENTAUR Type of mythical creature
128 CENTILLION Ten to the six-hundredth power (British system)
129 CENTIPEDE Variety of insect
130 CENTRAL AFRICAN REPUBLIC Flag of central African republic
131 CENTRE Middle point
132 CENTURION Roman officer
133 CENTURY Style of letterform
134 CEPHALOPOD Tentacled mollusc
135 CEPHALOPTEROUS Having a winged head
136 CERBERUS Three-headed mythological dog

137 CESTUS Ancient studded boxing glove
138 CHACO Style of military hat
139 CHAD Flag of central African republic
140 CHAFFINCH Variety of bird
141 CHAIN Series of connected metal links
142 CHALCEDONY Semi-precious stone (includes carnelian)
143 CHALICE Drinking cup
144 CHAMELEON Variety of lizard able to change colour
145 CHAMOIS Variety of European antelope
146 CHAMPSOCEPHALUS Variety of fish
147 CHANGE Coins of small value
148 CHANTERELLE Top string of instrument

149 CHAP Jaw
150 CHAPE Metal tip of scabbard
151 CHAPTER (Crack the code and find it)
152 CHAR Variety of fish
153 CHARACTER Letter
154 CHARGE Device depicted on shield
155 CHASING Ornamental engraving
156 CHASSIS Base-frame of vehicle
157 CHASUBLE Ecclesiastical vestment
158 CHECK Position in chess
159 CHECK Pattern of squares
160 CHECKERED Patterned with a check
161 CHECKY Type of heraldic device
162 CHEEK Side of face
163 CHEEKBONE Bone of the cheek
164 CHEESE Foodstuff made from curds
165 CHEETAH Variety of animal
166 CHEIROPOD Mammal with hands
167 CHELA Lobster or crab claw
168 CHEMICAL Substance used in chemistry
169 CHERRY Variety of fruit
170 CHERUB Winged child
171 CHESS Type of board game
172 CHESS-BOARD Board on which chess is played
173 CHESS-MEN Movable pieces used in chess
174 CHESSROOK Type of heraldic device
175 CHEST Large box
176 CHEST Front upper body
177 CHESTNUT Callosity on horse's leg
178 CHEVELURE Luminous core of comet
179 CHEVRON Type of heraldic device
180 CHEVRONEL Type of heraldic device

181 CHEVRONY Type of heraldic device
182 CHI-RHO Christian monogram
183 CHICKEN Variety of domestic bird
184 CHIEF Type of heraldic device
185 CHILD Immature human
186 CHILE Flag of South American republic
187 CHIME Rim on a cask
188 CHIMPANZEE Variety of ape
189 CHIN Lowest point of the face
190 CHINA Flag of communist east Asian country
191 CHINA Flag of non-communist east Asian country (Taiwan)
192 CHIPMUNK Variety of small rodent
193 CHITAL Variety of deer
194 CHOIL Indentation on knife blade
195 CHOKER Neck ornament
196 CHOPPER Axe
197 CHORD Line joining two points on curve
198 CHORD String of musical instrument
199 CHRIST Founder of Christianity
200 CHRISTIAN Member of Christian church
201 CHRISTIAN NAME Fore-name
202 CHROMATIC Coloured
203 CHRONOGRAM Phrase which conceals a date (add up the roman numeral red characters)
204 CHURCH Christian religious building
205 CHURCHWARDEN Long-stemmed clay pipe
206 CICISBEO Decorative ribbon on sword hilt
207 CIGAR Rolled tobacco leaf
208 CIGARETTE Shredded tobacco encased in paper
209 CILIA Eyelashes
210 CINCH Saddle girth
211 CINCTURE Moulding around column
212 CINDER Fragment of ash
213 CINQUEFOIL Five-cusped circle
214 CION Septum
215 CIPHER Code
216 CIRCLE Ring
217 CIRCLET Head ornament
218 CIRCULAR Round
219 CIRCUMFERENCE Perimeter of a circle
220 CIRCUMFLEX Type of diacritical mark
221 CIRCUMROTATION Revolving on an axle
222 CIRCUMSOLAR Revolving round the sun
223 CIRRUS Type of cloud formation
224 CITTERN Type of stringed instrument
225 CIVILIAN One not in armed forces
226 CLARENDON Style of letterform
227 CLARINET Type of woodwind instrument
228 CLARION Type of heraldic device
229 CLASP Fastener
230 CLAVICLE Collar-bone
231 CLAW Animal's horny nail
232 CLAY-PIPE Tobacco pipe made of clay
233 CLEAR Unclouded
234 CLEF Musical notation sign
235 CLENCH Close fist tightly
236 CLERESTORY Upper part of nave wall
237 CLERGYMAN Priest
238 CLERIC Clergyman
239 CLIFF Escarpment
240 CLIMBER One who climbs
241 CLIMBING Act of ascending
242 CLOCK Timepiece
243 CLOCK-FACE Dial of a clock

244 CLOCKWORK Operated by spring and pendulum
245 CLOCKWISE In the direction of clock hands
246 CLOG Wooden shoe
247 CLONE Identical genetic copy
248 CLOTH Woven fabric
249 CLOTHES Garments
250 CLOUD Mass of airborne water vapour
251 CLOVE-HITCH Type of knot
252 CLOVEN Divided in two
253 CLOVER Variety of plant
254 CLOWN Comic entertainer
255 CLUB One suit in playing cards
256 CLUE Informative hint (*use it to crack the code*)
257 COACH Carriage
258 COACH-BOX Coachman's seat
259 COACHMAN Coach driver
260 COACHWORK Craftsmanship of coach body
261 COAT OF ARMS Shield bearing heraldic devices
262 COBRA Variety of venomous snake
263 COBWEB Spider's web
264 COCK Male chicken
265 COCK-OF-THE-ROCK Variety of bird
266 COCKADE Feathered hat ornament
267 COCKATIEL Variety of bird
268 COCKATOO Variety of bird
269 COCKATRICE Mythical bird-snake
270 COCKED-HAT Style of hat
271 COCKLESHELL Variety of shell
272 COCKSCOMB Cock's head-crest
273 COCKSPUR Spur on cock's leg
274 COD Variety of fish
275 CODE Secret message
276 COG Toothed wheel
277 COIL Spiral or helix
278 COIN Metal money
279 COLD-BLOODED Having blood temperature less than surroundings
280 COLLAR Band worn around neck
281 COLLAR-BONE Prominent bone at neck; clavicle
282 COLLARINO Moulding on column
283 COLLIE Breed of dog
284 COLOMBIA Flag of South American republic
285 COLON Type of diacritical mark (:) (here in Morse code)
286 COLOPHON Publisher's imprint

Colophons

Pavilion Books   Henry Holt   Penguin Books

287 COLOSSAL Very large
288 COLOSSUS Giant
289 COLOUR Visual effect of various wavelengths of light
290 COLOURFUL Brightly coloured
291 COLUMN Cylindrical architectural support
292 COMB Crest of cock
293 COMB Toothed hairdressing implement
294 COMBUSTION Process of burning

295 COMESTIBLE Food
296 COMET Heavenly body with tail
297 COMMA Diacritical mark (,)
298 COMMA Diacritical mark (here in Morse code)
299 COMMONER Not of noble birth
300 COMMONWEALTH British community of nations (member)
301 COMOROS Flag of African island group
302 COMPASS Direction-finding instrument

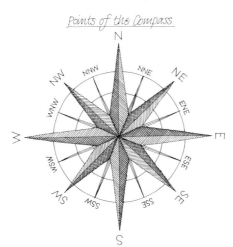

Points of the Compass

303 COMPONY Heraldic device
304 CONCAVE Curving inwards
305 CONCENTRIC Having the same centre
306 CONCERTINA Type of musical instrument
307 CONCH Variety of shell
308 CONDENSED Compressed style of letterform
309 CONDOM Contraceptive sheath
310 CONDOR Variety of large bird
311 CONE Solid geometrical shape
312 CONE Fruit of pine and fir tree
313 CONFEDERATE Flag of former Confederate States of America
314 CONGER-EEL Variety of fish
315 CONGO Flag of West African republic (Brazzaville)
316 CONIFER Cone-bearing tree
317 CONSONANT Letter other than vowel
318 CONSTELLATION Group of stars
319 CONSTRUCTION Building; thing constructed
320 CONTAINER That which contains
321 CONTRACEPTIVE Device for preventing conception
322 CONTRAPTION Machine or gadget
323 CONTUSION Bruise
324 CONVEX Curving outwards
325 CONVEYANCE Vehicle
326 COPPER Type of reddish metal
327 COPPERPLATE Style of handwriting
328 COPY Reproduction
329 COPYRIGHT Symbol denoting copyright
330 CORD Light rope
331 CORINTHIAN Style of capital on column
332 CORK Bottle stopper
333 CORKSCREW Device for removing cork
334 CORNEA Part of eye
335 CORNER Angle where two surfaces meet

336 CORNET Type of brass musical instrument
337 CORNETFISH Variety of fish
338 CORONA Halo around light source
339 CORONET Small crown
340 CORONET Part of horse's foot
341 CORPORAL Non-commissioned officer
342 CORPSE Dead body
343 CORRAL Enclosure for horses or cattle
344 COSMETIC Face paint
345 COSTA RICA Flag of Central American republic
346 COSTE Heraldic device
347 COSTUME Outer garments
348 COUGAR Variety of animal
349 COUNTERCHANGE Heraldic device
350 COUNTER-CLOCKWISE Opposite direction to hands of clock
351 COUNTRY Nation
352 COUPLE Two
353 COURT-CARD Jack, Queen or King
354 COVERED CUP Heraldic device
355 COVERING That which covers
356 COVERT-FEATHERS Type of feathers
357 COW Variety of domestic animal
358 COWBOY American cattle herdsman
359 COYOTE Variety of animal
360 CRAB Variety of crustacean
361 CRACK Fissure
362 CRAG Steep pointed rock
363 CRAKE Variety of bird
364 CRAMP Device for holding things together
365 CRANE Variety of bird
366 CRANE Hoisting machine
367 CRANIUM Skull
368 CRANNY Small hole or crack
369 CRAPS Game played with two dice
370 CRATER Hollow at top of volcano
371 CRAWFISH Variety of crustacean
372 CRAYFISH Crawfish
373 CREASE Ridge on material caused by folding
374 CREATURE Living being
375 CREESE Wavy Malayan dagger
376 CRENELLATION Notched top to battlement
377 CREPUSCULAR Like twilight
378 CRESCENT Stage of the moon
379 CREST Device above shield on coat of arms
380 CREST Tuft on bird's head
381 CREST Part of animal's neck
382 CREVICE Small fissure or cleft

383 CRIMINAL One guilty of crime
384 CRIMSON Deep red colour
385 CRIPPLE Maimed or disabled being
386 CROAKER Variety of fish
387 CROCODILE Variety of large amphibious reptile
388 CROOKED Bent or twisted
389 CROP Pouch in bird's gullet
390 CROSS Upright with crosspiece

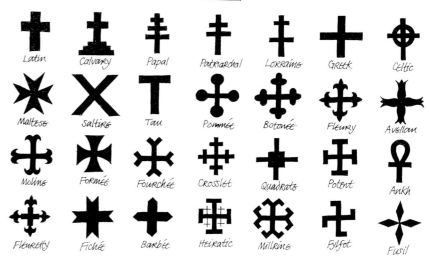

CROSSES

Latin   Calvary   Papal   Patriarchal   Lorraine   Greek   Celtic
Maltese   Saltire   Tau   Pommée   Botonée   Fleury   Avellan
Moline   Formée   Fourchée   Crosslet   Quadrate   Potent   Ankh
Fleuretty   Fiché   Barbée   Heiratic   Millrine   Fylfot   Fusil

391 CROSS-BILL Variety of bird
392 CROSSBOW Type of weapon
393 CROSSLET Heraldic device
394 CROTCH Point where legs meet body
395 CROTCHET Symbol in musical notation; quarter note
396 CROUP Horse's rump
397 CROW Variety of bird
398 CROWING Uttering cry
399 CROWN Sovereign's head-dress
400 CROZIER Bishop's staff
401 CRUCIFIXION Former method of execution
402 CRUMB Tiny portion or scrap

403 CRUPPER Horse's hind quarters
404 CRUSH Compress violently
405 CRUSTACEAN Animal such as crab or lobster
406 CRWTH Type of musical instrument
407 CRYSTAL Fifteenth anniversary
408 CRYSTAL-BALL Fortune-telling sphere
409 CUB Young lion
410 CUBA Flag of Caribbean island republic
411 CUBE Regular square-shaped solid figure

412 CUCHIA Variety of fish
413 CUCKOO Variety of bird
414 CUFF Wrist end of sleeve
415 CUMMERBUND Waist sash
416 CUP Drinking vessel
417 CUPID Poetic personification of love
418 CURASSOW Variety of bird
419 CURL Twisted hair
420 CURLEW Variety of bird
421 CURRENCY Money
422 CURTAIN Window covering
423 CURVE Bend
424 CUSP Point formed by two curves meeting
425 CUT Incision
426 CUTICLE Skin at base of finger-nail
427 CUTLASS Type of short sword
428 CUTTLEFISH Variety of mollusc
429 CYAN Shade of blue
430 CYCLOPS Mythological one-eyed giant
431 CYLINDER Geometric shape
432 CYMBAL Type of musical instrument
433 CYPRESS Variety of tree
434 CYPRUS Flag of Mediterranean island republic
435 CYRILLIC Slavonic alphabet
436 CZECHOSLOVAKIA Flag of East European state

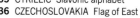

Conifer Cones

Pine   Silver Fir   Douglas Fir   Spruce   Cedar   Hemlock   Larch

D

1 D Fourth letter of the alphabet
2 D Braille alphabet
3 D International signal flag
4 D Manual alphabet – Anglo/Australian system
5 D Manual alphabet – American system
6 D Morse code alphabet
7 D Musical notation
8 D Semaphore alphabet
9 DACE Variety of fish
10 DACHSHUND Breed of dog
11 DADDY-LONG-LEGS Variety of insect; crane fly
12 DADO Part of pedestal
13 DAFFODIL Variety of flowering plant
14 DAGGER Short-bladed knife
15 DAGON Ancient Philistine fish-tailed god
16 DAHLIA Variety of flowering plant
17 DAISY Variety of flowering plant
18 DALETH Fourth letter of the Hebrew alphabet
19 DALMATIC Type of ecclesiastical vestment
20 DALMATIAN Breed of dog
21 DAMES-VIOLET Variety of plant
22 DAMSEL-FISH Variety of fish
23 DAMSEL-FLY Variety of flying insect
24 DAMSON Variety of plum
25 DANCER One who dances
26 DANCETTE Heraldic device
27 DANCETTY Heraldic device
28 DANCING Co-ordinated rhythmical movement
29 DANDELION Variety of plant
30 DAPPLED Variegated with spots
31 DARE Variety of fish
32 DART Variety of fish
33 DART Pointed hand-launched missile
34 DARTBOARD Target for dart
35 DASH Short drawn line
36 DATE Statement of time
37 DATE Variety of palm tree
38 DAVENPORT Type of compact desk
39 DAWN Daybreak
40 DAY-BOOK Diary

Days of the Week – symbols

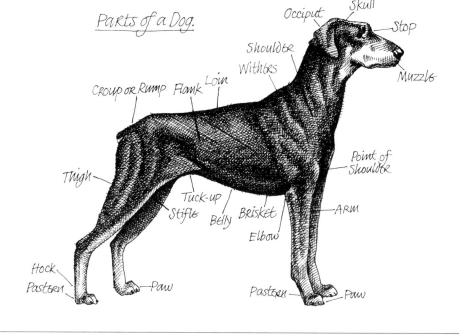

Sunday Monday Tuesday Wednesday
Thursday Friday Saturday

41 DAYBREAK Dawn
42 DAYLIGHT Sunlight
43 DEAD-EYES Part of a block
44 DEATH'S-HEAD A skull
45 DEATH'S-HEAD MOTH Variety of moth
46 DECAGON Ten-sided figure
47 DECANTER Ornamental wine vessel
48 DECAPITATION Cutting off of the head
49 DECASTYLE Classical architectural style with ten columns
50 DECILLION Ten to the 60th power (British numerical system)
51 DECKCHAIR Portable folding chair
52 DECOLLATED Beheaded
53 DECOLLETAGE Low-cut dress
54 DECORATION Ornamentation
55 DECORATION Medal
56 DECRESCENDO Mark used in musical notation
57 DECUMBITURE Lying down
58 DEDICATION Dedicatory inscription
59 DEER Variety of animal
60 DEER-HOUND Breed of dog
61 DEERSTALKER Style of hat
62 DEITY A god
63 DEINOTHERE Extinct elephant-like animal
64 DELACRIMATION Weeping
65 DELEATUR Proof correction mark for deletion
66 DELINEATION A sketch
67 DELTA Fourth letter of the Greek alphabet
68 DEMICIRCLE Half circle
69 DEMIJOHN Type of large bottle
70 DEMISEMIQUAVER Type of note in musical notation; thirty-second note
71 DEMOISELLE Variety of bird
72 DENMARK Flag of Scandinavian country
73 DENOMINATOR Figure below line in fraction
74 DENT Hollow caused by blow
75 DENTIL Style of moulding
76 DEPICTION Graphic representation
77 DEPOSIT Stain left by natural process
78 DEPRESSION A hollow
79 DERBY Style of hat
80 DERM Outer skin
81 DERMATOGLYPHICS Skin markings
82 DERRICK Lifting device
83 DERRINGER Type of small pistol
84 DESCENDER Tail of a letter
85 DESERT Barren place
86 DESERT RAT Variety of small animal; jerboa
87 DESIGN Drawn device
88 DESK Writing table with drawers
89 DESMAN Variety of small animal
90 DESMOSTYLUS Extinct hippopotamus-like animal
91 DESOLATION Barren wasteland
92 DETONATOR Contrivance for instigating explosions
93 DEVICE Mechanical contraption
94 DEVICE Emblematic design
95 DEVIL Satan
96 DEVIL-FISH Variety of fish
97 DEWLAP Loose fold of skin at throat
98 DHOW Single-masted Arab vessel
99 DIBATAG Variety of animal
100 DIADEM Arch of crown
101 DIAGONAL Slanting from corner to corner

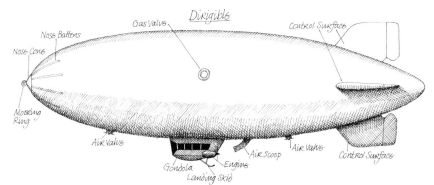

Dirigible

Nose Battens · Gas Valve · Control Surfaces · Nose Cone · Mooring Ring · Air Valve · Gondola · Landing Skid · Engine · Air Scoop · Air Valve · Control Surfaces

102 DIAMETER Total width of circle
103 DIAMOND Lozenge
104 DIAMONDBIRD Variety of bird
105 DIAPER Heraldic device; all-over diamond pattern
106 DIARY Book for recording daily events
107 DIATRYMA Variety of extinct bird
108 DICE Cubes marked with numerical spots
109 DIGAMMA Sixth letter of original Greek alphabet
110 DIGGER Variety of insect
111 DIGIT Numeral
112 DIGIT Finger or toe
113 DIMENSION Indication of measurement
114 DIMETRODON Variety of prehistoric reptile
115 DIMINUENDO Type of musical notation mark
116 DIMINUTIVE Shortened version of name
117 DIMPLE Small natural hollow in the flesh
118 DINOSAUR Huge extinct reptile
119 DIODE Electrical symbol for diode
120 DIPLODOCUS Variety of extinct dinosaur
121 DIPPER Variety of bird
122 DIPTHONG Union of two vowels
123 DIPTYCH Painting on two hinged panels
124 DIRIGIBLE Airship
125 DIRNDL Style of skirt with bodice
126 DISC Round, flat object
127 DISCOBOLUS Discus thrower
128 DISCUS Throwing disc
129 DISCUS Variety of fish
130 DISH Shallow vessel for holding food
131 DISSECTION Cut in half
132 DISTANCE Far away
133 DITTO Mark indicating repetition
134 DITTOGRAPH Unintentional repetition of a letter
135 DIVIDERS Measuring instrument
136 DIVING BEETLE Variety of insect
137 DIVISION Mathematical symbol
138 DOBERMANN Breed of dog
139 DODGEM Fairground car
140 DODO Variety of extinct bird
141 DOE Female deer
142 DOG Variety of domestic animal
143 DOG'S-EAR Folded corner of page
144 DOG-COLLAR Band worn around dog's neck
145 DOGFISH Variety of fish
146 DOGTAG Identification disc
147 DOLICHOPTERYX Variety of fish
148 DOLL Toy representing human figure

149 DOLLAR Symbol for currency unit
150 DOLMEN Prehistoric standing-stone
151 DOLPHIN Variety of aquatic mammal
152 DOLPHIN FISH Variety of fish
153 DOME Convex curved roof
154 DOMICILE Dwelling-place
155 DOMINICAN REPUBLIC Flag of Caribbean republic
156 DOMINO Small slab marked with numerical spots
157 DONJON Keep
158 DONKEY Variety of domestic animal
159 DOOR Hinged barrier in entrance
160 DOOR-FRAME Surround to a door
161 DOORKNOB Handle to a door
162 DOORMAT Mat set before a door
163 DOORSTEP Step at threshold
164 DOORWAY Entrance to room or building
165 DOPPLEGANGER A double
166 DOR Variety of insect; dung beetle
167 DORADO Variety of fish
168 DORIC Style of Greek architecture
169 DORIS Variety of butterfly

170 DORMANT Sleeping
171 DORMER Type of window
172 DORMOUSE Varety of small animal
173 DOROTHY-BAG Type of small bag
174 DORSAL-FIN Back fin of fish
175 DOT Small drawn spot
176 DOT Variety of moth
177 DOTTEREL Variety of bird
178 DOUBLE Person exactly like another
179 DOUBLE Two at dice
180 DOUBLE DART Variety of moth
181 DOUBLE-BREASTED Style of jacket
182 DOUBLET Formerly, men's upper garment
183 DOUGHNUT Ring-shaped cake
184 DOUGLAS FIR Variety of tree
185 DOVE Variety of bird
186 DOVECOTE Nesting hutch for pigeons
187 DOVETAIL Type of carpentry joint
188 DOWN Opposite direction to up
189 DOWN Feathers of young duck
190 DOZEN Twelve
191 DRAGON Mythical winged beast
192 DRAGON'S HEAD Symbol for ascending node of moon's orbit
193 DRAGON'S TAIL Symbol for descending node of moon's orbit
194 DRAGONFLY Variety of winged insect
195 DRAGONET Variety of fish
196 DRAGONTAIL Variety of butterfly
197 DRAGOON Type of soldier armed with short musket
198 DRAGOON Type of short musket
199 DRAIN Channel to carry away waste
200 DRAKE Male duck
201 DRAPERY Hanging fabric
202 DRAUGHT-BOARD Board for playing draughts
203 DRAUGHTS Type of board game
204 DRAW-BRIDGE Hinged bridge
205 DRAWER Sliding tray

Parts of a Dog.

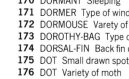

Occiput · Skull · Stop · Muzzle · Shoulder · Withers · Croup or Rump · Flank · Loin · Point of Shoulder · Thigh · Tuck-up · Stifle · Belly · Brisket · Arm · Elbow · Hock · Pastern · Paw · Pastern · Paw

206 DRAWING Graphic delineation; sketch
207 DRAWING-PIN Flat-headed pin
208 DRAWSHAVE Type of tool
209 DRAWSTRING String fastening for garment
210 DRESS Type of women's garment
211 DRESSING Bandage
212 DRIBBLE Flow of saliva
213 DRILL Boring tool
214 DRINKING HORN Drinking vessel made from a horn
215 DRIP Small drop of liquid
216 DRIVER Controller of vehicle
217 DRIZZLE Meteorological symbol
218 DROMEDARY Arabian camel
219 DROOL Allow saliva to trickle
220 DROP Globule of liquid
221 DROPPER Instrument for releasing drops of liquid
222 DRUM Musical percussion instrument
223 DRUM Variety of fish
224 DRUM Circular wall, supporting a dome

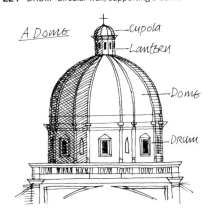

A Dome
— Cupola
— Lantern
— Dome
— Drum

225 DRUMHEAD Taut skin stretched across drum
226 DRUMSTICK Rod for beating drum
227 DRUPE Fleshy fruit with single stone
228 DRY Lacking moisture
229 DUCK Type of water bird
230 DUCKLING Young duck
231 DUEL Formal fight between two opponents
232 DUELLING PISTOL Handgun used in duel
233 DUELLIST Combatant in duel
234 DUG-OUT Canoe made from hollowed-out tree
235 DUGONG Variety of aquatic mammal
236 DUIKER Variety of antelope
237 DULCIMER Type of musical instrument
238 DUMBBELL Exercise weights
239 DUMMY Manikin
240 DUN Dull grey-brown colour
241 DUNCE Stupid person
242 DUNCE'S CAP Hat signifying dunce
243 DUNDREARY Style of whiskers
244 DUNE Sandhill
245 DUNG Animal's excrement
246 DUNG-BEETLE Variety of insect
247 DUODECUPLE Multiply by twelve
248 DUPLICATE Double; copy
249 DURIAN Variety of tropical fruit
250 DWARF Person of very small stature
251 DWELLING Habitation; abode
252 DYSPROSIUM Element; atomic number 66

1 E Fifth letter of the alphabet
2 E Braille alphabet
3 E International signal flag
4 E Manual alphabet – Anglo/Australian system
5 E Manual alphabet – American system
6 E Morse code alphabet
7 E Musical notation
8 E Semaphore alphabet
9 EAGLE Variety of bird
10 EAGLE-OWL Variety of bird
11 EAGLE-RAY Variety of fish
12 EAGLET Young eagle
13 EAR Organ of hearing
14 EAR Head of corn
15 EAR TRUMPET Trumpet-shaped hearing aid
16 EARFLAP Earlobe
17 EARLOBE Pendant part of the ear
18 EARPHONE Small loudspeaker worn over the ear
19 EARLESS Without ears
20 EARRING Ornament worn in the ear
21 EARTH The world
22 EARTH Planetary symbol
23 EARTH Electrical symbol
24 EARTHCREEPER Variety of bird
25 EARTHENWARE Pottery
26 EARTHLING Inhabitant of Earth
27 EARTHWORM Common worm
28 EARWIG Variety of insect
29 EASEL Artist's support for picture
30 EASY CHAIR Padded armchair
31 EATABLE Fit to be eaten
32 EAU-DE-NIL Pale green colour
33 EAVES Overhanging part of roof
34 ECCENTRIC Not having the same centre
35 ECCLESIASTIC Clergyman
36 ECDERON Outer part of the skin
37 ECHIDNA Variety of animal
38 ECHINACEA Variety of plant
39 ECLIPSE Obscuring of a heavenly body
40 ECORCHE Flayed anatomical figure
41 ECTOMORPH Tall, skinny physical type
42 ECUADOR Flag of South American republic
43 EDAM Type of Dutch cheese
44 EDELWEISS Variety of flowering plant
45 EDGE Outer extremity
46 EDH An old English letter
47 EDIBLE Fit to eat
48 EDIFICE Large building
49 EDUCATOR Teacher
50 EEL Variety of fish
51 EFFIGY Three-dimensional representation of person
52 EFFLORESCENT Flowering

53 EGG Ovum of bird
54 EGG AND DART Style of ornament
55 EGGPLANT Type of vegetable; aubergine
56 EGGSHELL Shell which encloses egg
57 EGG-TIMER Type of small sandglass
58 EGGCUP Small cup to hold cooked egg
59 EGGFLY Variety of butterfly
60 EGRESS Way out
61 EGRET Variety of bird
62 EGYPT Flag of North African republic
63 EGYPTIAN Native of Egypt
64 EGYPTIAN Style of letterform
65 EIDER-DUCK Variety of water bird
66 EIGHT Cardinal number between seven and nine
67 EIGHT-SQUARE Octagon
68 EIGHTEEN Eight more than ten
69 EIGHTY Eight times ten
70 EIRE Flag of Eire; republic of Ireland
71 EINSTEINIUM Element; atomic number 99
72 EL SALVADOR Flag of central American republic
73 ELAENIA Variety of bird
74 ELAND Variety of animal
75 ELBOW Joint between forearm and upper arm
76 ELDERLY Old
77 ELECTRIC-FISH Variety of fish
78 ELECTRIC-GUITAR Amplifiable stringed instrument
79 ELECTRIC-LIGHT Lamp powered by electricity
80 ELECTRIC-RAY Variety of fish
81 ELECTRICITY Electric power source

89 ELEVATOR Movable aerofoil on aircraft tailplane
90 ELEVEN One more than ten
91 ELF Small mythological being
92 ELF OWL Variety of bird
93 ELK Variety of large deer; wapiti
94 ELKHOUND Breed of dog
95 ELLIPSE Oval
96 ELLIPSOID Three-dimensional eliptical figure
97 ELM Variety of tree (leaf shown here)
98 ELONGATION Extension
99 EMASCULATED Deprived of manhood
100 EMBATTLED Heraldic device
101 EMBELLISHMENT Ornamentation
102 EMBER Glowing cinder
103 EMBLAZON Adorn with heraldic devices
104 EMBLEM Symbolic device
105 EMBOUCHURE Mouthpiece of brass instrument
106 EMBRYO Foetus
107 EMERALD Green precious gemstone
108 EMINENCE High ground
109 EMISSION Discharge
110 EMMARBLED Sculpted in marble
111 EMPENNAGE Tail-plane
112 EMPEROR Ruler of an empire
113 EMPEROR GOOSE Variety of water bird
114 EMPEROR PENGUIN Variety of large penguin
115 EMPEROR SWALLOWTAIL Variety of butterfly
116 EMPEROR MOTH Variety of moth
117 EMPHASIS Stress
118 EMPICTURED Portrayed in a picture

Electrical Symbols

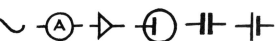

Alternating Current · Ammeter · Amplifier · Anode · Capacitor · Cell

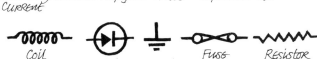

Coil · Diode · Earth · Fuse · Resistor

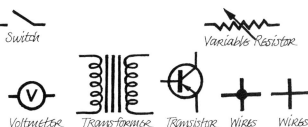

Switch · Variable Resistor · Voltmeter · Transformer · Transistor · Wires Joining · Wires Cross

82 ELECTROLIER Cluster of electric lamps
83 ELEMENT Fundamental substance
84 ELEPHANT Variety of large animal
85 ELEPHANT-BIRD Variety of large extinct bird
86 ELEPHANT-FISH Variety of fish
87 ELEPHANT-SHREW Variety of animal
88 ELEVATION Plan of one side of building

119 EMPTY-HANDED Holding nothing
120 EMU Variety of large flightless bird
121 EMU-WREN Variety of bird
122 ENAMEL Outer surface of tooth
123 ENCHANTER'S NIGHTSHADE Variety of plant
124 ENCORBELLEMENT Projecting brick courses
125 ENDGRAIN Grain at the end of wood

E

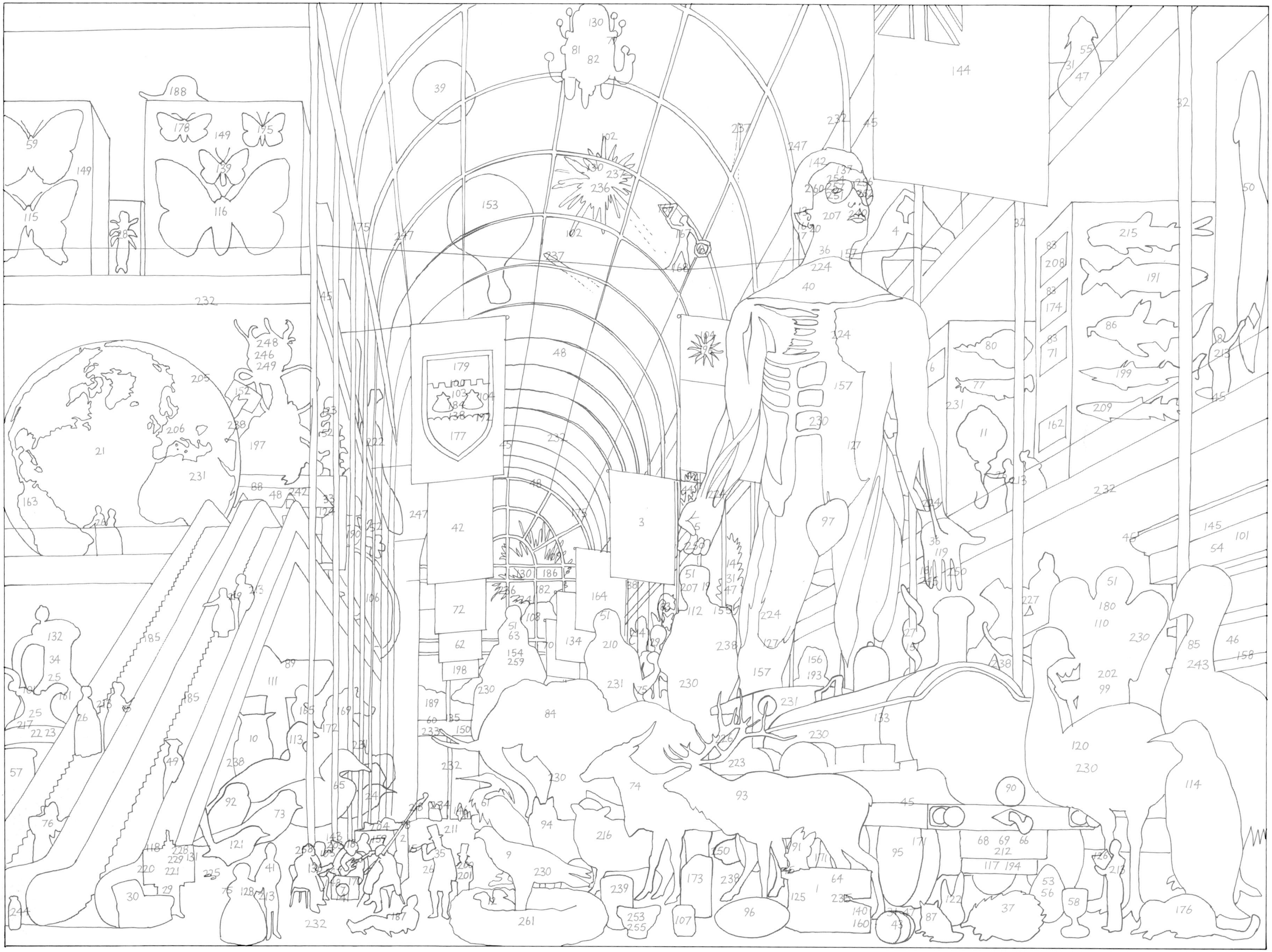

126 ENDPAPER Paper immediately inside book cover
127 ENDERON Layer of skin
128 ENDOMORPH Short, rounded body type
129 ENDOSKELETON Internal skeleton
130 ENERGY Power source
131 ENFRAMED Mounted within a frame
132 ENGHALSKRUG German narrow-necked ewer
133 ENGINE Locomotive
134 ENGLAND Flag of Western European country
135 ENGLISH The language spoken in England
136 ENGLISH-HORN Type of musical instrument
137 ENGLISHMAN Male of English birth
138 ENGRAIL Heraldic device
139 ENGRAILED-MOTH Variety of moth
140 ENGRAVING Incised design
141 ENNEAGON Nine-sided figure
142 ENORMOUS Very large
143 ENSEMBLE Group of performers
144 ENSIGN British naval flag
145 ENTABLATURE Cornice, frieze and architrave

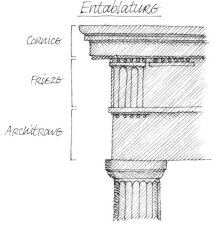

Entablature

Cornice

Frieze

Architrave

146 ENTERING Coming in
147 ENTERTAINER Performer
148 ENTERTAINING Performing
149 ENTOMOLOGY Study of insects
150 ENTRANCE Way in
151 ENTWINEMENT Twisting together
152 ENVELOPE Paper pouch for letter
153 ENVELOPE Gas container of balloon
154 EPALPERBRATE Without eyebrows
155 EPAULETTE Ornamental shoulder-piece
156 EPICANTHIC FOLD Fold of Mongoloid upper eyelid
157 EPIDERMIS Outer layer of skin
158 EPISTYLE Architrave
159 EPITRITE Ratio of 4:3
160 EPSILON Fifth letter of the Greek alphabet
161 EQUALS Mathematical sign
162 EQUATION Mathematical statement of equality
163 EQUATOR Region of Earth midway between poles
164 EQUATORIAL GUINEA Flag of West African republic
165 EQUESTRIAN Horseman
166 EQUILATERAL Having equal sides

167 EQUILIBRIST Tightrope walker
168 EQUILIBRIUM State of balance
169 EQUINE Like a horse
170 EQUIPMENT Necessary tools or apparatus
171 EQUIROTAL Having all wheels of equal size
172 EQUITATION Horseriding
173 ERASER Indiarubber
174 ERBIUM Element; atomic number 68
175 ERECTION Building
176 ERMINE Variety of animal
177 ERMINE Heraldic device
178 ERMINE-MOTH Variety of moth
179 ERMINES Heraldic device
180 EROS Ancient Greek god of love
181 ERROR Mistake
182 ERUPTION Volcanic explosion
183 ERYTHRONIUM Variety of plant
184 ESCALLOP Heraldic shell
185 ESCALATOR Moving staircase
186 ESCAPING Outward flow
187 ESCAPOLOGIST Performer specializing in escaping feats
188 ESCARGOT Snail
189 ESCARPMENT Cliff
190 ESCHSCHOLTZIA Variety of plant
191 ESCOLAR Variety of fish
192 ESCUTCHEON Shield bearing coat of arms
193 ESKIMO North American Arctic Indian
194 ESQUIRE Respectful suffix to man's name (abbreviation)
195 ESSEX EMERALD Variety of moth
196 ESTOILE Heraldic star
197 ET CETERA And so on (abbreviation)
198 ETHIOPIA Flag of East African country
199 ETMOPTERUS SPINAX Variety of fish
200 ETON COLLAR Style of wide collar
201 ETON JACKET Style of short jacket
202 EUNUCH Castrated man
203 EUPHONIUM Type of musical instrument
204 EUPHONON Type of musical instrument
205 EURASIA Europe and Asia
206 EUROPE Continent contiguous with Asia
207 EUROPEAN Native of Europe
208 EUROPIUM Element; atomic number 63

Keystone

Extrados
Intrados

Voussoir
Springer
Impost

Pier

209 EUSTHENOPTERON Variety of extinct fish
210 EVE Biblical first woman
211 EVEN Flat
212 EVEN Number divisible by two
213 EVENING-DRESS Formal clothes worn in the evening
214 EVENING PRIMROSE Variety of plant
215 EVERMANNELLA Variety of fish
216 EWE Female sheep
217 EWER Type of water jug
218 EXAGGERATION Representation greater than is true
219 EXARTICULATION Amputation
220 EXCAVATING Digging out
221 EXCAVATOR Digging machine
222 EXCEPTION That which is different (banana begins with B)
223 EXCLAMATION Symbol denoting interjection
224 EXCORIATION Flaying
225 EXCREMENT Bodily waste matter
226 EXCURVED Curved outwards
227 EXECUTIONER Inflicter of capital punishment
228 EXHAUST Waste gas from engine
229 EXHAUST-PIPE Waste gas conduit
230 EXHIBIT Object publicly shown
231 EXHIBITION Display of objects
232 EXHIBITION-HALL Large space where objects are exhibited
233 EXIT Way out
234 EXITING Going out
235 EXPANDED Wide letterform
236 EXPLOSION Violent outburst
237 EXPLOSIVE Substance which explodes
238 EXPOSITION Exhibition
239 EXPOSURE METER Instrument for measuring light intensity
240 EXPRESSION Facial aspect
241 EXPULSION Action of expelling
242 EXTERIOR Outside
243 EXTINCT Died out
244 EXTINGUISHER Apparatus for putting out fires
245 EXTRA Additional
246 EXTRA-HUMAN Extraterrestrial
247 EXTRADOS Outside curve of arch

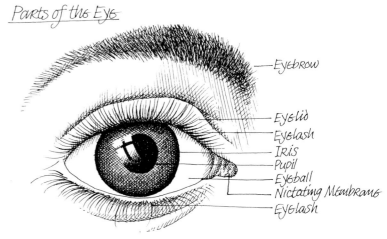

Parts of the Eye

Eyebrow
Eyelid
Eyelash
Iris
Pupil
Eyeball
Nictating Membrane
Eyelash

248 EXTRAMUNDANE Not of this world
249 EXTRATERRESTRIAL From another world
250 EXTREMITY Hands and feet
251 EYE Organ of sight
252 EYEBALL Ball of the eye
253 EYEBATH Vessel for bathing the eye
254 EYEBROW Ridge above the eye
255 EYECUP Eyebath
256 EYEGLASSES Spectacles
257 EYELASH Hairs fringing eyelid
258 EYESHADE Visor for shielding eyes from light
259 EYELESS Without eyes
260 EYELID Moveable flesh lids over eye
261 EYRIE Eagle's nest

F

1 F Sixth letter of the alphabet
2 F Braille alphabet
3 F International signal flag
4 F Manual alphabet – American system
5 F Morse code alphabet
6 F Musical notation
7 F Semaphore alphabet
8 F-HOLE Shaped hole in violin body
9 FABRIC Woven material
10 FABULOUS Legendary
11 FAÇADE Front of a building
12 FACE Front of head
13 FACE Dial of clock
14 FACE MASK Diver's eye protection
15 FACE-GUARD Fencer's eye protection
16 FACING Contrasting collar and cuffs
17 FACTORY Building where goods are manufactured
18 FAECES Excrement
19 FAG Cigarette
20 FAGGOT Bound bundle of twigs
21 FAIR Light complexion
22 FAIR Clement weather
23 FAIR ISLE Type of knitting design
24 FAIRY Small supernatural being
25 FAIRY-ARMADILLO Variety of animal
26 FAKIR Hindu ascetic
27 FALCHION Type of sword
28 FALCON Variety of bird of prey
29 FALDSTOOL Folding chair
30 FALKLAND ISLANDS Flag of South Atlantic island group
31 FALLING Freely descending
32 FALLING Meteorological symbol
33 FALLOW-DEER Variety of deer
34 FALLS Waterfall
35 FALSE SCORPION Variety of insect
36 FAN Folding device for cooling the face
37 FANLIGHT Window over door
38 FANAL Lighthouse
39 FANDANGLE Fantastic ornament
40 FANTAIL Variety of bird
41 FARD Face-paint
42 FARE Food
43 FARLOWELLA Variety of fish
44 FARM Land devoted to agriculture
45 FARMER Agriculturalist
46 FARTHINGALE Style of dress
47 FASCES Ancient Roman symbol of authority
48 FASCIATED Striped
49 FASCIATION Bandaged
50 FASTENING Device for holding clothing together
51 FASTIGIATE Sloping up to a point

52 FASTIGIUM Gable end of a roof
53 FASTNESS Fortress
54 FAT Corpulent
55 FATHOM Six feet
56 FAUCET Tap
57 FAUN Type of mythological creature
58 FAUNA Animals
59 FAWN Young deer
60 FEATHER Body covering of bird

Parts of a Feather

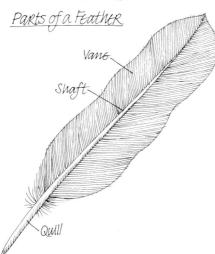

Vane
Shaft
Quill

61 FEATHER DUSTER Cleaning utensil made from feathers
62 FEATHER STAR Variety of starfish
63 FEDORA Style of hat
64 FEEDING Eating
65 FEET Lower extremities of body
66 FELINE Like a cat
67 FELLOE Wheel rim
68 FELLY Wheel rim
69 FELUCCA Lateen-rigged Mediterranean vessel
70 FEMALE Woman
71 FEMALE Symbol for woman
72 FEMINIE Amazon
73 FEMUR Thigh-bone
74 FENCE Boundary barrier
75 FENCER Swordsman
76 FENDER Metal guard on automobile
77 FENESTRATED Windowed
78 FENNEC Variety of animal
79 FERMATA Musical notation symbol
80 FERMIUM Element; atomic number 100
81 FERN Variety of plant
82 FERRET Variety of animal
83 FERRIS WHEEL Large fairground wheel
84 FERRULE Metal retaining band
85 FESSE Heraldic device
86 FETISH Idol
87 FETLOCK Part of horse's leg
88 FETTER Restraint for animal's feet
89 FEZ Style of hat
90 FIBONACCI NUMBERS Sequence of numbers $(1 + 1 = 2, 1 + 2 = 3, 2 + 3 = 5, 3 + 5 = 8, 5 + 8 = 13, 8 + 13 = 21$ etc.)
91 FIBULA Shin-bone
92 FICHEE Heraldic device

93 FICHU Triangular neck-cloth
94 FIDDLE Violin
95 FIDDLE-STRING String of violin
96 FIDDLEHEAD Fern frond
97 FIDDLER Violinist
98 FIDDLER-CRAB Variety of crustacean
99 FIDDLESTICK Violin bow
100 FIDDLING Playing the violin
101 FIELD Pasture
102 FIELD Plain background
103 FIELD-GLASSES Binoculars
104 FIELD-MOUSE Variety of small rodent
105 FIELDFARE Variety of bird
106 FIFE Small flute
107 FIFER Fife player
108 FIFTEEN Five more than ten
109 FIFTEEN Roman numeral for 15
110 FIFTY Five times ten
111 FIFTY Roman numeral for 50
112 FIG Variety of fruit
113 FIG LEAF Leaf of the fig
114 FIGBIRD Variety of bird
115 FIGHTER Type of military aircraft
116 FIGHTER Boxer
117 FIGURATIVE Representational art
118 FIGURE Human body
119 FIGURE Numeral
120 FIGURE-OF-EIGHT Variety of butterfly (wings shown are)
121 FIGURE-OF-EIGHT Type of knot
122 FIGURINE Statuette
123 FIJI Flag of South Pacific island group
124 FILBERT Type of paintbrush
125 FILE Cutting and smoothing tool
126 FILE Row
127 FILE FISH Variety of fish
128 FILLET Narrow headband
129 FILLING That which fills
130 FILM Light sensitive photographic material
131 FILTER-TIP Cigarette with filter
132 FIN Fish's flat swimming organ

Parts of a Fish

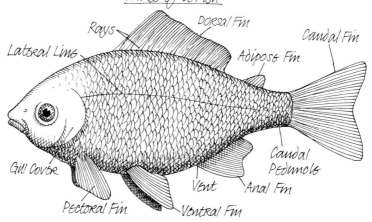

Rays
Lateral Line
Dorsal Fin
Adipose Fin
Caudal Fin
Caudal Peduncle
Gill Cover
Pectoral Fin
Vent
Ventral Fin
Anal Fin

133 FINE Clement weather
134 FINERY Elaborate clothes and jewels
135 FINGER Digit on hand
136 FINGER-GUARD Protective cup on sword

137 FINGER-HOLE Stop on wind instrument
138 FINGER-POST Signpost
139 FINGER-STALL Protective sheath for finger
140 FINGERTIP End of finger
141 FINGERBOARD Part of stringed instrument
142 FINGERING Use of fingers in playing an instrument
143 FINGERNAIL Horny growth at end of finger
144 FINIAL Ornament at apex of gable
145 FINLAND Flag of Scandinavian republic
146 FIPPLE FLUTE Type of flute; flageolet
147 FIR Variety of tree
148 FIRE Burning
149 FIRE-ALARM Audible warning signal of fire
150 FIRE-EATER Entertainer who swallows fire
151 FIRE-ENGINE Fire-fighting appliance
152 FIREWOOD Wood for fuel
153 FIREARM Gun
154 FIREDRAKE Dragon
155 FIRELOCK Musket
156 FIREMAN Fire-fighter
157 FIREWORK Pyrotechnic device
158 FIRKIN Small cask
159 FIRST Earliest in order
160 FIRST-AID Immediate medical attention
161 FIRST-QUARTER Lunar symbol
162 FISH Aquatic creature
163 FISHER Variety of animal
164 FISHERMAN Angler
165 FISHERMAN'S BEND Type of knot
166 FISHING-ROD Pole for catching fish
167 FISHMONGER Fish merchant
168 FISHNET Open-weave stocking
169 FISSIPEDAL With separated toes
170 FISSURE Crack
171 FIST Clenched hand
172 FIST Printer's symbol
173 FITCHET Ferret
174 FIVE Cardinal number between four and six
175 FIVE Roman numeral for 5
176 FIZGIG Whipping top

177 FLAG Banner signifying nationality etc.
178 FLAG-STAFF Pole for displaying flag
179 FLAGELLUM Whip
180 FLAGEOLET Type of musical instrument

181 FLAGON Vessel for serving wine
182 FLAGSTONE Paving stone
183 FLAIL Utensil for threshing corn
184 FLAME Glowing gas from burning matter
185 FLAMINGO Variety of bird
186 FLAMMIVOMOUS Fire-breathing
187 FLAN Open pie
188 FLANG Miner's pick
189 FLANK Side
190 FLAP Flexible cover over opening
191 FLARE Signal light
192 FLASHBULB Photographer's momentary light source
193 FLASHLAMP Device for firing flashbulb
194 FLASHLIGHT Electric torch
195 FLASK Small container for liquids
196 FLAT Level
197 FLATFISH Fish flat in shape
198 FLATIRON Implement for ironing clothes
199 FLATWARE Flat household items
200 FLAUNCHES Heraldic device
201 FLAUTINO Type of musical instrument; flageolet
202 FLAX Variety of plant
203 FLAYED Stripped of flesh
204 FLEA Variety of insect
205 FLEDGED Feathered
206 FLEECE Wool covering of sheep
207 FLEET Organized collection of warships
208 FLEMISH BOND Style of bricklaying
209 FLESH Surface covering of body
210 FLETCHED Fitted with feathers
211 FLEUR-DE-LIS Heraldic device
212 FLEURETTY Heraldic device
213 FLEURON Flower-shaped ornament
214 FLEWS Hanging chaps of dog
215 FLEX Electric cable
216 FLIGHT Passage through the air
217 FLIGHT Feathers on arrow
218 FLIGHT Series of stairs
219 FLINT Stone used to produce sparks
220 FLINT-LOCK Flint ignited musket
221 FLIPPER Swim-fin
222 FLOAT Small buoy on fishing line
223 FLOAT Buoyant undercarriage
224 FLOATING Buoyant
225 FLOCK Group of sheep
226 FLOE Sheet of floating ice
227 FLOODLIGHT Powerful electric lamp
228 FLOOR Level base of room
229 FLOORED Knocked to the ground
230 FLORA Plants
231 FLORIN Two shillings
232 FLORY Heraldic device
233 FLOUNDER Variety of fish
234 FLOWING Smoothly moving
235 FLOWER Coloured head of plant
236 FLOWERPOT Container for flowering plant
237 FLUID Liquid
238 FLUID OUNCE Apothecaries' symbol
239 FLUID DRAM Apothecaries' symbol
240 FLUKE Tale fin of whale
241 FLUNKEY Liveried servant
242 FLUORINE Element; atomic number 9
243 FLUTE Type of musical instrument
244 FLUTE Vertical groove on column
245 FLY Variety of flying insect

F

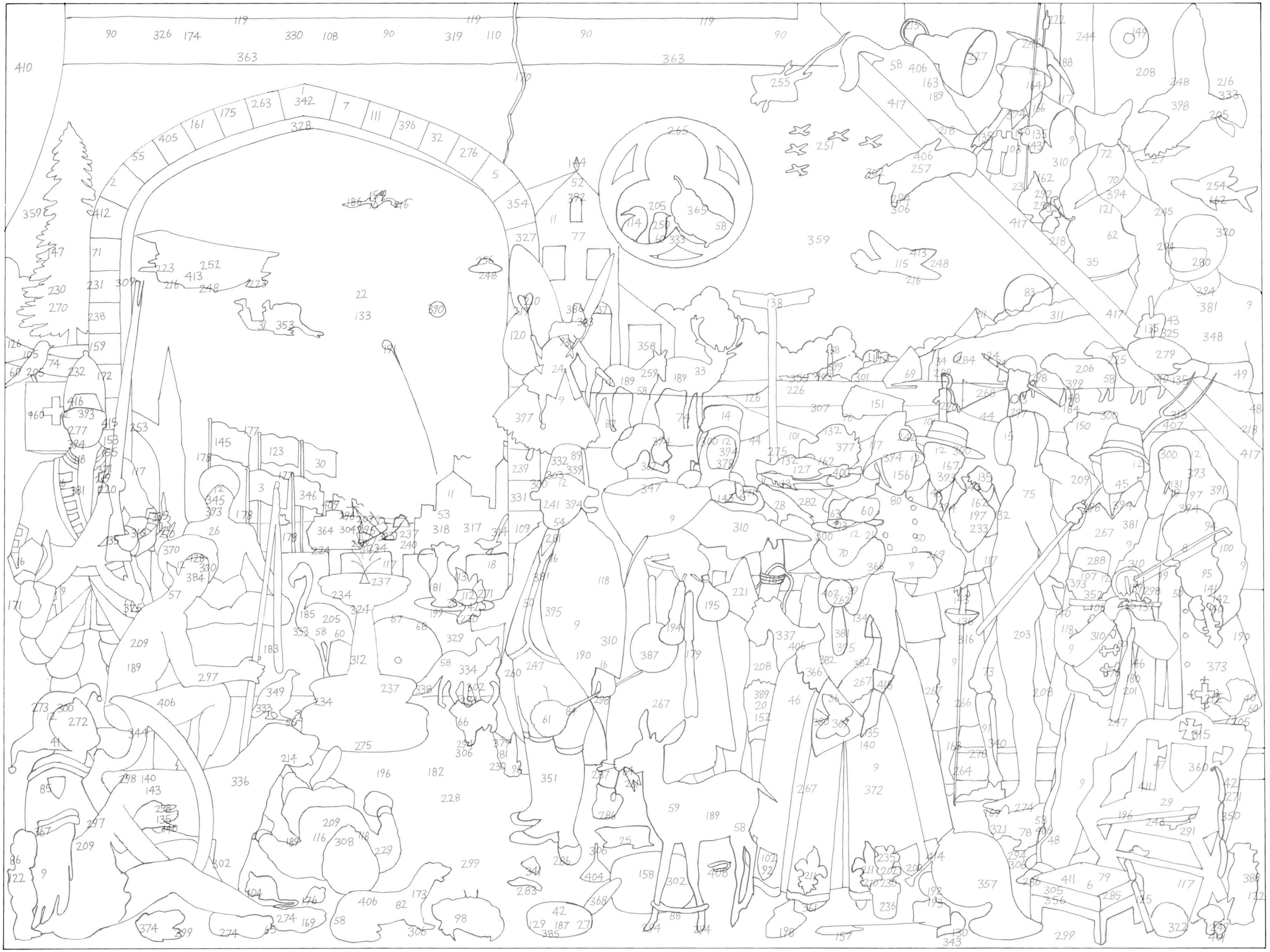

Parts of a Flag

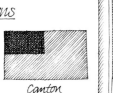

Upper Hoist   Upper Fly

Lower Hoist   Lower Fly

Basic Flag Designs

  Border

  Canton

Cross

Greek Cross

  Quarterly

  Saltire

Scandinavian Cross

Serration

Triangle

Tricolour

246 FLY Fishing lure
247 FLY Opening at front of trousers
248 FLY Sustained passage through the air
249 FLY-AGARIC Variety of fungus
250 FLY-CATCHER Variety of bird
251 FLY-PAST Formal aircraft display
252 FLYING BOAT Aircraft that lands and takes off from water
253 FLYING BUTTRESS Type of wall support
254 FLYING FISH Variety of fish
255 FLYING LIZARD Variety of reptile
256 FLYING SAUCER Unidentified flying object
257 FLYING SQUIRREL Variety of animal
258 FO'C'SLE Forward part of ship (forecastle)
259 FOAL Young horse
260 FOB-CHAIN Watch-chain
261 FODDER Animal foodstuff
262 FOETUS Embryo
263 FOG Meteorological symbol
264 FOIBLE Sword blade from middle to point
265 FOIL Arc between cusps

Foils

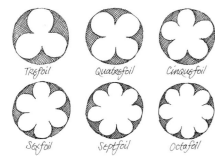

Trefoil   Quatrefoil   Cinquefoil

Sexfoil   Septfoil   Octafoil

266 FOIL Light fencing sword
267 FOLD Crease
268 FOLD Sheep pen

269 FOLDED Crossed arms
270 FOLIAGE Leaves of plant
271 FOOD Solid nutriment
272 FOOL Jester
273 FOOL'S-CAP Jester's hat
274 FOOT Lower bodily extremity
275 FOOT Base
276 FOOT Twelve inches
277 FOOT SOLDIER Infantryman
278 FOOT-RAIL Bar for supporting the feet
279 FOOTBALL Inflated leather ball
280 FOOTBALLER Football player
281 FOOTMAN Liveried servant
282 FOOTPATH Pedestrian pathway
283 FOOTPRINT Mark made by foot
284 FOOTRILL Tunnel entrance
285 FOOTSTOOL Low stool for the feet
286 FOOTWEAR Shoes, boots etc
287 FORAGE Animal foodstuff
288 FORAGE-CAP Type of military cap
289 FORCE Waterfall
290 FORCE-PUMP Hand-operated water pump
291 FORCEPS Small medical pincers
292 FORCEPS-FISH Variety of fish
293 FORCIPIGER Variety of fish; forceps fish
294 FOREFOOT Front foot of animal
295 FORESTAY Stay on foremast
296 FORETOP Platform on foremast
297 FOREARM Arm betwen elbow and hand
298 FOREFINGER Finger next to thumb
299 FOREGROUND Scene nearest to viewer
300 FOREHEAD Area of face between hairline and eyes
301 FORELAND Promontory
302 FORELEG Animal's front leg
303 FORELOCK Lock of hair above forehead
304 FOREMAST Mast nearest bows
305 FORENAME First name
306 FOREPAW Animal's front paw
307 FORESHORE Shore between high and low water mark

308 FORESHORTEN Appearance shortened by perspective
309 FORESIGHT Front gun sight
310 FORESLEEVE Part of sleeve nearest hand
311 FOREST Extensive tree covered area
312 FORFEX Scissors
313 FORK Pronged utensil
314 FORKTAIL Variety of bird
315 FORMY Heraldic device
316 FORTE Upper part of sword blade
317 FORTIFICATIONS Defensive works
318 FORTRESS Stronghold
319 FORTY Four times ten
320 FORTY Roman numeral for 40
321 FOSSA Variety of animal
322 FOSSIL Preserved remains of organism
323 FOUNDER Sink
324 FOUNTAIN Ornamental structure which spouts water
325 FOUNTAIN-PEN Refillable pen incorporating ink reservoir
326 FOUR Cardinal number between three and five
327 FOUR Roman numeral for 4
328 FOUR-CENTRED ARCH Style of arch
329 FOURSCORE Eighty
330 FOURTEEN Four more than ten
331 FOURTEEN Roman numeral for 14
332 FOURTH A quarter
333 FOWL Bird
334 FOX Variety of animal
335 FOXGLOVE Variety of plant
336 FOXHOUND Breed of dog
337 FOXTERRIER Breed of dog
338 FOXTAIL Tail of fox
339 FRACTION Numerical quantity less than one
340 FRACTURE Break in a bone
341 FRAGMENT Part broken off
342 FRAKTUR Style of letterform
343 FRAME Single portion of photographic film
344 FRAME HARP Type of musical instrument
345 FRAMES Retaining structure for lenses
346 FRANCE Flag of West European republic
347 FRANCISCAN Friar of the Order of St Francis
348 FRANCIUM Element; atomic number 87
349 FRANCOLIN Variety of bird
350 FRANKFURTER Type of sausage
351 FREAK Person with abnormal appearance
352 FRECKLE Small brownish skin spot
353 FREE-FALL Fall before opening of parachute
354 FREEZING RAIN Meteorological symbol
355 FREIGHTER Cargo ship
356 FRENCH Language spoken in France
357 FRENCH-HORN Type of musical instrument
358 FRENCH-WINDOW Glazed door
359 FRESCO Mural painted on to plaster
360 FRET Heraldic device
361 FRET Style of ornamentation
362 FRIAR Monk
363 FRIEZE Ornamental band just below ceiling
364 FRIGATE Type of warship
365 FRIGATE-BIRD Variety of sea-bird
366 FRILL Ornamental flounced edging
367 FRINGE Ornamental edging of hanging threads
368 FRISBEE Plastic throwing disc
369 FRITILLARY Variety of butterfly
370 FRIZZ Unmanageable mass of curls

371 FRIZZLE Striking steel of musket
372 FROCK Woman's long outer garment
373 FROCK-COAT Knee-length man's coat
374 FROG Variety of amphibian
375 FROG Sword support
376 FROG Ornamental loop on garment
377 FROG-FISH Variety of fish
378 FROGMAN Skin diver
379 FROND Fern leaf
380 FRONS Space between insect's eyes
381 FRONT Foremost part
382 FRONT Meteorological symbol
383 FRONTLET Forehead ornament
384 FROWN Disapproving expression
385 FRUIT Sweet seedcase of plant
386 FRUSTUM Truncated cone
387 FRYING-PAN Shallow cooking utensil
388 FU HSING Chinese Star God of Happiness
389 FUEL Combustible material
390 FULL MOON Moon with whole disc illuminated
391 FULL-BOTTOM WIG Wig with large bottom
392 FULL-CENTRE ARCH Semicircular arch
393 FULL-FACED Face turned fully towards spectator
394 FULL-GROWN Mature; adult
395 FULL-LENGTH Showing whole figure
396 FULL-MOON Astrological symbol
397 FULL-SKIRT Large flowing skirt
398 FULMAR Variety of sea-bird
399 FUME Pungent vapour or smoke
400 FUNDULUS Variety of fish
401 FUNGUS Variety of plant
402 FUNICULUS Umbilical cord
403 FUNNEL Smoke-stack
404 FUNNEL Utensil for directing poured liquid
405 FUNNEL CLOUDS Meteorological symbol
406 FUR Soft, close animal hair
407 FURCATION Division into a fork
408 FURCULA Wish-bone
409 FURL Roll up and bind
410 FURNISHING Domestic fittings
411 FURNITURE Household equipment
412 FUSE Electrical symbol for fuse
413 FUSELAGE Main body of aircraft
414 FUSIL Heraldic device
415 FUSIL Light musket
416 FUSILIER Soldier armed with fusil
417 FUTHORC Runic alphabet
418 FYLFOT Swastika

G

1 G Seventh letter of the alphabet
2 G Braille alphabet
3 G Guitar chord
4 G International signal flag
5 G Manual alphabet – Anglo/Australian system
6 G Manual alphabet – American system
7 G Morse code alphabet
8 G Musical notation
9 G Semaphore alphabet
10 G-STRING Guitar string tuned to G
11 G-STRING Woman's brief lower undergarment
12 GABLE Triangular part of end wall beneath ridged roof
13 GABLE-END End wall surmounted by gable
14 GABON Flag of West African republic
15 GADOLINIUM Element; atomic number 64
16 GADROON Type of ornamentation
17 GAG Mouth covering
18 GAGGLE Group of geese
19 GAITER Lower leg covering
20 GALAGO Variety of animal; bush-baby
21 GALAH Variety of bird
22 GALAPAGOS PENGUIN Variety of penguin
23 GALAXIAS Variety of fish
24 GALEATED Helmeted
25 GALEENY Variety of bird; guinea fowl
26 GALIMATIAS Gibberish; nonsense
27 GALLEON Large sailing ship
28 GALLITO Variety of bird
29 GALLIUM Element; atomic number 31
30 GALLOWS Scaffold
31 GALOSH Rubber overshoe
32 GAMBIA Flag of West African republic
33 GAME-BIRD Bird shot for sport
34 GAMMA Third letter of Greek Alphabet
35 GAMP Large umbrella
36 GANDER Male goose
37 GANESHA Elephant-headed Hindu god
38 GANNET Variety of sea-bird
39 GAP Space
40 GAPE Yawn
41 GAR-PIKE Variety of fish
42 GARB Wheat-sheaf
43 GARB Clothing
44 GARGOYLE Grotesquely carved rain spout
45 GARLAND Wreath
46 GARLIC Variety of vegetable
47 GARMENT Article of clothing
48 GARTER Support for stocking
49 GAS-BAG Gas envelope of blimp
50 GAS-MASK Respirator
51 GASKET Rope binding furled sail to yard
52 GASKIN Horse's hind thigh
53 GASTROCNEMIUS Calf muscle

Gastropod

Eyes · Shell · Mantle · Tentacles · Foot

54 GASTROPOD Mollusc
55 GATE Hinged barrier
56 GATEPOST Post supporting gate
57 GAUDY Brilliantly coloured
58 GAUNTLET Long glove
59 GAVEL Chairperson's mallet
60 GAZELLE Variety of antelope
61 GEAR-WHEEL Toothed wheel
62 GECKO Variety of lizard
63 GEESE Plural of goose
64 GEISHA Japanese hostess
65 GEMINI Astrological symbol; the twins
66 GEMSBOK Variety of antelope
67 GENDER Sex
68 GENET Variety of animal
69 GENEVA BANDS Style of neck-cloth
70 GENITALS Reproductive organs
71 GENOUILLÈRE Armour covering the knee
72 GENTILE Non-Jew
73 GENTLEMAN Adult male
74 GEOMETRIC Regular; symmetrical
75 GEOSAURUS Variety of extinct crocodile-like animal
76 GERBIL Variety of animal
77 GERMAN SHEPHERD Breed of dog
78 GERMANIUM Element; atomic number 32
79 GERMANY Flag of East European country (East Germany)
80 GERMANY Flag of West European country (West Germany)
81 GERMINATION Sprouting
82 GESTURE Expressive movement of body
83 GET-UP Costume
84 GHANA Flag of West African republic
85 GHARIAL Variety of crocodile-like animal
86 GHOST Spirit of dead person
87 GIBBERISH Nonsense words
88 GIBBET Gallows
89 GIBBON Variety of ape
90 GIBRALTAR Flag of southern European British colony
91 GIGAKU MASK Type of Japanese theatrical mask
92 GIGANTURA Variety of fish
93 GILA MONSTER Variety of venomous lizard
94 GILL Breathing organ of fish
95 GIMBALS Suspension rings for gyroscope
96 GIMEL Third letter of the Hebrew alphabet
97 GIMLET Boring tool
98 GIPON Tunic
99 GIPSER Pouch suspended from belt
100 GIPSY Romany
101 GIRAFFE Variety of animal
102 GIRDLE Belt

103 GIRDLE Band around column
104 GIRDLE TIE Type of ancient Egyptian amulet
105 GIRL Young female
106 GIRTH Band securing saddle to horse
107 GITTERN Type of stringed musical instrument
108 GLABELLA Space between the eyebrows
109 GLABRATE Bald
110 GLADIATOR Ancient Roman public fighter
111 GLADIUS Variety of fish; sword fish
112 GLAIVE Broadsword
113 GLAND Secretory organ
114 GLAND Acorn
115 GLASSES Spectacles
116 GLEEMAN Minstrel
117 GLENGARRY Style of Scots highland cap
118 GLIDER Variety of animal
119 GLINT Gleam
120 GLOBE Spherical model of the Earth
121 GLOCKENSPIEL Type of musical instrument
122 GLORIOLE Halo
123 GLOVE Covering for the hand
124 GLUTTON Variety of animal; wolverine
125 GLYPH Sculpted symbol
126 GLYPTODON Variety of extinct armadillo-like animal
127 GNAT Variety of flying insect
128 GNOMON Pin of sundial
129 GNOMON Type of geometric figure
130 GNU Variety of antelope; wildebeest
131 GO-AWAY BIRD Variety of bird
132 GOAT Variety of animal
133 GOATEE Style of beard
134 GOBBLEDEGOOK Nonsense words
135 GOBLET Drinking vessel
136 GOBLIN Mischievous supernatural being
137 GOBY Variety of fish
138 GOD Supernatural being worshipped by men
139 GOLD Chemical symbol (Au)
140 GOLD Element; atomic number 79
141 GOLD Bull on archery target
142 GOLDEN EAGLE Variety of bird of prey
143 GOLDEN ORIOLE Variety of bird
144 GOLDEN SECTION Area proportionally divided
145 GOLDFINCH Variety of bird
146 GOLF-BALL Ball used in game of golf
147 GOLF-CLUB Club used in game of golf
148 GOLFER Player of golf
149 GOLLYWOG Black-faced doll
150 GONDOLA Venetian canal-boat
151 GONDOLA Car of airship
152 GONFALON Hanging banner
153 GONFANON Small pennon
154 GONG Type of musical instrument
155 GOOBER Peanut
156 GOOSE Variety of bird
157 GOPHER Variety of animal
158 GORAL Variety of antelope
159 GORDIAN KNOT Classical complicated knot
160 GORGE Throat
161 GORGET Armour protecting throat
162 GORGIO Non-gypsy
163 GORGON Mythical snake-haired creature
164 GORILLA Variety of large ape
165 GOSHAWK Variety of bird of prey
166 GOSLING Young goose
167 GOUGE Curved chisel
168 GOWN Loose full-length garment

169 GOY Gentile
170 GRACES Ancient Greek goddesses of fertility
171 GRADATORY Flight of steps
172 GRADIENT Slope
173 GRAIN Fibre pattern in wood
174 GRANDFATHER CLOCK Long-case clock
175 GRANNY'S KNOT Type of knot
176 GRAPE Fruit of the vine
177 GRAPHITO Scrawling on wall
178 GRASP Clutch
179 GRASS Variety of plant
180 GRASSHOPPER Variety of insect
181 GRATING Perforated cover over drain
182 GRAVE Burial place
183 GRAVEN Carved; sculpted
184 GRAVER Engraver's tool; burin
185 GRAVESTONE Grave marker
186 GRAVEYARD Burial-ground
187 GRAVY-BOAT Container for sauces
188 GREAT DANE Breed of dog
189 GREATCOAT Military overcoat
190 GREAVE Armour protecting lower leg
191 GREBE Variety of bird
192 GREECE Flag of southern European republic
193 GRECQUE Style of ornamentation
194 GREEK Belonging to Greece

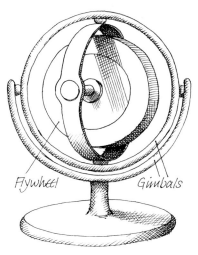

The Greek Alphabet

Α Β Γ Δ Ε Ζ Η Θ
Alpha Beta Gamma Delta Epsilon Zeta Eta Theta

Ι Κ Λ Μ Ν Ξ Ο Π
Iota Kappa Lambda Mu Nu Xi Omicron Pi

Ρ Σ Τ Υ Φ Χ Ψ Ω
Rho Sigma Tau Upsilon Phi Chi Psi Omega

195 GREEN Colour between yellow and blue
196 GREENERY Green vegetation
197 GREENFINCH Variety of bird
198 GREENLAND Large Arctic island
199 GRENADA Flag of Caribbean country
200 GRENADE Small hand-thrown bomb
201 GREY Colour between black and white
202 GREYHOUND Breed of dog
203 GRID Grating
204 GRIFFIN Type of mythological beast
205 GRIN Smile
206 GRIP Handle
207 GRISON Variety of animal
208 GRIZZLY BEAR Variety of large bear
209 GROIN Point where legs meet abdomen
210 GROOVE Channel
211 GROSBEAK Variety of bird
212 GROSS 144

213 GROTESQUE Bizarre; fantastic
214 GROTESQUE Style of letterform
215 GROUND Surface of land; floor
216 GROUND ROLLER Variety of bird
217 GROUND-HOG Variety of animal; marmot
218 GROUNDNUT Peanut
219 GROUPER Variety of fish
220 GROUSE Variety of bird
221 GROWN-UP Adult
222 GRUB Insect larva
223 GUAN Variety of bird
224 GUANACO Variety of llama-like animal
225 GUANO Bird's droppings
226 GUARA Variety of bird; scarlet ibis
227 GUARDSMAN Soldier in the Brigade of Guards
228 GUATEMALA Flag of Central American republic
229 GUGLIO Obelisk
230 GUIDE-DOG Seeing-eye dog
231 GUIDON Swallow-tailed cavalry standard
232 GUILLEMOT Variety of sea-bird
233 GUILLOCHE Style of ornamentation
234 GUILLOTINE Device for beheading people
235 GUINEA One pound and one shilling
236 GUINEA Flag of West African republic
237 GUINEA-FOWL Variety of bird
238 GUINEA-PIG Variety of small animal

239 GUITAR Type of musical instrument
240 GUITARIST Guitar player
241 GULL Variety of sea-bird
242 GUM-BOOT Tall waterproof boot
243 GUMS Flesh around the teeth
244 GUN Fire-arm
245 GUN-BARREL Tubular part of gun
246 GUN-DECK Deck of ship containing cannon
247 GUN-PORT Holes through which cannon fire
248 GUN-STOCK Wooden part of gun supporting barrel
249 GUNWALE Upper part of ship's side
250 GUPPY Variety of fish
251 GURNARD Variety of fish
252 GUSLA Variety of musical instrument
253 GUTTER Water channel
254 GUTTIFORM Drop-shaped
255 GUYANA Flag of South American republic

256 GYMNAST Person skilled in physical exercise
257 GYRON Heraldic device
258 GYRONNY Heraldic device
259 GYROSCOPE Freely rotating spinning wheel

Gyroscope

Flywheel · Gimbals

H

1 H Eighth letter of the alphabet
2 H Braille alphabet
3 H International signal flag
4 H Manual alphabet – American system
5 H Morse code alphabet
6 H Semaphore alphabet
7 HABILIMENT Clothing
8 HABIT Monk's garment
9 HABITACLE Dwelling-place
10 HABITATION Dwelling-place
11 HACKBUT Early type of gun; harquebus
12 HACKLE Neck feathers of chicken
13 HACKLE Top of haystack
14 HACKSAW Saw for cutting metal
15 HADDOCK Variety of fish
16 HAEMORRHAGE Escape of blood
17 HAFNIUM Element; atomic number 72
18 HAFT Hilt; handle
19 HAIL Meteorological symbol
20 HAIR Growth on human head
21 HAIRDRYER Machine for drying the hair
22 HAIRLINE Limit of hair growth
23 HAIRBRUSH Utensil for brushing the hair
24 HAITI Flag of Caribbean republic
25 HAKE Variety of fish
26 HALBERD Long-handled battle-axe
27 HALBERDIER Soldier armed with halberd
28 HALF Fraction expressing 50 per cent
29 HALF-BEAK Variety of fish
30 HALF-BINDING Type of book-binding
31 HALF-BOOT Boot reaching half-way to knee
32 HALF-CROWN Two shillings and sixpence (Imperial currency)
33 HALF-DOZEN Six
34 HALF-FACE Profile
35 HALF-HITCH Type of knot
36 HALF-TIMBERED Infilled timber-frame building
37 HALIBUT Variety of fish
38 HALLUX The big toe
39 HALO Aura of light
40 HALTER Leash
41 HAMBURGER Type of foodstuff
42 HAMES Horse collar
43 HAMILTONSTOVARE Breed of dog
44 HAMMER Striking tool
45 HAMMERHEAD Metal head of hammer
46 HAMMERHEAD Variety of bird
47 HAMMERHEAD SHARK Variety of large fish
48 HAMPER Large lidded basket
49 HAMSTER Variety of animal
50 HAMSTRING Tendon behind horse's hock
51 HAND End of arm with fingers and thumb
52 HAND HORN Hand-held horn
53 HAND-AXE Axe wielded with one hand

54 HAND-RAIL Rail for the hands
55 HAND-SAW Hand-operated saw
56 HANDBELL Small hand-operated bell
57 HANDCUFFS manacles
58 HANDGRIP Grip for the hand
59 HANDGUN Pistol
60 HANDKERCHIEF Square of fabric for wiping nose
61 HANDLE Part of object to be grasped by hand
62 HANDLEBAR Style of large moustache
63 HANDLESS Without hands
64 HANDPRINT Mark left by hand
65 HANDWRITING Writing executed by hand
66 HANGING Suspended
67 HANGTAG Tag attached by string
68 HANSOM CAB Light two-wheeled carriage
69 HARE Variety of animal
70 HARE-LIP Split upper lip
71 HARLEQUIN Pantomime character
72 HARLEQUIN-BEETLE Variety of insect
73 HARMONICA Variety of musical instrument; mouth organ
74 HARNESS Horse's straps and trappings
75 HARP Type of musical instrument
76 HARP-SEAL Variety of aquatic mammal
77 HARPIST Harp player
78 HARPOON Barbed spear for catching fish
79 HARPY Mythological creature
80 HARPY-EAGLE Variety of bird of prey
81 HARQUEBUS Early type of gun
82 HARQUEBUSIER Person armed with harquebus
83 HARRIER Breed of dog
84 HART Adult male deer
85 HARTEBEEST Variety of antelope
86 HARVEST MOUSE Variety of rodent
87 HASP Hinged fastening for lid
88 HAT Covering for the head
89 HATBAND Decorative band around crown of hat
90 HATCH Trapdoor
91 HATCHET Light axe
92 HATLESS Without a hat
93 HATTED Wearing a hat
94 HATTER Maker of hats (this one comes from Wonderland)
95 HAUBERK Coat of chain-mail
96 HAULING Pulling
97 HAUNCH Hind quarters
98 HAURIENT Heraldic device
99 HAVELOCK Type of hat covering
100 HAVERSACK Canvas shoulder-bag
101 HAWAIIAN Native of Hawaii
102 HAWK Variety of bird of prey
103 HAWK-MOTH Variety of moth
104 HAY Dried grass
105 HAYSTACK Stack of hay
106 HAZE Meteorological symbol
107 HE Fifth letter of Hebrew alphabet
108 HEAD Topmost part of body
109 HEAD Cutting part of a tool
110 HEADBAND Band worn around head
111 HEAD-DRESS Covering for the head
112 HEADGEAR Covering for the head
113 HEAD-ON Viewed directly
114 HEADPHONES Small loudspeakers fitted to head
115 HEADPIECE Covering for the head

116 HEADLESS Without a head
117 HEAP Pile
118 HEARING AID Small electric amplifier
119 HEART Symbol of suit of playing cards
120 HEAVEN The sky
121 HEBREW Jewish language

The Hebrew Alphabet

א Aleph ב Beth ג Gimel ד Daleth ה He ו Waw ז Zayin ח Heth ט Teth
י Yod כ Kaph ל Lamed מ Mem נ Nun ס Samekh
ע Ayin פ Pe צ Sadhe ק Qoph ר Resh ש Sin ש Shin ת Taw

122 HEDGEHOG Variety of animal
123 HEDGE Barrier of dense shrubs
124 HEDGEROW Hedge
125 HEEL Back part of foot
126 HEEL Raised part at rear of shoe
127 HEEL-PLATE Plate on butt-end of gun
128 HELICIFORM Spiral
129 HELICON Type of musical instrument
130 HELICOPTER Rotary-winged aircraft
131 HELIOGRAPH Signalling device using sun's rays
132 HELIOGRAPHER Heliograph signaller
133 HELIUM Element; atomic number 2
134 HELIX Spiral
135 HELMET Armour protecting head
136 HELTER-SKELTER Fairground tower with chute
137 HELVE Axe handle
138 HEM Double-back edge of cloth
139 HEMICYCLE Half circle
140 HEMIDEMISEMIQUAVER Sixty-fourth note
141 HEMIOCTAHEDRON Geometric solid figure; tetrahedron
142 HEMIRHAMPHINE Short upper-jawed
143 HEMISPHERE Half a sphere
144 HEN Adult female chicken
145 HENDECAGON Eleven-sided polygon
146 HEPTAGON Seven-sided polygon
147 HERALD Medieval official
148 HERALDRY Heraldic devices
149 HERBIVORE Plant-eating animal
150 HERMAPHRODITE Person with both male and female sexual characteristics
151 HERMIT Religious recluse
152 HERMIT-CRAB Variety of crustacean
153 HERON Variety of bird
154 HERRING Variety of fish
155 HERRINGBONE Pattern of chevrons
156 HERSE Heraldic device
157 HESSIAN BOOT Style of boot
158 HETEROCHIRAL Mirror-image hands; normal hands
159 HETEROGRAPHY Wrong spelling

160 HETEROSOMATOUS Fish deviating from normal body type
161 HETH Eighth letter of the Hebrew alphabet
162 HEXADACTYLOUS Having six fingers
163 HEXAGON Six-sided polygon
164 HEXAGRAM Six-sided star
165 HEXAPOD Having six feet
166 HIDE Animal's skin
167 HIGHLAND FLING Type of Scottish dance
168 HIGHLANDER Scotsman from the Highlands
169 HIGHLIGHT Light reflected on shiny object
170 HILL Elevated ground
171 HILLSIDE Side of hill
172 HILLTOP Top of hill
173 HILT Sword handle
174 HIND Adult female deer
175 HIND Posterior
176 HINDI Language of Northern India
177 HINDSIGHT Rear sight on gun
178 HINDU Aryan non-Muslim of Northern India
179 HINGE Moveable joint

180 HIP Projecting part of middle of body
181 HIPPOPOTAMUS Variety of large animal
182 HIRELING Person who plies for hire
183 HIRSUTE Hairy
184 HIVE Place where bees are kept
185 HOAR Grey-haired
186 HOATZIN Variety of bird
187 HOAX Jokey deception (this creature does not exist)
188 HOB Mythological being; puck
189 HOBBLE Fetter
190 HOBBY Variety of bird of prey
191 HOBBY-HORSE Type of children's toy
192 HOCK Joint in animal's hind leg
193 HOCKEY-STICK Stick used in game of hockey
194 HOE Type of gardening utensil
195 HOG Pig
196 HOGAN Type of North American Indian dwelling
197 HOIST Part of flag nearest staff
198 HOLD Grasp
199 HOLE Cavity
200 HOLLAND Flag of the Netherlands
201 HOLLOW-WARE Hollow vessels
202 HOLMIUM Element; atomic number 67
203 HOLSTER Container for pistol
204 HOLY Saintly
205 HOMBURG Style of hat
206 HOMINID Family of man
207 HOMO SAPIENS Human being
208 HOMOCENTRIC Concentric
209 HOMOCHIRAL Two right hands or two left hands
210 HOMONCULUS Very small man
211 HONDURAS Flag of Central American republic
212 HONG KONG Flag of British Asian colony
213 HOOD Cowl
214 HOODED SEAL Variety of aquatic mammal

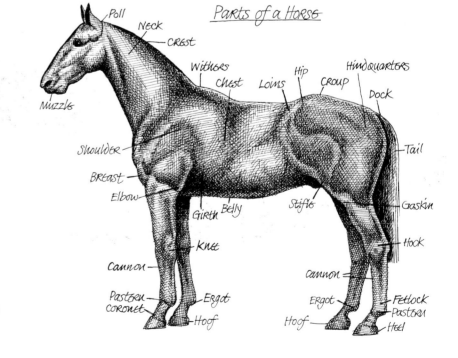
Parts of a Horse

Poll, Neck, Crest, Withers, Hip, Hindquarters, Croup, Dock, Loins, Chest, Muzzle, Shoulder, Breast, Elbow, Girth, Belly, Stifle, Gaskin, Tail, Knee, Hock, Cannon, Pastern, Coronet, Ergot, Hoof, Fetlock, Heel

215 HOODWINK Blindfold
216 HOOF Horny sheath on foot of animal
217 HOOFLET Half of a cloven hoof
218 HOOK Curved metal hanging device
219 HOOKAH Arabian water-cooled pipe
220 HOOP Circular ring
221 HOOPER Variety of swan
222 HOOPOE Variety of bird
223 HOPLOPODOUS Hoofed
224 HORIZON Meeting-point of earth and sky
225 HORIZONTAL Parallel to the horizon
226 HORN Hard, pointed growths on animal's head
227 HORN Type of musical instrument
228 HORN-OWL Variety of bird of prey; eagle-owl
229 HORNBILL Variety of bird
230 HORNET Variety of flying insect
231 HORSE Variety of animal
232 HORSE-MACKEREL Variety of fish
233 HORSESHOE Protective metal shoe fitted to horse
234 HORSEWHIP Whip for driving horses
235 HORUS Ancient Egyptian hawk-headed god
236 HOSE Flexible water-pipe
237 HOSE Stockings
238 HOT-DOG Type of foodstuff
239 HOUDAH Litter mounted on animal's back
240 HOUND Hunting dog
241 HOUND'S-TOOTH CHECK Type of pattern
242 HOURGLASS Timing device, sand-glass
243 HOUSE Dwelling-place
244 HOWLING Uttering mournful cry
245 HOWLER-MONKEY Variety of animal
246 HU Type of Chinese vessel
247 HU-CH'IN Type of musical instrument
248 HUARACHE Type of Mexican sandal
249 HUB Central part of wheel
250 HUBBLE-BUBBLE Hookah
251 HUGE Very large
252 HULA Type of Hawaiian dance
253 HULA-SKIRT Style of Hawaiian grass skirt
254 HUMAN Member of mankind
255 HUMANOID Having human form
256 HUMMING-BIRD Variety of bird
257 HUMMING-BIRD HAWK-MOTH Variety of moth
258 HUNDRED Ten times ten
259 HUNDRED Roman numeral for 100
260 HUNDREDWEIGHT 112 pounds (abbreviation)
261 HUNGARY Flag of Eastern European country
262 HURDY-GURDY Type of musical instrument
263 HURRICANE Meteorological symbol
264 HURRICANE-LAMP Shielded oil-lamp
265 HURT Wound
266 HUSKY Breed of dog
267 HUSSAR Type of light cavalryman
268 HUTIA Variety of animal
269 HYBRID Thing derived from several sources
270 HYDRIA Ancient Greek water vessel
271 HYDROGEN Element; atomic number 1
272 HYENA Type of dog-like animal
273 HYPHEN Dash linking two parts of word
274 HYPODERMIC SYRINGE Device for injecting drugs
275 HYPOCOLY Variety of bird
276 HYPOTENUSE Longest side of right-angled triangle
277 HYRAX Variety of animal

I

1 I Ninth letter of the alphabet
2 I Braille alphabet
3 I International signal flag
4 I Manual alphabet – American system
5 I Morse code alphabet
6 I Semaphore alphabet
7 IANTHINE Violet coloured
8 IBERIAN BARBEL Variety of fish
9 IBERIAN NASE Variety of fish
10 IBEX Variety of animal
11 IBIS Variety of bird
12 IBISBILL Variety of bird
13 IBIZAN HOUND Breed of dog
14 ICE Frozen water
15 ICE HOCKEY Type of sport played on ice
16 ICE NEEDLES Meteorological symbol
17 ICE-AXE Mountaineer's ice-cutting tool
18 ICE-BOUND Hemmed in by ice
19 ICE-BREAKER Boat for clearing passage through ice
20 ICE-CREAM Frozen confection
21 ICE-FLOE Mass of floating ice
22 ICE-SKATE Metal runner attached to shoe
23 ICE-YACHT Wind-powered vehicle with runners
24 ICE-YACHTSMAN Pilot of an ice-yacht
25 ICEBLINK Glare reflected from ice on horizon
26 ICEBOAT Ice-yacht
27 ICELAND Flag of North Atlantic island republic
28 ICELAND POPPY Variety of flowering plant
29 ICHNEUMON Variety of animal; mongoose
30 ICHNEUMON Variety of insect
31 ICHTHYOMORPH Mermaid
32 ICHTHYOPHAGIST Fish-eater
33 ICHTHYOPHAGY The eating of fish
34 ICHTHYORNIS Variety of extinct bird
35 ICHTHYOSAURUS Variety of extinct fish
36 ICICLE Hanging mass of ice
37 ICING Sweet decorative coating for cakes
38 ICON Religious image
39 ICONOGRAPH Book illustration
40 ICOSAHEDRON Geometric solid figure with twenty equal faces
41 ICOSITETRAHEDRON Icosahedron
42 IDE Variety of fish
43 IDEOGRAPH Character expressing idea
44 IDES Fifteenth of March, May, July or October; or the 13th day of the other months (Roman calendar)
45 IDIOGRAPH Personal signature
46 IDIOPHONE Gong and other such instruments
47 IDOL Worshipped effigy
48 IGLOO Small hut built from ice
49 IGUANA Variety of lizard

50 IGUANODON Variety of extinct dinosaur
51 IIWI Variety of bird
52 ILIUM Upper part of the pelvis
53 ILLAQUEATED Caught in a noose
54 ILLEGIBLE Impossible to read
55 ILLUMINATION Lighting up
56 ILLUSTRATION Picture in a book
57 IMAGE Representation
58 IMAGO Mature insect
59 IMBIBER Drinker
60 IMBIBITION Drinking
61 IMBREX Overlapping tile
62 IMBRICATE Covered with scales
63 IMBRICATION Pattern with overlapping elements
64 IMMANACLED Handcuffed
65 IMMURED Imprisoned
66 IMP Mischievous sprite
67 IMPALA Variety of antelope
68 IMPALED Pierced with something pointed
69 IMPALM Held in the palm
70 IMPERIAL British standard weight or measurement
71 IMPERIAL Style of whiskers
72 IMPERIAL ANGELFISH Variety of fish
73 IMPICTURED Portrayed in picture
74 IMPLEMENT Tool
75 IMPOST Block on which arch rests
76 IMPRINT Mark made by pressure
77 IMPRISONMENT Being locked in prison
78 IMPUBERAL Immature
79 INACCURATE Not accurate (study the ruler closely)
80 INAURATE Gilded
81 INBOND Style of bricklaying
82 INCARCERATION Imprisonment
83 INCARVED Engraved
84 INCATENATION Enchained
85 INCENSE Fragrant smoke
86 INCENSORY Censor
87 INCH One-twelfth of a foot
88 INCH Symbol for an inch
89 INCISED Engraved
90 INCISION Cut
91 INCISOR Front cutting tooth
92 INCISURE Notch; cleft
93 INCLINE Slope
94 INCORONATE Wearing a crown
95 INCORRECT Not accurate
96 INCROTCHET Enclosed within brackets
97 INDENTATION Further from margin than rest of paragraph
98 INDEX Indication of position of contents
99 INDEX Printer's symbol
100 INDEX FINGER Finger next to thumb
101 INDIA Flag of Southern Asian republic
102 INDIAN Native of India
103 INDIAN Native North American
104 INDIAN CANE Bamboo
105 INDIAN CLUB Club used in gymnastic exercise
106 INDIAN ELEPHANT Variety of large Indian mammal
107 INDIAN HOG Variety of Indian animal; babirussa
108 INDIAN LEAF Variety of butterfly
109 INDIAN PIPE Variety of plant; corpse plant
110 INDIGO Deep blue colour

111 INDIUM Element; atomic number 49
112 INDIVIDUAL Single person
113 INDONESIA Flag of South-east Asian republic
114 INDOORS Within a building
115 INDOSTOMUS PARADOXUS Variety of fish
116 INDRI Variety of animal; lemur
117 INESCUTCHEON Heraldic device
118 INFANT Child
119 INFANTA Spanish princess
120 INFANTE Spanish prince
121 INFANTRYMAN Foot-soldier
122 INFIBULATED Fastened with a clasp
123 INFINITY Symbol for limitless quantity
124 INFIRMARY Hospital
125 INFIRMITY Disablement
126 INFLORESCENCE Flowering
127 INFULA Lappets of a bishop's mitre
128 INGESTION Eating
129 INGOT Block of precious metal
130 INGRESS Entering
131 INHUMAN Not of the human race
132 INITIAL First letter of name used as abbreviation
133 INITIAL TEACHING ALPHABET Alphabet used as teaching aid
134 INJURY Physical hurt
135 INKY CAP Variety of fungus
136 INLET Creek
137 INMATE Prisoner
138 INN Hostelry
139 INNKEEPER Host of an inn
140 INRO Small Japanese medical case worn on belt
141 INSCRIPTION Inscribed lettering
142 INSCULPTURE Carved inscription
143 INSECT Small invertebrate animal with six legs

Parts of an Insect (Beetle)

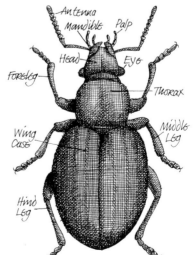

144 INSECTIVORE Animal that feeds on insects
145 INSIDE Within
146 INSIGNIA Badge

147 INSTEP Part of a shoe
148 INSTRUMENT Music-making device
149 INSTRUMENTALIST Performer on a musical instrument
150 INTAGLIO Engraving
151 INTEGER Whole number
152 INTERIOR Inside
153 INTERTIE Horizontal connecting two vertical timbers
154 INTERTWINE Twist together
155 INTERTWIST Intertwine
156 INTESTINE Alimentary canal
157 INTI Ancient Inca sun god; Apu-Punchau
158 INTOXICANT Alcoholic beverage
159 INTOXICATED Drunk
160 INTRADOS Lower curve of arch
161 INVALID Chronically ill or injured person
162 INVERNESS Style of overcoat
163 INVERSION Turning upside down
164 IODINE Element; atomic number 53
165 IONIC Style of ancient Greek architecture
166 IORA Variety of bird
167 IOTA Ninth letter of the Greek alphabet
168 IPNOPS Variety of fish
169 IRAN Flag of South-west Asian country
170 IRAQ Flag of South-west Asian country
171 IRELAND Flag of European island republic
172 IRID Iris of the eye
173 IRIDIUM Element; atomic number 77
174 IRIS Coloured part around pupil of the eye
175 IRIS Variety of flowering plant
176 IRISH HARP Type of musical instrument
177 IRISH SETTER Breed of dog
178 IRISH TERRIER Breed of dog
179 IRISH WOLFHOUND Breed of dog
180 IRON Element; atomic number 26
181 IRON Chemical symbol (Fe)
182 IRON Type of golf club
183 IRON Utensil for pressing clothes
184 IRON Manacle
185 IRON ANNIVERSARY Anniversary celebrated after six years
186 IRONCLAD Warship protected by iron plates
187 IRONER Person using an iron
188 IRONING Pressing clothes
189 IRONING BOARD Board on which clothes are pressed
190 ISATIS Type of animal; arctic fox
191 ISCHIUM Lower section of pelvis
192 ISIS Ancient Egyptian goddess
193 ISLAND Land surrounded by water
194 ISLE Island
195 ISLET Small island
196 ISOMETRIC Type of drawing projection
197 ISOSCELES Triangle with two equal sides
198 ISRAEL Flag of South-west Asian republic
199 ITALIAN LOACH Variety of fish
200 ITALIC Sloping letterform
201 ITALY Flag of European republic
202 ITEM Single article
203 IVORY Material of elephant's tusks
204 IVORY COAST Flag of West African republic
205 IVORY-BILLED WOODPECKER Variety of bird
206 IVY Variety of climbing plant

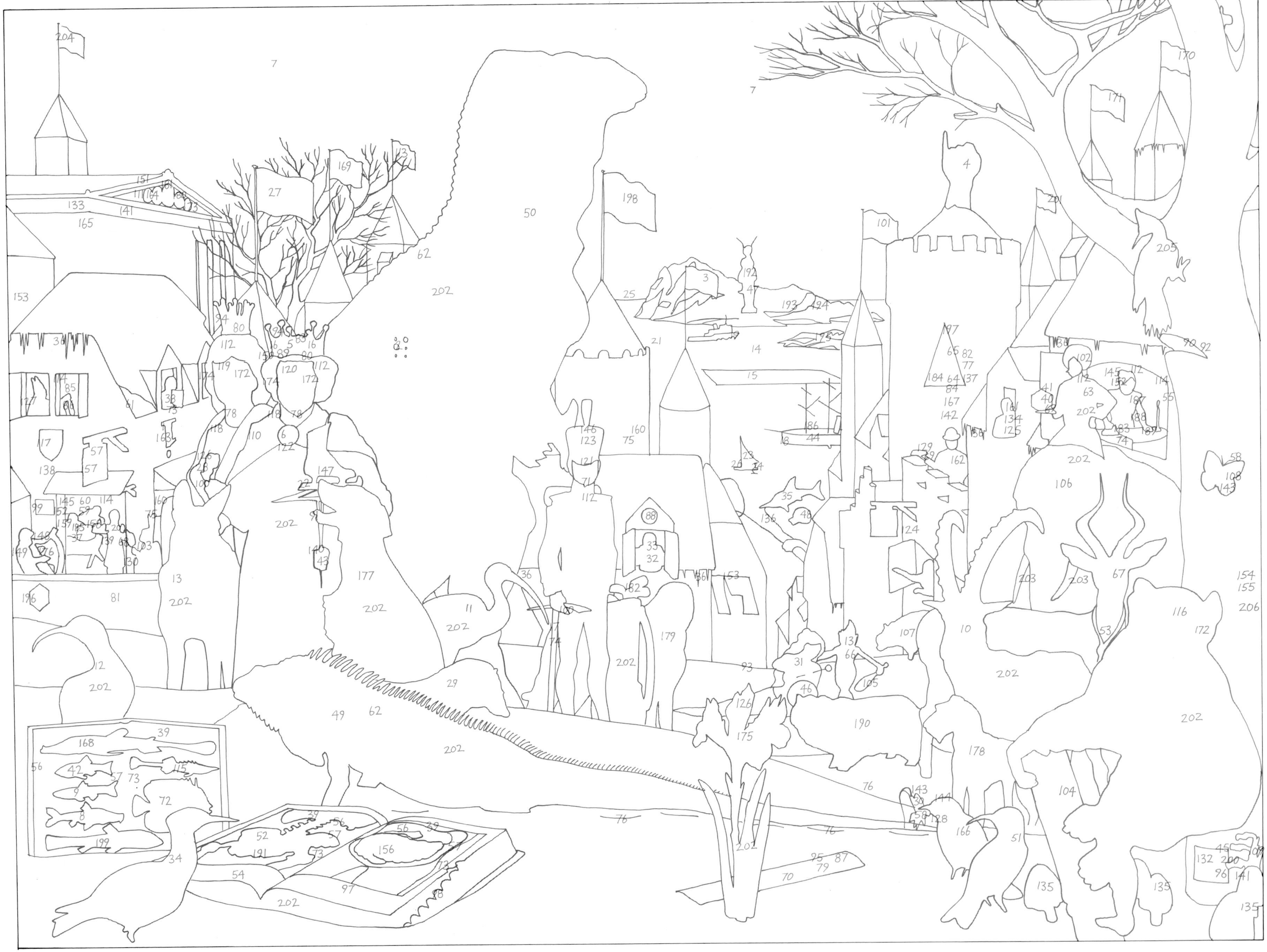

J

1 J Tenth letter of the alphabet
2 J Braille alphabet
3 J International signal flag
4 J Morse code alphabet
5 J Semaphore alphabet
6 JABIRU Variety of bird
7 JABOT Decorative frill on shirt-front
8 JACAMAR Variety of bird
9 JACANA Variety of bird
10 JACK Court playing-card
11 JACK DEMPSEY Variety of fish
12 JACK-CHAIN Chain with twisted links
13 JACK-IN-THE-BOX Type of child's toy
14 JACK-KNIFE Type of folding pocket-knife
15 JACK-LADDER Type of nautical ladder
16 JACK-O'-LANTERN Grotesque lantern made from a pumpkin
17 JACK-RABBIT Variety of animal
18 JACKAL Variety of animal
19 JACKBOOT Style of tall military boot
20 JACKDAW Variety of bird
21 JACKET Short coat
22 JACKET Book wrapper
23 JACOB SHEEP Variety of domestic animal
24 JAEGER Variety of sea-bird
25 JAG Slash in garment revealing material beneath
26 JAGGED Edge of a garment irregularly cut

27 JAGUAR Variety of animal
28 JAGUARUNDI Variety of animal
29 JAM Fruit preserve; jelly
30 JAMAICA Flag of Caribbean island country
31 JAMBEAU Armour protecting the leg
32 JANISSARY Type of Turkish soldier
33 JANUS Ancient Roman two-faced god
34 JAPAN Flag of East Asian island country
35 JAPANESE Native of Japan
36 JAPANESE CHIN Breed of dog
37 JAPANESE SPITZ Breed of dog
38 JAR Cylindrical glass container
39 JARDINIÈRE Ornamental flowerpot on a stand
40 JASPERWARE Type of unglazed stoneware pottery
41 JASTROW FIGURE Type of optical illusion (lower portion seems bigger than upper, both are same size)
42 JAVA SPARROW Variety of bird
43 JAVELIN Light throwing-spear
44 JAVELIN Variety of fish
45 JAW Mouth and lower face area
46 JAWLINE Outline of lower jaw
47 JAY Variety of bird
48 JEANS Style of denim work-trousers
49 JEEP Type of light military truck
50 JELLY Fruit preserve, jam
51 JERBOA Variety of animal; desert rat
52 JERKIN Short, close-fitting leather jacket
53 JERRYCAN Water or petrol container
54 JESS Short strap securing bird
55 JESTER Buffoon; fool
56 JESUS Founder of Christianity
57 JET Jet-propelled aircraft
58 JETSAM Things jettisoned from ship
59 JETTY Landing-stage
60 JEW Member of the Jewish race
61 JEWEL Precious stone
62 JEWEL BUTTERFLY Variety of butterfly
63 JEWELLERY Ornament set with precious stones

64 JEWISH YEAR Year reckoned by the Jewish calendar (5744 = year beginning 8 September 1983)
65 JEW'S-HARP Type of musical instrument
66 JIB Sail set between foremast and bowsprit
67 JIB Lifting arm of crane
68 JIB-STAY Stay on which the jib is set
69 JIBUTI Flag of East African country
70 JIGSAW PUZZLE Puzzle made from interlocking pieces
71 JINGLING JOHNNY Type of musical instrument
72 JOCKEY Professional racehorse rider
73 JOCKEY-CAP Cap worn by jockey
74 JOCULATOR Jester
75 JODHPURS Riding-breeches
76 JOHN BULL Personification of England
77 JOHN DORY Variety of fish
78 JOINT Joining structure of two pieces of wood
79 JOINT Drugged cigarette
80 JOKER Odd card in pack of playing cards
81 JOLLY ROGER Pirate flag
82 JONGLEUR Juggler

83 JORDAN Flag of South-west Asian country
84 JOSS-STICK Incense-stick
85 JOTTER Note-pad
86 JOUGS Iron-collared instrument of punishment
87 JOUSTING Formal horseback combat with lance
88 JOUSTER One engaged in jousting
89 JOWL Flabby flesh around jaws
90 JUDGE Legal official
91 JUG Vessel for containing liquids
92 JUGGLER Performer of tricks of manual dexterity
93 JUGGLING Tricks performed by a juggler
94 JUMBUCK A sheep
95 JUNGLE Densely overgrown tropical forest
96 JUNGLE FOWL Variety of bird
97 JUNGLE GLORY Variety of butterfly
98 JUNK Type of Chinese vessel
99 JUPITER Largest planet of the solar system
100 JUPITER Astrological symbol for Jupiter
101 JUSTICE Personification of justice
102 JUVENILE Young person

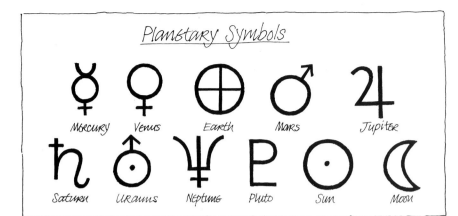

Planetary Symbols

Mercury   Venus   Earth   Mars   Jupiter
Saturn   Uranus   Neptune   Pluto   Sun   Moon

Joints

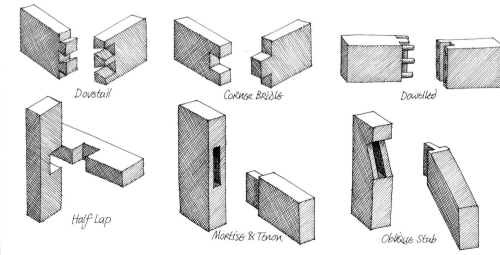

Dovetail   Corner Bridle   Dowelled

Half Lap   Mortise & Tenon   Oblique Stub

K

1 K Eleventh letter of the alphabet
2 K Braille alphabet
3 K International signal flag
4 K Manual alphabet – American system
5 K Morse code alphabet
6 K Semaphore alphabet
7 KACHINA DOLL American Indian religious figurine
8 KAFFIR CAT Variety of animal
9 KAGU Variety of bird
10 KAISER-I-HIND Variety of butterfly
11 KAKA Variety of bird
12 KAKAPO Variety of bird
13 KALLIMA Variety of butterfly
14 KAMANJA Type of musical instrument
15 KAMPUCHEA Flag of South-east Asian country; Cambodia
16 KANGAROO Variety of marsupial animal
17 KANGAROO-RAT Variety of animal
18 KANTHAROS Variety of ancient Greek vessel
19 KAPH Eleventh letter of the Hebrew alphabet
20 KAYAK Eskimo canoe
21 KEA Variety of bird
22 KEEL Projection from bottom of boat's hull
23 KEEP Central tower of castle
24 KEG Small barrel

31 KETTLEDRUM Type of musical instrument
32 KEY Device for closing and opening lock
33 KEY Lever on musical instrument
34 KEY-RING Ring to retain keys
35 KEYBOARD Set of piano keys
36 KEYHOLE Hole for admitting key into lock
37 KEYSTONE Locking stone at crown of an arch
38 KHAKI Dull yellow-brown colour
39 KHAROSTI Early North-west Indian script
40 KID Young goat
41 KILIMANJARO COLOBUS Variety of monkey
42 KILLER WHALE Variety of aquatic mammal; grampus
43 KILT Scotsman's skirt
44 KIMONO Style of Japanese robe
45 KING Male ruler of a nation
46 KING Principal chess-piece
47 KING Court playing-card
48 KING CHARLES SPANIEL Breed of dog
49 KING-FISH Variety of fish
50 KING-SALMON Variety of fish
51 KING-VULTURE Variety of bird
52 KINGCROW Variety of bird
53 KINGFISHER Variety of bird
54 KIRIBATI Flag of South Pacific island country
55 KISKADEE Variety of bird
56 KISS Affectionate touching of lips
57 KIT Variety of musical instrument
58 KITE Fabric covered flying contraption
59 KITE Variety of bird of prey
60 KITTEN Young cat
61 KITTIWAKE Variety of sea-bird
62 KIWI Variety of flightless bird
63 KLEIN BOTTLE Theoretical three-dimensional object with only one surface
64 KLIPDAS Variety of animal; Cape dassie
65 KLIPSPRINGER Variety of antelope
66 KNAPSACK Back-pack
67 KNAVE Court playing-card; Jack

Knots

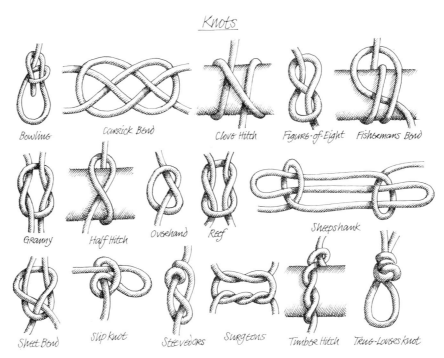

Bowline   Carrick Bend   Clove Hitch   Figure-of-Eight   Fishermans Bend

Granny   Half Hitch   Overhand   Reef   Sheepshank

Sheet Bend   Slip Knot   Stevedors   Surgeons   Timber Hitch   True-Lovers Knot

74 KNIGHT Type of chess-piece
75 KNITTING Piece of knitted work
76 KNITTING-NEEDLE Needle used to make knitting
77 KNOB Small round handle
78 KNOBKERRIE Type of African club
79 KNOT Entwined fastening made in cord
80 KNOT Cross-grained lump in timber
81 KNOT Variety of bird
82 KNUCKLE Joint of finger
83 KOALA Variety of marsupial animal
84 KOB Variety of antelope
85 KODIAK BEAR Variety of large animal
86 KOKAKO Variety of bird
87 KONGONI Variety of animal
88 KORE Ancient Greek female statue
89 KOREA Flag of East Asian country; North Korea
90 KOREA Flag of East Asian country; South Korea
91 KORI BUSTARD Variety of bird
92 KOUROS Ancient Greek male statue
93 KRATER Type of ancient Greek vessel
94 KRILL Variety of small marine crustacean
95 KRISHNA A Hindu god
96 KRYPTON Element; atomic number 36
97 KU Type of ancient Chinese vessel
98 KUANG Type of ancient Chinese vessel
99 KUDU Variety of antelope
100 KUEI Type of ancient Chinese vessel
101 KUKRI Type of Gurkha knife
102 KUSIMANSE Variety of animal
103 KUWAIT Flag of South-west Asian country
104 KYLIE Boomerang
105 KYLIX Type of ancient Greek vessel

Types of Cask

Firkin 8 gals.   Anker 8½ gals.   Keg 8–10 gals.   Barrel 10 gals.   Kilderkin 16 gals.   Hogshead 52 gals.   Butt 108 gals.   Puncheon 120 gals.

25 KENNEL Small hut for dog
26 KENYA Flag of East African republic
27 KEPI Style of military cap
28 KESTREL Variety of bird of prey
29 KETCH Type of small two-masted sailing vessel
30 KETTLE Metal vessel for boiling water

68 KNEE Joint between upper and lower leg
69 KNEE-HOLE Space beneath desk to accommodate user's legs
70 KNICKERBOCKERS Style of knee-breeches
71 KNIFE Short-bladed cutting tool
72 KNIFE-CASE Cutlery container
73 KNIGHT Armoured mounted soldier

L

1 L Twelfth letter of the alphabet
2 L Braille alphabet
3 L International signal flag
4 L Manual alphabet – American system
5 L Morse code alphabet
6 L Semaphore alphabet
7 LABEL Tag
8 LABEL Heraldic device
9 LABIATE Having lips
10 LABRADOR Breed of dog
11 LACE Ornamental openwork fabric
12 LACE Fastening thong
13 LACERATION Cut
14 LACERTILIAN Lizard
15 LACEWING Variety of insect
16 LACHRYMATION Weeping
17 LACHRYMIST Weeper
18 LACKEY Liveried manservant
19 LAD Boy
20 LADDER Climbing device
21 LADEN Burdened
22 LADLE Long-handled scoop
23 LADY Woman
24 LADY-FISH Variety of fish
25 LADYBIRD Variety of insect
26 LADYBUG Ladybird
27 LAG Barrel stave
28 LAITY Persons not in Holy Orders
29 LAKE Large body of enclosed water
30 LAMA Tibetan priest
31 LAMB Young sheep
32 LAMBDA Eleventh letter of the Greek alphabet
33 LAMBDACISM Unnecessary repetition of letter L
34 LAMBREQUIN Helmet covering
35 LAMED Twelfth letter of the Hebrew alphabet
36 LAMINA Expanded part of a leaf
37 LAMP Device for providing light
38 LAMP-POST Pillar supporting street-lamp
39 LAMPER-EEL Variety of fish; lamprey
40 LAMPLIGHT Light shed by a lamp
41 LAMPREY Variety of fish
42 LANCE Long-shafted weapon with sharp head
43 LANCE-CORPORAL Military rank between private and corporal
44 LANCER Soldier armed with a lance
45 LANCER CAP Style of military cap worn by lancer
46 LANCET-ARCH Narrow pointed arch
47 LANCET-FISH Variety of fish
48 LANCET-WINDOW Narrow pointed window
49 LAND Solid dry part of Earth's surface
50 LAND-SNAIL Variety of mollusc
51 LANDING CRAFT Amphibious military vehicle

52 LANDING-STAGE Jetty
53 LANDMARK Conspicuous feature of landscape
54 LANDRAIL Variety of bird
55 LANDSCAPE Painting representing scenery
56 LANGUAGE System of communicaton
57 LANGUR Variety of animal
58 LANIARY Canine tooth
59 LANIFEROUS Wool bearing
60 LANTERN Light chamber of lighthouse
61 LANTERN Structure on top of dome
62 LANTERN-FISH Variety of fish
63 LANTERN-LIGHT Light shed by a lantern
64 LANTHANUM Element; atomic number 57
65 LANYARD Retaining cord hung around neck
66 LAOS Flag of South-east Asian country
67 LAP Upper thighs of seated person
68 LAPEL Doubled back part of coat
69 LAPIDARY STYLE Style of letterform
70 LAPIDESCENT Becoming stone
71 LAPPET Ear lobe
72 LAPPET Variety of moth
73 LAPWING Variety of bird
74 LARBOARD Left side of ship; port
75 LARGEMOUTH BASS Variety of fish
76 LARIAT Rope with noose; lasso
77 LARK Variety of bird
78 LARVA Pre-adult stage of insect

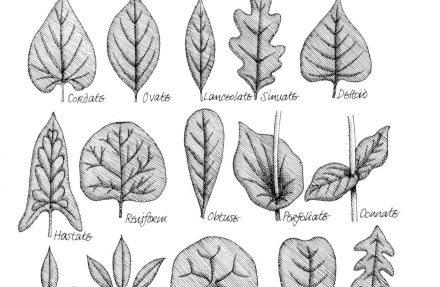

Some Types of Leaf

Cordate   Ovate   Lanceolate   Sinuate   Deltoid

Reniform   Obtuse   Perfoliate   Connate

Hastate

Trifoliate   Palmate   Peltate   Cuneate   Runcinate

79 LARVATE Masked
80 LARVE Mask
81 LASH Fine hair around eye
82 LASS Girl

83 LASSO Lariat
84 LAST Shoemaker's form
85 LATEEN Type of triangular sail
86 LATERAL-FIN Fish's side fin
87 LATIMERIA Variety of extinct fish
88 LATIN CROSS Style of cross
89 LATITUDE Lines marking distance north or south of Equator
90 LATTICE Diagonal criss-cross structure
91 LAUGH Expression of happiness
92 LAUGHING THRUSH Variety of bird
93 LAUGHING-GAS Nitrous oxide (N_2O)
94 LAUNCH Motor-boat
95 LAURE Crown woven of laurel leaves
96 LAUREATE Crowned with laurel leaves
97 LAUREL Variety of plant
98 LAVA Molten rock
99 LAVENDER Light purple colour
100 LAWN Flat, close-mown grass
101 LAWRENCIUM Element; atomic number 103
102 LAY FIGURE Artist's model of the human figure
103 LAYMAN Person not in Holy Orders
104 LEAD Type of heavy metal; symbol Pb
105 LEAD Element; atomic number 82
106 LEAD Leash
107 LEAD Electrical flex
108 LEAF Unit of plant's foliage
109 LEAF Sheet of paper
110 LEAF-FISH Variety of fish
111 LEAFBIRD Variety of bird
112 LEAK Hole permitting liquid to escape

113 LEAKAGE Escaping liquid
114 LEAN Incline
115 LEAP-YEAR Year with 366 days
116 LEASH Restraining strap for dog; lead
117 LEATHER Tanned skin of animal
118 LEATHERHEAD Variety of bird
119 LEBANON Flag of South-west Asian country
120 LECHWE Variety of antelope
121 LEDGE Rock shelf
122 LEEK Variety of vegetable
123 LEG Lower body extremity
124 LEG Support of table or chair etc
125 LEGGING Protective covering for lower leg
126 LEGIBLE Clear enough to read
127 LEIOTHRIX Variety of bird
128 LEKYTHOS Type of Greek vessel
129 LEMMING Variety of small animal
130 LEMON Variety of fruit
131 LEMUR Variety of animal
132 LENS Corrective glass in spectacles
133 LEO Fifth sign of the zodiac; the lion
134 LEOPARD Variety of animal
135 LEOPARD MOTH Variety of moth
136 LEOPARD SHARK Variety of fish
137 LEPIDOPTERA Butterflies and moths
138 LEPRECHAUN Type of small supernatural being
139 LESION Injury
140 LESOTHO Flag of Southern African country
141 LETTER Alphabetical symbol
142 LETTERING Letters used in an inscription
143 LETTUCE Variety of vegetable
144 LEVERET Young hare
145 LEVIN Lightning
146 LEVITATION Floating in the air
147 LEYDEN JAR Device for storing static electricity
148 LHASO APSO Breed of dog
149 LIBERIA Flag of West African republic
150 LIBERTY Personification of freedom
151 LIBRA Seventh sign of the zodiac; the scales
152 LIBRATE Balanced
153 LIBYA Flag of North African republic
154 LID Covering for top of vessel
155 LID Skin covering of the eye
156 LICHTENSTEIN Flag of Western European country
157 LIFEBELT Buoyant life-saving device
158 LIFE BOAT Small emergency boat carried by ship
159 LIFEGUARD Trained rescuer of drowning persons
160 LIFE-PRESERVER Life belt
161 LIFTING Raising
162 LIGAMENT Bandage
163 LIGHT Radiance
164 LIGHT BULB Device for illuminating
165 LIGHTER Device for producing flame
166 LIGHTHOUSE Tower with light as warning of danger
167 LIGHTNING Natural electrical discharge in the sky
168 LIGHTSHIP Anchored vessel with warning light
169 LIKENESS Portrait
170 LILY Variety of flowering plant
171 LILY-OF-THE-VALLEY Variety of flowering plant

172 LIMACEOUS Pertaining to slugs or snails
173 LIMB Arm or leg
174 LIME Variety of fruit
175 LIME BUTTERFLY Variety of butterfly
176 LIMNING Painting or drawing
177 LIMNER Painter or draughtsman
178 LIMPET Variety of mollusc
179 LIMPKIN Variety of bird
180 LINE Thin mark made by brush or pen etc
181 LINE Cord
182 LINER Large passenger vessel
183 LINE-DRAWING Drawing made with drawn lines
184 LINEN TESTER Small magnifying device
185 LING Variety of fish
186 LINING Material covering inner surface of garment
187 LINK Loop of a chain
188 LINNET Variety of bird
189 LINSANG Variety of animal
190 LION Variety of animal
191 LIONESS Female lion
192 LIONET Lion cub
193 LIP Fleshy edges of the mouth
194 LIP Rim of vessel
195 LIPSTICK Cosmetic lip colouring
196 LIPARIS Variety of fish
197 LIQUID Fluid
198 LIRA Type of musical instrument
199 LIST Inclination to one side
200 LITCHI Variety of fruit
201 LITEWKA Style of military tunic
202 LITHIUM Element; atomic number 3
203 LITTLE-OWL Variety of bird
204 LIVESTOCK Animals
205 LIVERY Servants' uniform
206 LIZARD Variety of reptile
207 LIZARD FISH Variety of fish
208 LLAMA Variety of animal
209 LOACH Variety of fish
210 LOAF Block of uncut bread
211 LOBE Lower part of ear
212 LOBSTER Variety of crustacean
213 LOBSTER MOTH Variety of moth
214 LOCH Lake
215 LOCK Fastening device
216 LOCK Mechanism for igniting firearm
217 LOCK Clump of hair
218 LOCKER Box with lock
219 LOCKET Metal band on scabbard
220 LOCKET Ornament worn around the neck
221 LOCUST Variety of insect
222 LOG Rough length of wood
223 LOIN Area on back of body between hips and ribs
224 LOINCLOTH Garment worn around the loins
225 LOLL To let dangle
226 LONDON Flag of the city of London
227 LONGBOW Powerful archery bow
228 LONG-EARED BAT Variety of flying mammal
229 LONGHAND Written out in full
230 LONGICORN Variety of beetle
231 LONGITUDE Lines marking distance east or west of Greenwich meridian
232 LONGSHIP Type of ancient sailing vessel
233 LOOKING Directing the eyes
234 LOOKING-GLASS Mirror

235 LOOM Shaft of an oar
236 LOOP Noose
237 LOOSE-LEAF Detachable page
238 LORGNETTE Spectacles on a long handle
239 LORIKEET Variety of bird
240 LORIOT Variety of bird
241 LORIS Variety of animal
242 LOUD-HAILER Megaphone
243 LOUP-GAROU Werewolf
244 LOUR Dark and gloomy
245 LOUVAR Variety of fish
246 LOVE-APPLE Tomato
247 LOVE-BIRD Variety of bird
248 LOVING-CUP Large drinking cup
249 LOW-BELL Cow or sheep-bell
250 LOWER CASE Non-capital letters
251 LOZENGE Heraldic device
252 LOZENGY Heraldic device
253 LUBRICANT Lubricating oil
254 LUBRICATOR Device for applying oil
255 LUCE Variety of fish; pike
256 LUCENT Shining
257 LUCERN Variety of animal; lynx
258 LUCIFER The Devil
259 LUFF Back of sail
260 LUG Flat handle
261 LUGGAGE Baggage
262 LUGGER Type of sailing vessel
263 LUGSAIL Square sail of a lugger
264 LUMBER Timber
265 LUMP-FISH Variety of fish
266 LUMPSUCKER Variety of fish; lump-fish
267 LUNT Smoke without flame
268 LUTE Type of musical instrument
269 LUTE-PIN Tuning peg of a lute
270 LUTENIST Lute player
271 LUTETIUM Element; atomic number 71
272 LUXEMBURG Flag of West European country
273 LYCANTHROPE Werewolf
274 LYING Recumbent
275 LYNX Variety of animal
276 LYRE Type of musical instrument
277 LYRE-BIRD Variety of bird
278 LYRIST Lyre player

M

1 M Thirteenth letter of the alphabet
2 M Braille alphabet
3 M International signal flag
4 M Manual alphabet – American system
5 M Morse code alphabet
6 M Semaphore alphabet
7 MACAQUE Variety of animal
8 MACAW Variety of bird
9 MACE Spiked war-club
10 MACHETE Type of large knife
11 MACHINE Mechanical instrument
12 MACHINE-GUN Automatic rapid-firing gun
13 MACKEREL Variety of fish
14 MACRON Mark over vowel indicating long sound
15 MACULATED Stained
16 MADONNA The Virgin Mary
17 MAELSTROM Whirlpool
18 MAGAZINE Ammunition clip
19 MAGE Magician
20 MAGELLAN GOOSE Variety of bird
21 MAGEN DAVID Star of David
22 MAGENTA Purple-red colour
23 MAGIAN Magician
24 MAGIC SQUARE Numbered matrix (any vertical, horizontal or diagonal line adds up to the same number)
25 MAGIC WAND Stage magician's prop
26 MAGICIAN Conjuror
27 MAGNESIUM Element; atomic number 12
28 MAGNET Device that attracts metal
29 MAGNIFICATION Enlarged appearance
30 MAGNIFYING GLASS Lens for enlarging appearance of objects
31 MAGNOLIA WARBLER Variety of bird
32 MAGPIE Variety of bird
33 MAGPIE-JAY Variety of bird
34 MAGPIE-LARK Variety of bird
35 MAGPIE-ROBIN Variety of bird
36 MAHL STICK Painter's hand-rest
37 MAHOMETAN Follower of Islam
38 MAHOUT Elephant driver
39 MAHSEER Variety of fish
40 MAIDEN Young unmarried woman
41 MAIMED Mutilated
42 MAIN-LOWER TOPSAIL Type of sail
43 MAIN-ROYAL STAYSAIL Type of sail
44 MAIN-ROYAL Type of sail
45 MAIN-SKYSAIL Type of sail
46 MAIN-STAYSAIL Type of sail
47 MAIN-TOPGALLANT STAYSAIL Type of sail
48 MAIN-TOPMAST STAYSAIL Type of sail
49 MAIN-UPPER TOPSAIL Type of sail
50 MAIN Ocean

51 MAIN-DECK Ships principal deck
52 MAIN-TOP Platform at head of lower mainmast
53 MAIN-TOPGALLANT Type of sail
54 MAIN-TOPGALLANT MAST Mast above main-topmast
55 MAIN-TOPMAST Mast above lower topmast
56 MAIN-TOPSAIL Type of sail
57 MAIN-YARD Yard on which mainsail is set
58 MAINMAST Principle mast of ship
59 MAINSAIL Type of sail
60 MAIZE Variety of vegetable; Indian corn
61 MAJORETTE Performing baton-twirler
62 MAJUSCULE Capital letter
63 MAKE-UP Cosmetic face colouring
64 MALADY Illness

65 MALAGASY REPUBLIC Flag of East African island republic
66 MALAWI Flag of East African republic
67 MALAYSIA Flag of South-east Asian country
68 MALCOHA Variety of bird
69 MALDIVE ISLANDS Flag of Indian Ocean island group
70 MALE Man
71 MALEO Variety of bird
72 MALI Flag of West African republic
73 MALKIN Scarecrow
74 MALLARD Variety of water-bird
75 MALLEE Variety of bird
76 MALLET Hammer with wooden head
77 MALTA Flag of Mediterranean island country
78 MALTESE CROSS Heraldic device
79 MAMILLA Nipple
80 MAMMARY-GLAND Milk-producing gland
81 MAMO Variety of extinct bird
82 MAMMOTH Extinct type of elephant
83 MAN Adult human male
84 MANHOLE Inspection hole in ground
85 MANACLE Handcuff
86 MANACLED Handcuffed
87 MANAKIN Variety of bird
88 MANATEE Variety of aquatic mammal

89 MANDARIN DUCK Variety of water-bird
90 MANDIBLE Jaw-bone
91 MANDIL Turban
92 MANDOLIN Type of musical instrument
93 MANDRILL Variety of animal
94 MANE Long hair on animal's neck
95 MANGABEY Variety of monkey
96 MANGANESE Element; atomic number 25
97 MANIFOLD Exhaust with several pipes
98 MANIKIN Dwarf
99 MANLING Little man, dwarf
100 MANTEAU Cloak
101 MANTICORE Type of mythical beast
102 MANTLE Cloak
103 MANUAL ALPHABET Sign language for deaf-mutes

104 MANUFACTORY Factory
105 MANURE Dung
106 MANX LOGHTAN RAM Variety of sheep
107 MANX-CAT Breed of tailless cat
108 MAP Printed representation of Earth's surface
109 MAP Variety of butterfly
110 MAPLE Variety of tree (leaf shown here)
111 MARA Variety of animal
112 MARACA Type of musical instrument
113 MAREMMA Breed of dog
114 MARGAY Variety of animal; tiger cat
115 MARIACHI Mexican street musician
116 MARINER Sailor
117 MARIONETTE String operated puppet
118 MARK Stain or blemish
119 MARKHOR Variety of animal
120 MARKINGS Pattern on animal's skin
121 MARLIN Variety of fish
122 MARMALADE Ginger (colouring of cat)
123 MAROON Dark red colour
124 MARQUEE Large tent
125 MARROW Variety of vegetable
126 MARS Astrological symbol for planet Mars
127 MARSUPIAL Animal which carries its young in a pouch
128 MARTEN Variety of animal

129 MARTIN Variety of bird
130 MARY Mother of Jesus
131 MASCULINE Of the male sex
132 MASK Bizarre head-covering
133 MASJID Mosque
134 MASONRY Stonework
135 MAST Pole supporting sails
136 MASTER Captain
137 MASTER Male teacher
138 MASTIFF Breed of dog
139 MATCH Device for producing flame
140 MATCHSTICK Wooden shaft of match
141 MATERIAL Fabric
142 MATERNAL Characteristic of a mother
143 MATTER Substance
144 MATTOCK Type of pickaxe

145 MATURE Fully developed
146 MAUL Mace
147 MAURITANIA Flag of West African country
148 MAURITIUS Flag of Indian Ocean island country
149 MAUVE Red-purple colour
150 MAW Open jaws of animal
151 MAXILLA Jaw
152 MAY Fifth month of the year (shown as Roman figure 5)
153 MAYPOLE Decorated festive pole
154 MAZAME Variety of animal; pronghorn antelope
155 MAZE Labyrinth
156 MEAGRE Variety of fish
157 MEASLES Illness accompanied by red rash
158 MEDAL Decoration commemorating an honour bestowed
159 MEDITERRANEAN Sea between Europe and Africa
160 MEERKAT Variety of animal; mongoose
161 MEERSCHAUM Type of tobacco pipe
162 MEGALITH Standing stone monument; menhir
163 MEGALOSAUR Variety of extinct dinosaur
164 MEGAPHONE Speaking-trumpet
165 MEGAPODE Variety of bird

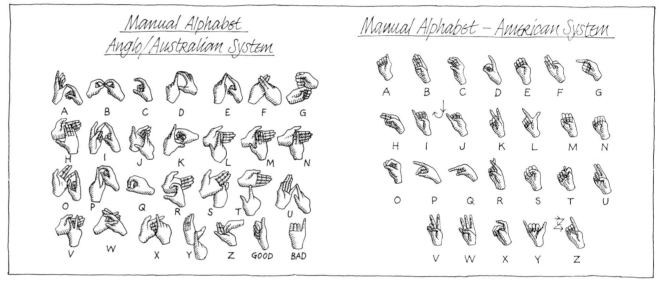

Manual Alphabet
Anglo/Australian System

A B C D E F G
H I J K L M N
O P Q R S T U
V W X Y Z GOOD BAD

Manual Alphabet – American System

A B C D E F G
H I J K L M N
O P Q R S T U
V W X Y Z

166 MEGATHERIUM Variety of extinct giant sloth
167 MELANIC Dark complexion
168 MELANOCOMOUS Black-haired
169 MELODY Succession of musical notes
170 MELON Variety of fruit
171 MEM Thirteenth letter of the Hebrew alphabet
172 MEMBER Limb
173 MEMENTO MORI Skull as a reminder of mortality
174 MENDELEVIUM Element; atomic number 101
175 MENHADEN Variety of fish
176 MENHIR Megalith
177 MENISCUS Crescent
178 MENORAH Jewish candelabrum
179 MENSWEAR Garments worn by men
180 MERCATOR'S PROJECTION Map with parallel lines of longitude and latitude
181 MERCHANDISE Wares
182 MERCHANTMAN Merchant ship
183 MERCURY Ancient messenger of the gods
184 MERCURY Astrological symbol for the planet Mercury
185 MERCURY Chemical symbol (Hg)
186 MERCURY Element; atomic number 80
187 MERGANSER Variety of water-bird
188 MERIDIAN Noon
189 MERIDIAN Line of longitude
190 MERLIN Variety of bird of prey
191 MERMAID Mythological creature
192 MERRY Cheerful
193 MERRY-GO-ROUND Carousel
194 MESITE Variety of bird
195 MESOMORPH Muscular physical type

196 MESSENGER Message carrier
197 MESSIAH Christ
198 METAL Iron, steel and other similar materials
199 METAMERE One of a similar segment of animal's body
200 METEOR Shooting-star
201 METRONOME Musician's time-keeping aid
202 MEXICAN Native of Mexico
203 MEXICO Flag of North American republic
204 MICE Plural of mouse
205 MICROMETER Type of measuring instrument
206 MICRONESIA Flag of South Pacific island group
207 MICROPHONE Electrical device to pick up sound
208 MICROSCOPE Magnifying instrument
209 MID-AIR Between the sky and the ground
210 MIDDAY Noon
211 MIDDLE-AGED Between forty and sixty years old
212 MIDDLE DISTANCE Between the foreground and the background
213 MIDDLE EAST Arabic-speaking area of the world
214 MIDDLE FINGER Longest finger
215 MIDGET Very small person
216 MIDRIFF Mid-region of human torso
217 MIDSHIPS Middle area of a ship
218 MIDWAY Avenue at a fair
219 MIGRANT Creature that migrates
220 MIKADO PHEASANT Variety of bird
221 MIKE Self-portrait of the artist
222 MILESTONE Distance marker

223 MILITARY Pertaining to soldiers
224 MILITARY CROSS Type of military medal
225 MILK Liquid secreted by female mammals
226 MILKWEED Variety of butterfly; monarch
227 MILL Factory for grinding grain
228 MILLWHEEL Waterwheel of mill
229 MILLER'S THUMB Variety of fish
230 MILLIARD 1,000,000,000
231 MILLINERY Hats
232 MILLION 1,000,000
233 MILLION Roman numeral for a million
234 MINARET Tower of a mosque
235 MINE Aquatic bomb
236 MINERAL Natural inorganic substance
237 MINI-SKIRT Style of short skirt
238 MINIKIN Midget

262 MIZEN-CROJACK Type of sail
263 MIZEN-LOWER TOPSAIL Type of sail
264 MIZEN-ROYAL Type of sail
265 MIZEN-TOPGALLANT STAYSAIL Type of sail
266 MIZEN-TOPGALLANT Type of sail
267 MIZEN-TOPMAST STAYSAIL Type of sail
268 MIZEN-UPPER TOPSAIL Type of sail
269 MIZEN-YARD Yard on which sail is set
270 MIZEN-MAST Rear mast on ship
271 MIZEN-TOP Platform on mizen-mast
272 MIZEN-TOPGALLANT MAST Top part of mizen-mast
273 MIZEN-TOPMAST Upper part of mizen-mast
274 MOA Variety of bird
275 MOB Crowd
276 MOBIUS STRIP One-sided surface

Möbius Strip

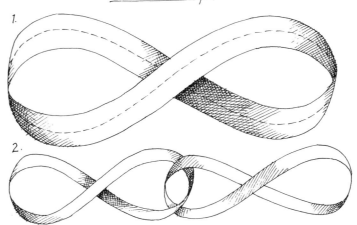

1.

2.

1. Make a Möbius strip from a band of paper and cut along dotted line. 2. The cut strip remains interlocked.

298 MONK Male member of religious order
299 MONK PARAKEET Variety of bird
300 MONKEY Variety of animal
301 MONKEY WRENCH Adjustable spanner
302 MONKEY-PUZZLE Variety of tree
303 MONOCEROS Unicorn
304 MONOCHROME Single-coloured
305 MONOCLE Single eye-glass
306 MONOCULE One-eyed being
307 MONOCYCLE One-wheeled self-propelled vehicle
308 MONOLITH Standing stone monument; menhir
309 MONOPLANE Single-winged aircraft
310 MONOSYLLABIC Having one syllable
311 MONSTER Bizarre or grotesque creature
312 MONTH One of year's twelve divisions
313 MONTSERRAT Flag of Caribbean island
314 MOON Astrological symbol for Moon
315 MOON MOTH Variety of moth
316 MOON-FISH Variety of fish
317 MOOR Arab
318 MOORISH IDOL Variety of fish
319 MOOSE Variety of animal
320 MOP Long-handled cleaning implement
321 MOP-HEAD Head of a mop
322 MOPSTICK Shaft of a mop
323 MORA MEDITERRANEA Variety of fish
324 MORBILLOUS Pertaining to measles
325 MORNING First part of the day
326 MOROCCO Flag of North African country
327 MORSE CODE Signalling system
328 MORSEL Small quantity
329 MORTAL Creature that can die
330 MORTAR Substance for binding bricks
331 MORTAR Grinding-bowl
332 MORTAR-BOARD Academic hat
333 MOSLEM Follower of Islam
334 MOSQUE Islamic temple
335 MOSQUITO FISH Variety of fish
336 MOTH Type of winged insect
337 MOTHER Female parent
338 MOTIF Ornamental pattern
339 MOTLEY Parti-coloured clothes
340 MOTMOT Variety of bird
341 MOTOR Engine
342 MOTOR CAR Automobile
343 MOTORCYCLE Motorized two-wheeled vehicle
344 MOTORCYCLIST Motorcycle driver
345 MOTORIST Motor car driver
346 MOTTLED Marked with irregular spots
347 MOUFFLON Variety of animal
348 MOUND Heap
349 MOUNTAIN Very high landmass
350 MOUNTED Seated on an animal
351 MOUNTAIN GOAT Variety of animal
352 MOUNTIE Royal Canadian Mounted Policeman
353 MOURNER Person in mourning
354 MOURNING CLOAK Variety of butterfly; Camberwell Beauty
355 MOURNING-BAND Arm-band worn by mourner
356 MOUSE Variety of small rodent
357 MOUSETRAP Spring-trap for mice
358 MOUSTACHE Whiskers on upper lip
359 MOUSTACHE PARAKEET Variety of bird

Somatotypes

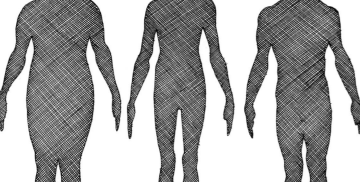

Endomorph   Ectomorph   Mesomorph

239 MINIM Type of musical note; half note
240 MINIM Medical symbol
241 MINIMUS Little finger
242 MINIVET Variety of bird
243 MINK Variety of animal
244 MINNOW Variety of fish
245 MINOTAUR Mythological creature
246 MINSTER Church
247 MINSTREL Itinerant singer
248 MINUS Subtraction symbol
249 MINUTE-HAND Clock hand indicating minutes
250 MIRROR Reflecting surface
251 MISDATE Incorrect date
252 MISS Young unmarried woman
253 MISSILE Guided rocket
254 MISSPELL Incorrect spelling
255 MISTAKE Error
256 MISTLETOE Variety of plant
257 MISTLETOE BIRD Variety of bird
258 MISTRESS Female teacher
259 MITRE Bishop's headdress
260 MITTEN Fingerless glove
261 MIXED NUMBER Sum of an integer and a fraction

277 MOCCASIN Style of soft shoe
278 MOCKING-BIRD Variety of bird
279 MODEL Small-scale reproduction
280 MODERN Style of letterform
281 MOHAMMEDAN Muslim
282 MOLE Variety of animal
283 MOLE Dark skin blemish
284 MOLEHILL Heap of earth caused by burrowing mole
285 MOLLIENESIA Variety of fish; molly
286 MOLLUSC Soft-bodied invertebrate animal
287 MOLLY Variety of fish
288 MOLINE CROSS Heraldic device
289 MOLYBDENUM Element; atomic number 42
290 MONA Variety of monkey
291 MONARCH Sovereign
292 MONARCH Variety of butterfly
293 MONACO Flag of European country
294 MONGOLIAN PEOPLE'S REPUBLIC Flag of Eastern Asian country
295 MONGOOSE Variety of animal
296 MONOGRAM Figure of interwoven letters (M & W)
297 MONIAS Variety of bird

360 MOUTH Opening in the face
361 MOUTH-PIECE Part of a musical instrument for the mouth
362 MOUTHLESS Without a mouth
363 MOZAMBIQUE Flag of East African country
364 MRDANGA Type of musical instrument
365 MU Twelfth letter of the Greek alphabet
366 MUD Wet earth
367 MUDGUARD Contraption to prevent mud splashes
368 MUFF Warm covering for the hands
369 MUFFLE Ruminant's upper lip and nose
370 MUFFLER Scarf
371 MUFFLER Silencer
372 MUG Type of drinking vessel
373 MULE Variety of cross-bred animal
374 MULE DEER Variety of animal
375 MULLET Variety of fish
376 MULLION Vertical bar in window
377 MULTIFOIL Foil of many divisions
378 MULTIPLICATION Mathematical symbol
379 MUMMY Wrapped and embalmed body
380 MUMMY-CLOTH Wrappings of a mummy
381 MUNITION Ammunition
382 MUNTJAK Variety of animal
383 MUREX Variety of shell
384 MUSCLE Parts of the body that produce movement
385 MUSCOVY DUCK Variety of water-bird
386 MUSCULAR Having well-developed muscles
387 MUSHROOM Edible fungus
388 MUSIC Score of musical symbols
389 MUSICIAN Maker of musical sounds
390 MUSK-DEER Variety of animal
391 MUSK-RAT Variety of rodent
392 MUSKET Type of firearm
393 MUSKET-REST Firing support for a musket
394 MUSKETEER Soldier armed with a musket
395 MUSLIM Follower of Islam
396 MUSMON Variety of animal; mouflon
397 MUSQUASH Variety of animal; musk-rat
398 MUSSEL Variety of shellfish
399 MUSSULMAN Muslim
400 MUTANT Freak
401 MUTE Person unable to speak
402 MUTE Device for reducing volume of trumpet
403 MUTE SWAN Variety of water-bird
404 MUTILATION Disfigurement
405 MUTTONCHOPS Style of whiskers
406 MUZZLE Snout of an animal
407 MUZZLE Mouth of a gun
408 MUZZLE-LOADER Gun loaded by the barrel
409 MUZZLE-SIGHT Front sight of gun
410 MYTHICAL Legendary or fictitious

1 N Fourteenth letter of the alphabet
2 N Braille alphabet
3 N International signal flag
4 N Manual alphabet – American system
5 N Morse code alphabet
6 N Semaphore alphabet
7 NABATEAN Ancient writing system
8 NAIANT Heraldic device
9 NAIL Horny growth at end of finger
10 NAIL Small fixing spike
11 NAIL-HEAD Flat head of a nail
12 NAKED Unclothed
13 NAME Words by which a person is known
14 NAMEPLATE Plaque with inscribed name
15 NAPE Back of the neck
16 NAPKIN Serviette
17 NAPKIN RING Small ring to hold rolled napkin
18 NARCISSUS Variety of flowering plant
19 NARES Nostrils
20 NARGILEH Oriental pipe; hookah
21 NARWHAL Variety of tusked whale
22 NASAL Nose bone
23 NASE Variety of fish
24 NASTURTIUM Variety of flowering plant
25 NATARAJA Hindu god Shiva as a cosmic dancer
26 NATES Buttocks
27 NATIONAL Pertaining to a nation
28 NATTERJACK Variety of toad
29 NATURAL Type of musical note
30 NAURU Flag of South Pacific island
31 NAVEL Pit in the centre of abdomen
32 NAVY-BLUE Dark blue
33 NEANDERTHAL Extinct type of man (skull shown here)
34 NEBULA Patch of interstellar gas
35 NEBULY Heraldic device
36 NECK Part of body between head and shoulders
37 NECK Part of musical instrument with fingerboard
38 NECK-TIE Strip of material worn around neck
39 NECK-WEAR Scarves and neck-ties
40 NECKERCHIEF Folded fabric square worn around neck
41 NECKLACE Ornamental beads worn at neck
42 NECTARINE Variety of fruit
43 NEEDLE Obelisk
44 NEEDLE-FISH Variety of fish
45 NEF Table vessel in the shape of a ship
46 NEGRESS Female of African origin
47 NEGRO Man of African origin
48 NEKHBET Ancient Egyptian vulture-headed goddess

49 NEMESIA Variety of plant
50 NEOCERATODUS Variety of fish; lungfish
51 NEODYMIUM Element; atomic number 60
52 NEON Element; atomic number 10
53 NEON TETRA Variety of fish
54 NEPAL Flag of Southern Asian country
55 NEPTUNE Ancient Roman water god
56 NEPTUNE Astrological symbol for the planet Neptune
57 NEPTUNIUM Element; atomic number 93
58 NERVURE Leaf vein
59 NEST Structure to shelter eggs and young birds
60 NESTLING Young bird unable to fly
61 NET Mesh of knotted twine
62 NETHERLANDS Flag of West European country
63 NETHERLANDS ANTILLES Flag of Caribbean island group
64 NETTLE Variety of plant
65 NEW MOON First discernible phase of the moon
66 NEW YORK Flag of the city of New York
67 NEW ZEALAND Flag of South-west Pacific country
68 NEWARA Variety of animal; mongoose
69 NEWFOUNDLAND Breed of dog
70 NEWT Variety of small amphibian
71 NIB Writing point of a pen

Musical Notation

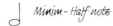

E F G A B C D E F

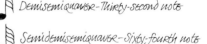

⊟ BREVE - Double note
○ SEMIBREVE - Whole note
♩ MINIM - Half note
♩ CROTCHET - Quarter note
♪ QUAVER - Eighth note
♬ SEMIQUAVER - Sixteenth note
♬ DEMISEMIQUAVER - Thirty-second note
♬ SEMIDEMISEMIQUAVER - Sixty-fourth note

Nibs

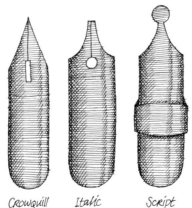

Crowquill   Italic   Script

72 NICARAGUA Flag of Central American country
73 NICHE Recess in wall
74 NICK Small notch
75 NICKEL Five cents
76 NICKEL Element; atomic number 28
77 NICKNAME Familiar form of person's first name
78 NICOTIAN Tobacco-smoker
79 NICOTIANA Variety of plant
80 NICTITATE To wink
81 NIGER Flag of West African republic
82 NIGERIA Flag of West African republic
83 NIGHT Dark period of the day
84 NIGHTCLOTHES Garments worn in bed
85 NIGHT-HAWK Variety of bird

86 NIGHT-HERON Variety of bird
87 NIGHTCAP Type of cap worn in bed
88 NIGHTPIECE Picture depicting night
89 NIGHTSHIRT Long gown worn in bed
90 NIGHTINGALE Variety of bird
91 NIGHTJAR Variety of bird
92 NIKE Ancient Greek goddess of victory
93 NIL Zero
94 NILGAI Variety of antelope
95 NIMBUS Halo
96 NINE Number between eight and ten
97 NINE Roman numeral for 9
98 NINETEEN Nine more than ten
99 NINETEEN Roman numeral for 19
100 NINETY Nine times ten
101 NINETY Roman numeral for 90
102 NIOBIUM Element; atomic number 41
103 NIPPLE Teat of woman's breast
104 NITROGEN Element; atomic number 7
105 NIUE Flag of South Pacific island
106 NOBELIUM Element; atomic number 102
107 NOCTULE Variety of bat
108 NOCTURNAL Active by night
109 NOCTURNE Work of art depicting night
110 NODDLE Head
111 NODE Knot
112 NOGGIN Mug or cup
113 NOMEUS Variety of fish
114 NONAGON Nine-sided figure
115 NONILLION Ten to the fifty-fourth power – British system
116 NONILLION Ten to the thirtieth power – American system
117 NONSENSE Meaningless words
118 NOOK Narrow corner
119 NOOSE Knotted loop of rope

120 NOPE Variety of bird; bullfinch
121 NORTH A cardinal point of the compass
122 NORTH-WEST Direction between north and west
123 NORTH-EAST Direction between north and east
124 NORTH-NORTH-EAST Direction between north and north-east
125 NORTH-NORTH-WEST Direction between north and north-west
126 NORTHERN IRELAND Flag of West European province
127 NORTHERN LIGHTS Aurora borealis
128 NORTHERN MARIANAS Flag of South Pacific island group
129 NORWAY Flag of Scandinavian country
130 NOSE Smelling organ
131 NOSE-PIECE Part of spectacles that rest on nose
132 NOSEGAY Bunch of flowers
133 NOSELESS Without a nose
134 NOSTRIL Opening in the base of the nose
135 NOTCH V-shaped cut
136 NOTE Musical symbol
137 NOTHOBRANCHUS Variety of fish
138 NOUGHT Zero
139 NOUN Naming word
140 NOURISHMENT Food
141 NOVEMDECILLION Ten to the 114th power – British numerical system
142 NOVEMDECILLION Ten to the 60th power – American numerical system
143 NOZZLE Socket for candle on a candlestick
144 NU Thirteenth letter of the Greek alphabet
145 NUBILE Of marriageable age
146 NUCHA Nape of the neck
147 NUDE Unclothed
148 NUMBAT Variety of animal
149 NUMBER Mathematical unit
150 NUN Woman member of a religious community
151 NUN Fourteenth letter of the Hebrew alphabet
152 NUNBIRD Variety of bird
153 NURSE Woman trained to care for the sick
154 NUT Dry fruit of certain plants
155 NUT Metal device used with a bolt
156 NUT Fixed bridge at top of violin fingerboard
157 NUTCRACKER Device for cracking nuts
158 NUTCRACKER Variety of bird
159 NUTHATCH Variety of bird
160 NUTRIA Variety of animal; coypu
161 NUTSHELL Outer casing of nut
162 NYALA Variety of antelope
163 NYMPH Immature form of insect

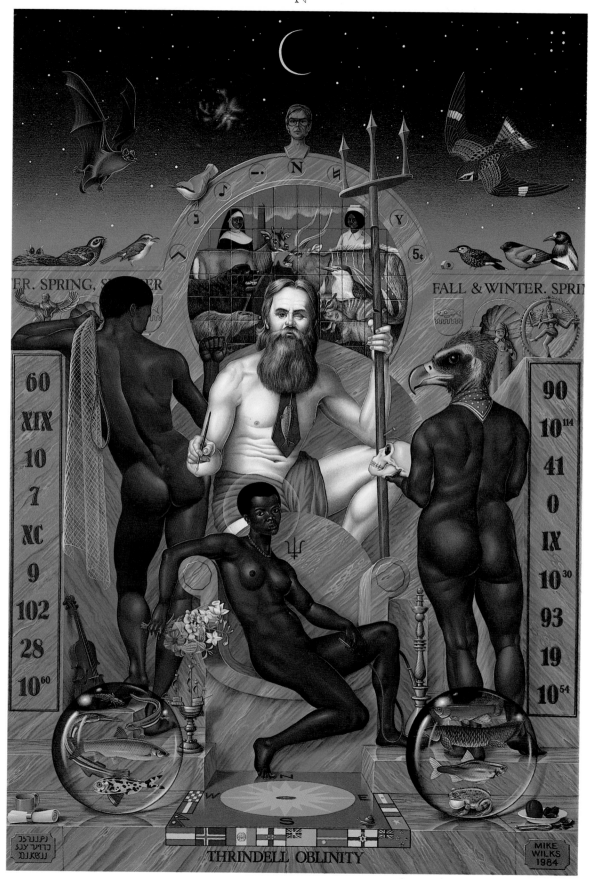

THRINDELL OBLINITY

1 O Fifteenth letter of the alphabet
2 O Braille alphabet
3 O International signal flag
4 O Morse code alphabet
5 O Semaphore alphabet
6 O-O Variety of bird
7 OAK Variety of tree (leaves and acorn shown here)
8 OAR-FISH Variety of fish; ribbonfish; King-of-the-Herrings
9 OAST-HOUSE Hop-drying kiln
10 OBCORDATE Inversely heart-shaped
11 OBELISK Tapering stone pillar, needle
12 OBELUS Symbol used to mark manuscripts
13 OBI Kimono sash
14 OBJECT Thing
15 OBJECT-GLASS Lens of optical instrument nearest to object
16 OBLIVION Forgetfulness (spelt out in Ogham)
17 OBLONG Rectangle
18 OBNUBILATION Cloudy
19 OBOE Type of musical instrument
20 OBOIST Oboe player
21 OBSERVATORY Building housing astronomical telescope
22 OBSTACLE Thing causing obstruction
23 OBSTRUCTION Hindrance
24 OBTURATION Obstruction of an opening
25 OBTURATOR Something that stops up
26 OCARINA Type of musical instrument
27 OCCIDENTAL Westerner
28 OCCIPUT Back of the head
29 OCCLUDED FRONT Meteorological symbol
30 OCCLUSION Stopping up
31 OCCLUSOR Stopper
32 OCEAN Large body of sea
33 OCEAN SURGEON Variety of fish
34 OCEAN-GOING Designed for ocean travel
35 OCELLATED TURKEY Variety of bird
36 OCELLUS Ringed spot on animal's coat
37 OCELOT Variety of animal
38 OCHRE Yellow-brown colour
39 OCTAGON Eight-sided figure
40 OCTANGLE Octagon
41 OCTANT Eighth part of a circle
42 OCTASTYLE Eight-columned classical architectural style
43 OCTAVE Two musical notes eight diatonic degrees apart
44 OCTOFOIL Foil with eight lobes
45 OCTOPED Octopus
46 OCTOPOD Octopus
47 OCTOPUS Variety of sea-creature
48 OCULATE With eyes

49 OCULUS Circular window
50 OCULUS Ocellus
51 ODD Uneven numbers (1, 3, 5, 7, 9)
52 OEIL-DE-BOEUF Circular window
53 OFF-SHORE Distant from the shore
54 OFFING Distant sea visible from shore
55 OFFSHOOT Branch
56 OGAC Variety of fish; Greenland cod
57 OGDOAD Eight
58 OGEE S-shaped curve
59 OGHAM Ancient Irish alphabet system

Ogham

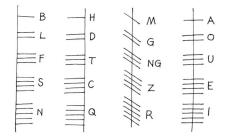

60 OGIVE Pointed arch
61 OGLE Eye
62 OIL BEETLE Variety of insect
63 OIL SLICK Mass of floating oil
64 OIL-RIG Moored oil drilling platform
65 OIL-TANKER Vessel for transporting oil
66 OKAPI Variety of animal
67 OLD ENGLISH SHEEPDOG Breed of dog
68 OLD GLORY The flag of the United States of America
69 OLD LADY MOTH Variety of moth
70 OLEANDER HAWKMOTH Variety of moth
71 OLFACTORY Nose
72 OLIGOSYLLABLE Word with less than four syllables
73 OLIVE Variety of plant (leaves and fruit shown here)
74 OLIVE Dull green colour
75 OLYMPIC Flag of the International Olympic Movement
76 OM Hindu sacred syllable
77 OMAN Flag of South-west Asian country
78 OMEGA Twenty-fourth and last letter of the Greek alphabet
79 OMICRON Fifteenth letter of the Greek alphabet
80 OMISSION Something left out
81 OMNIVORE Creature that feeds on all kinds of food
82 OMOPHAGIST Creature that feeds on raw flesh
83 ONE The first integer; 1
84 ONION Variety of vegetable
85 ONYCHOPHOROUS Having nails or claws
86 ONYMOUS Having a name
87 OPAH Variety of fish; moonfish
88 OPAQUE Not transparent
89 OPEN-AIR Out of doors
90 OPEN-EYED Awake
91 OPENBILL Variety of bird

92 OPENING Hole
93 OPERA-GLASSES Small binoculars
94 OPHRYON Point between the eyes
95 OPPOSITION Astrological symbol
96 OPPOSUM Variety of animal
97 OR Heraldic gold
98 ORANG-OUTANG Variety of ape
99 ORANGE Variety of fruit
100 ORANGE Colour between red and yellow
101 ORANGE CHROMIDE Variety of fish
102 ORB Article of regalia, symbol of sovereignty
103 ORBIT Eye socket
104 ORDINARY Heraldic division
105 ORDURE Excrement
106 ORFE Variety of fish
107 ORGAN Functional unit of body
108 ORGAN Type of musical instrument
109 ORGAN-PIPE Pipe of an organ
110 ORGANISM Living individual
111 ORGANIST Organ player
112 ORIBI Variety of antelope
113 ORIEL Style of bay window
114 ORIENTAL Easterner
115 ORIFICE Opening
116 ORIFLAMME Type of banner
117 ORIOLE Variety of bird
118 ORLE Heraldic device

Heraldic Ordinaries

Chief Fess Pale Palet Bend Bendlet

Chevron Pall Saltire Cross Base Pile

Coste Bordure Canton Lozenge Label Fret

Inescutcheon Gyron Flaunches Rondel Orle Billet

119 ORNAMENT Decoration
120 ORNATE BICHIR Variety of fish
121 ORNATE HAWK-EAGLE Variety of bird of prey
122 ORTHOGONAL Rectangular
123 ORTHOGRAPHIC Correctly spelt
124 ORYX Variety of antelope
125 OSCAR Academy award
126 OSCAR Variety of fish
127 OSIRIS Ancient Egyptian god of the dead

128 OSMIUM Element; atomic number 76
129 OSPREY Variety of bird of prey
130 OSSIFRAGE Osprey
131 OSTRICH Variety of large flightless bird
132 OTTAVA Octave
133 OTTER Variety of animal
134 OTTERHOUND Breed of dog
135 OUNCE Apothecaries' symbol
136 OUNCE Variety of animal; snow leopard
137 OUROBOROS Ancient symbol of self-devouring serpent
138 OUTDOORS Not in a building
139 OUTER EAR Visible part of the ear
140 OUTLINE Line defining outer edge of an object
141 OUTSIDE Not in a building; outdoors
142 OVAL Flattened ellipse
143 OVEN-BIRD Variety of bird
144 OVERCAST Cloudy
145 OVERCLOUDED Overcast
146 OVERCOAT Topcoat
147 OVERGARMENT Outer garment
148 OVERHANG Projecting rock
149 OVERHAND KNOT Type of knot
150 OVERLAP Where one thing partly covers another
151 OVERLIP Upper lip
152 OVERSIZED Larger than normal

153 OWL Variety of bird
154 OWL BUTTERFLY Variety of butterfly
155 OWL MOTH Variety of moth
156 OX Variety of domestic animal
157 OXEYE Variety of flowering plant
158 OXLIP Variety of flowering plant
159 OXPECKER Variety of bird
160 OXYGEN Element; atomic number 8
161 OYSTER-CATCHER Variety of bird

1 P Sixteenth letter of the alphabet
2 P Braille alphabet
3 P International signal flag
4 P Manual alphabet – American system
5 P Morse code alphabet
6 P Semaphore alphabet
7 PABULUM Food
8 PACA Variety of animal
9 PACK Small parcel; package
10 PACK Set of playing cards
11 PACK Mass of compressed ice
12 PACKAGE Small parcel
13 PACKET Small parcel; package
14 PACKSACK Backpack
15 PAD Bound sheets of paper
16 PADDLE Short broad oar
17 PADDLE Propulsion blade of vessel
18 PADDLE-STEAMER Vessel propelled by paddles
19 PADDLE-WHEEL Propulsion wheel of vessel
20 PADLOCK Small movable lock
21 PADRE Clergyman
22 PAGAN Heathen
23 PAGE Trainee knight
24 PAGE Leaf of a book
25 PAGODA Oriental temple
26 PAGOD Idol
27 PAIL Bucket
28 PAINT Substance used to colour surfaces
29 PAINT-BOX Box containing artist's colours
30 PAINTBRUSH Artist's brush for applying paint
31 PAINTED JEZEBEL Variety of butterfly
32 PAINTED LADY Variety of butterfly
33 PAINTED PARAKEET Variety of bird
34 PAINTED STORK Variety of bird
35 PAINTER Artist specializing in painting
36 PAINTER Mooring-rope
37 PAINTING Applying paint
38 PAINTING Painted work of artist
39 PAINTING KNIFE Artist's tool for applying paint
40 PAIR Two
41 PAJAMAS Loose two-piece sleeping garments
42 PAKISTAN Flag of Southern Asian republic
43 PALACE Large magnificent house
44 PALADIN Knightly hero
45 PALE Upright wooden stake
46 PALE Heraldic device
47 PALETTE Board for mixing paint
48 PALETTE Armour protecting armpit
49 PALETTE KNIFE Artist's tool for mixing paint
50 PALFREY Saddle-horse
51 PALINDROME Phrase which reads the same backwards and forwards

52 PALING Fence of pales
53 PALISADE Defensive fence of pales
54 PALL Heraldic device
55 PALLADIAN Style of neo-classical architecture
56 PALLADIUM Element; atomic number 46
57 PALLET Mattress
58 PALLET Paddle blade
59 PALLET Heraldic device
60 PALM Variety of tree
61 PALM Inner surface of hand
62 PALM Oar or paddle blade
63 PALM CHAT Variety of bird
64 PALMATE Webbed
65 PALMIPEDE Web-footed bird
66 PALOMINO Breed of horse
67 PALPEBRA Eyelid
68 PALY Heraldic device
69 PAMPANO Variety of fish
70 PAMPLEMOUSSE Grapefruit
71 PAN Shallow cooking vessel
72 PAN Small container for solid paint
73 PAN Ancient Greek rural god
74 PAN In-filled part of half-timbered building
75 PAN-PIPE Type of musical instrument
76 PANACHE Plume on knight's helmet
77 PANAMA Flag of Central American republic
78 PANAMA-HAT Style of man's straw hat
79 PANATELA Long cigar
80 PANDA Variety of animal
81 PANE Sheet of glass
82 PANE Flat side of nut or bolt
83 PANEL Distinct section of a surface
84 PANEL Contrasting section of fabric
85 PANELLING Series of panels
86 PANGOLIN Variety of animal; scaly ant-eater
87 PANHANDLE Handle of a pan
88 PANOPLY Complete suit of armour
89 PANTALETTES Long frilly drawers
90 PANTALOONS Long tight trousers
91 PANTHER Variety of animal; black leopard
92 PANTHER CAP Variety of fungus
93 PANTIES Brief lower undergarment
94 PANTS Trousers
95 PAPACHKA Cossak hat
96 PAPAL CROSS Cross with three bars
97 PAPAL CROWN Style of crown worn by the Pope
98 PAPER Substance made in thin sheets from pulp
99 PAPER-CLIP Clip for holding papers together
100 PAPERBACK Book bound in soft covers
101 PAPILIONACEOUS Pertaining to butterflies
102 PAPILLA Nipple
103 PAPILLON Breed of dog
104 PAPIST Roman Catholic
105 PAPOOSH Style of turkish slipper
106 PAPUA NEW GUINEA Flag of South-west Pacific island group
107 PARABOLA Geometrical curve
108 PARACHUTE Canopy to check speed of fall
109 PARACHUTIST Person using a parachute
110 PARAFOIL Shaped sporting parachute
111 PARAGRAPH Distinct section of written words
112 PARAGRAPH Typographer's symbol for paragraph
113 PARAGUAY Flag of South American republic
114 PARAKEET Variety of bird

115 PARALLEL Equidistant for whole length
116 PARALLELEPIPED Geometric solid with six parallelogram faces
117 PARALLELOGRAM Geometric figure with parallel opposite sides
118 PARAMOUR The lady-love of a knight
119 PARAPET Barrier around balcony
120 PARASOL Sunshade
121 PARASOL MUSHROOM Variety of fungus
122 PARCEL Small wrapped package
123 PARD Panther
124 PARENT Father or mother
125 PARENTHESIS Brackets
126 PAREU Polynesian wraparound garment
127 PARFAIT GLASS Glass vessel for serving parfaits
128 PARFAIT Layered cold dessert
129 PARGETING Ornamental plaster-work
130 PARIS Flag of the capital of France
131 PARK Public garden
132 PARKING METER Meter limiting car parking time
133 PARROT Variety of bird
134 PARROT-FISH Variety of fish
135 PARROTBILL Variety of bird
136 PARSNIP Variety of vegetable
137 PARSON Clergyman
138 PARTICIPANT One that participates
139 PARTICIPATING To take part
140 PARTICIPATOR One taking part
141 PARTICOLOURED Differently coloured in different parts
142 PARTING Dividing line in hair
143 PARTITION Dividing of one thing into parts
144 PARTNER One who shares in an act
145 PARTRIDGE Variety of game bird
146 PARTY Division of a whole
147 PARULA Variety of bird
148 PARVATI A Hindu goddess
149 PASS Passage between mountains
150 PASS-BOAT Punt
151 PASSENGER Traveller in a vehicle
152 PASSER-BY Casual passer
153 PASSERES Type of birds
154 PASTEL Type of artist's crayon
155 PASTEL Soft pale colour
156 PASTERN Horse's foot between fetlock and hoof
157 PASTICCIO Pastiche
158 PASTICHE Work of art imitating another artist
159 PASTOR Clergyman
160 PASTRY Baked dough
161 PASTURE Grazing land
162 PATAGIUM Bat's wing membrane
163 PATAS Variety of monkey
164 PATCH Piece of material repairing a hole
165 PATCH Material protecting empty eye socket
166 PATCH-POCKET Pocket applied to outside of garment
167 PATCHWORK Work of various cloths sewn together
168 PATE Head
169 PATEE Type of heraldic device
170 PATEN Plate
171 PATONCE Type of heraldic cross
172 PATH Pedestrian track
173 PATHWAY Path

174 PATIBLE Horizontal bar of a cross
175 PATINA Green oxide coating on bronze
176 PATRIARCH Orthodox Christian archbishop
177 PATRIARCH CROSS Cross with two cross bars
178 PATRON-SAINT Protecting saint of person or country (St George of England shown here)
179 PATTERN Repeating ornamental design
180 PAUNCH Large stomach
181 PAUSE Musical notation symbol
182 PAVEMENT Footway; sidewalk
183 PAVILION Type of tent
184 PAVING Stones of a pavement
185 PAVONINE Pertaining to a peacock
186 PAW Animal's foot
187 PAWN Chessman of least value
188 PAYSAGE Landscape
189 PE Seventeenth letter of the Hebrew alphabet
190 PEA Variety of vegetable
191 PEA-SHOOTER Child's blowpipe for peas
192 PEACE SIGN 'V' sign made with the hand
193 PEACE-OFFICER Policeman
194 PEACH Variety of fruit
195 PEACOCK Male peafowl
196 PEACOCK Variety of butterfly
197 PEAFOWL Variety of bird
198 PEAK Pointed mountaintop
199 PEAK Visor of a cap
200 PEAK Point of anchor fluke
201 PEANUT Variety of nut; groundnut
202 PEAR Variety of fruit
203 PEASANT Rural labourer
204 PEASECOD Pod of the pea
205 PEAVY Tool used in log handling
206 PEBBLE Small rounded stone
207 PECCARY Variety of animal
208 PECTORAL Breast-plate
209 PECTORAL-FIN Fin behind fish's gills
210 PEDAL Foot-operated propulsion lever on a bicycle
211 PEDALLING Propelling a bicycle by foot
212 PEDESTAL Base for a statue
213 PEDESTRIAN Walker
214 PEDIGEROUS Having feet
215 PEDIMENT Classical triangular gable end

216 PEEL Skin of a fruit
217 PEELER Policeman
218 PEEWIT Variety of bird; lapwing
219 PEG Split wooden pin for securing clothes to a line
220 PEG-LEG Rudimentary artificial limb
221 PEGASUS Mythological winged horse
222 PELAGE Animal's coat
223 PELAMID Variety of fish
224 PELICAN Variety of bird
225 PELISSE Hussar's overgarment
226 PELLET Heraldic device
227 PELLOCK Porpoise
228 PELMET Cloth concealing curtain rod
229 PELT Animal's skin
230 PELUDO Variety of animal; hairy armadillo
231 PELVIS Part of the skeleton
232 PEN Enclosure for animals
233 PEN Porcupine quill
234 PEN Instrument for drawing or writing in ink
235 PENCEL Small pennon or streamer
236 PENCIL Graphite drawing instrument
237 PENCIL FISH Variety of fish
238 PENCIL-SHARPENER Device for sharpening pencils
239 PENDULE Pendulum-clock
240 PENDULUM Swinging weight in clock mechanism
241 PENDULUM-BOB Weight on the end of pendulum
242 PENDULUM-CLOCK Clock regulated by a pendulum
243 PENGUIN Variety of flightless bird
244 PENHOLDER Barrel to hold pen nib
245 PENIS Male sex organ
246 PENITENTIARY Prison
247 PENKNIFE Small folding knife
248 PENNANT Long tapering flag
249 PENNIFEROUS Feathered
250 PENNON Long triangular flag
251 PENNONCEL Small pennon attached to a lance
252 PENNY-FARTHING Style of early bicycle
253 PENTACERATOPS Variety of extinct dinosaur

254 PENTACHORD Five-stringed musical instrument
255 PENTACLE Five-pointed star; pentagram
256 PENTADACTYL Five fingered
257 PENTAGON Geometric figure with five sides
258 PENTAGRAM Five-pointed star
259 PENTAHEDRON Geometrical solid with five faces
260 PENTALPHA Five-pointed star
261 PENTANGLE Five-pointed star
262 PENTASTYLE Classical architectural style with five columns
263 PENULTIMA Last but one syllable of a word
264 PEOPLE Persons
265 PEPLUM Short section attached to waistline of garment
266 PEPO Pumpkin
267 PEPPER Variety of vegetable
268 PEPPER-MILL Device for grinding peppercorns
269 PEPPERCORN Dried berry of black pepper
270 PEPPERSHRIKE Variety of bird
271 PER CENT Mathematical symbol
272 PERAMBULATION Walking
273 PERAMBULATOR Baby-carriage
274 PERCH Variety of fish
275 PERCH Bird's resting place
276 PERCHERON Breed of draught-horse
277 PERCHER That which perches
278 PERCOLATOR Coffee-maker
279 PEREGRINE FALCON Variety of bird of prey
280 PERFECT Numbers as 6 or 15
$(1 + 2 + 3 = 6)$
$(1 + 2 + 3 + 4 + 5 = 15)$
281 PERFECT SQUARE Nine (3^3)
282 PERFORATION Hole made by piercing
283 PERFORMANCE A stage entertainment
284 PERFORMER Entertainer
285 PERFORMING Entertaining
286 PERIANTH Outer part of a flower
287 PERIOD Full stop
288 PERISCOPE Submarine's viewing device
289 PERIWIG Wig
290 PERIWINKLE Variety of shellfish; winkle
291 PERPENDICULAR Vertical
292 PERPENDICULAR Gothic architectural style
293 PERPETUA Style of letterform
294 PERSIAN Breed of cat
295 PERSON Human individual
296 PERSONAGE Person
297 PERSPECTIVE Artistic illusion of distance
298 PERTUSE Perforated
299 PERU Flag of South American republic
300 PERUKE Wig
301 PES Hind foot of an animal
302 PEST Destructive animal
303 PESTLE Pounding implement used with a mortar
304 PET Tame animal kept as a companion
305 PETAL Section of a flower corolla
306 PETASOS Style of ancient Greek hat
307 PETUARIST Flying mammal such as phalanger
308 PETREL Variety of bird
309 PETTICOAT Woman's underskirt
310 PHAETON Type of carriage
311 PHAINOPEPLA Variety of bird
312 PHALANGER Variety of animal

Pediments

Triangular   Segmental

Broken   Open

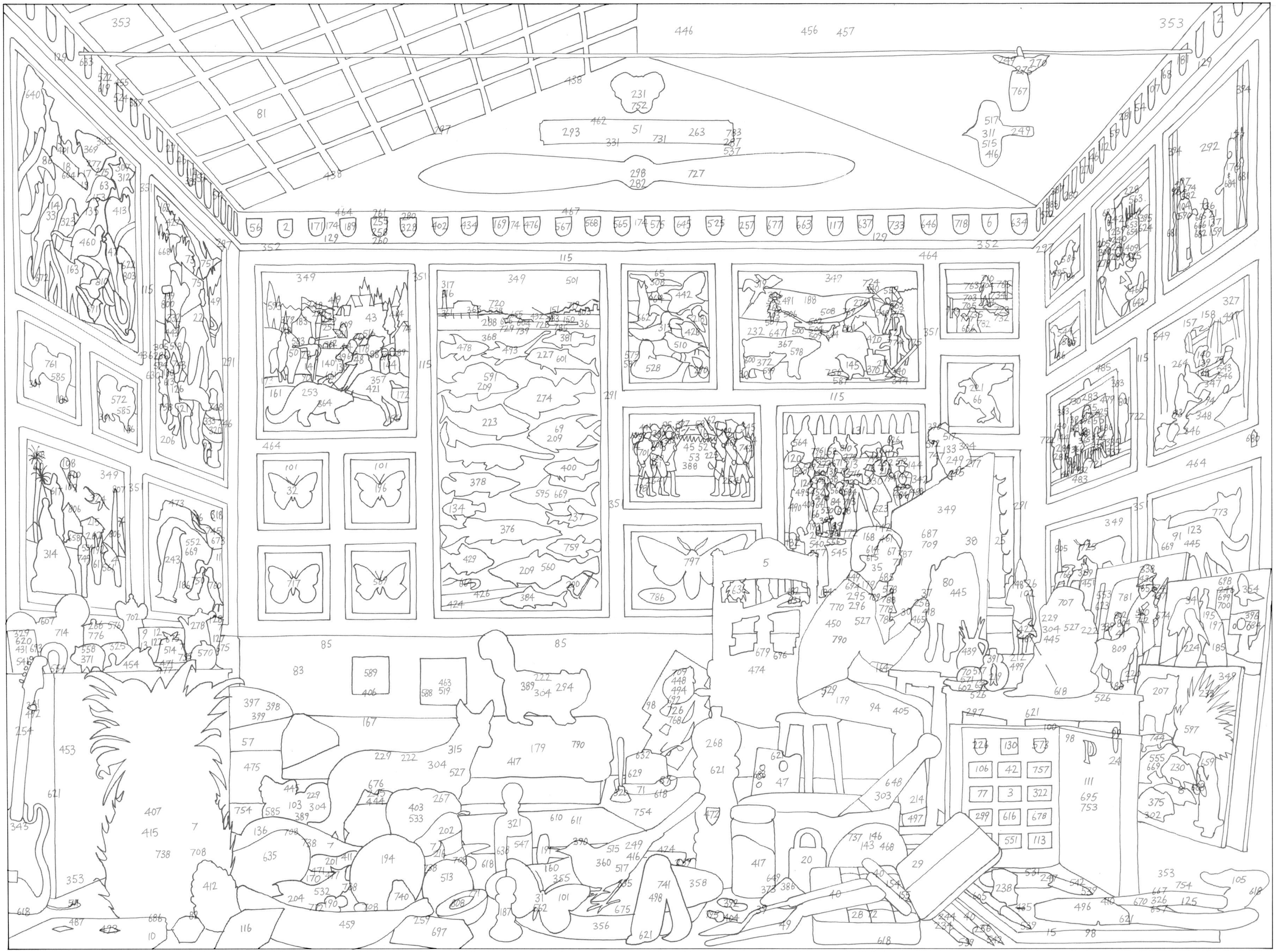

SUBI DURA A RUDIBUS.

313 PHALAROPE Variety of bird
314 PHARAOH Ancient Egyptian King
315 PHARAOH HOUND Breed of dog
316 PHARE Lighthouse
317 PHAROS Lighthouse
318 PHASIS New moon
319 PHEASANT Variety of game bird
320 PHI Twenty-first letter of the Greek alphabet
321 PHIAL Small glass vessel
322 PHILIPPINES Flag of South-east Asian republic
323 PHOEBE Variety of bird
324 PHOENICOPTER Variety of bird; flamingo
325 PHONE Communication instrument; telephone
326 PHONETIC Representing the sounds of speech (signature is spelt phonetically)
327 PHONEY Fake
328 PHOSPHORUS Element, atomic number 15
329 PHOTOGRAPH Picture made with a camera
330 PHOTOGRAPHER Maker of photographic pictures
331 PHRASE Group of words
332 PHRYGIAN CAP Style of cap
333 PI Sixteenth letter of the Greek alphabet
334 PIANIST Piano player
335 PIANO Type of musical instrument
336 PIANO-STOOL Pianist's seat
337 PIANOFORTE Piano
338 PICAROON Pirate
339 PICCOLO Type of musical instrument
340 PICK Digging tool
341 PICK Plectrum
342 PICK-A-BACK Child's game where one carries another
343 PICK-UP Microphone of a sound reproduction system
344 PICKAXE Digging tool; pick
345 PICKELHAUBE Style of Prussian spiked military helmet
346 PICNIC Casual meal eaten in the open air
347 PICNICKERS People eating a picnic
348 PICKNICKING Eating a picnic
349 PICTURE Two-dimensional work of art
350 PICTURE-HAT Wide-brimmed woman's hat
351 PICTURE-FRAME Wooden frame surrounding picture
352 PICTURE-MOULDING Moulding from which pictures are hung
353 PICTURE-PLANE The surface of a painting
354 PIE Variety of bird; magpie
355 PIE Foodstuff covered with baked pastry
356 PIE-DISH Dish in which pie is baked
357 PIEBALD Light-coloured horse with dark markings
358 PIECRUST baked pastry portion of a pie
359 PIED ANTELOPE Variety of animal; bontebok
360 PIED WAGTAIL Variety of bird
361 PIER Sea-front jetty
362 PIER Column supporting bridge
363 PIER-HEAD Part of pier furthest from the shore
364 PIERCED Stabbed
365 PIERETTE A female character in French pantomime
366 PIERROT A male character in French pantomime

367 PIG Variety of domestic animal
368 PIGBOAT Submarine
369 PIGEON Variety of bird
370 PIGGIN Type of pail
371 PIGGY-BANK Money-box in the shape of a pig
372 PIGLET Young pig
373 PIGMENT Powdered colouring matter
374 PIGTAIL Plait of hair at back of head
375 PIKA Variety of animal
376 PIKE Variety of fish
377 PIKE Type of long-handled spear
378 PIKE CICHLID Variety of fish
379 PIKE HORN Style of medieval woman's hat
380 PIKEMAN Soldier armed with a pike
381 PIKEPERCH Variety of fish
382 PIKESTAFF Handle of a pike
383 PILASTER Shallow pier projecting from wall
384 PILCHARD Variety of fish
385 PILCROW Paragraph mark
386 PILE Heap
387 PILE Heraldic device
388 PILE Pointed stake
389 PILE Fine soft hair
390 PILEUM Top of a bird's head
391 PILGRIM BOTTLE Style of vessel
392 PILL Small medicinal tablet
393 PILL-BOX Style of woman's hat
394 PILLAR Supporting column
395 PILLAR-BOX Post-box
396 PILLORY Antique method of punishment
397 PILLOW Cushion to support the head
396 PILLOW-CASE Fabric sleeve enclosing pillow
399 PILLOW-SLIP Pillow-case
400 PILOT FISH Variety of fish
401 PILOTHOUSE Deckhouse for ship's pilot
402 PILY Heraldic device
403 PIMENTO Red pepper
404 PIN Small slender metal spike
405 PIN-STRIPE Pattern with a thin stripe
406 PIN-UP Picture pinned on a wall
407 PINA Pineapple
408 PINAFORE Sleeveless apron
409 PINCE-NEZ Glasses attached to the nose
410 PINCERS Grasping tool
411 PINDAR Peanut
412 PINE-CONE Woody fruit of the pine
413 PINE-MARTEN Variety of animal
414 PINE-TREE Variety of tree
415 PINEAPPLE Variety of fruit
416 PINION Wing feather
417 PINK Pale red colour
418 PINKIE The little finger
419 PINNACLE Small pointed turret
420 PINSCHER Breed of dog
421 PINTO Piebald
422 PINWHEEL Lightweight toy windmill
423 PIP Spot on a playing card
424 PIPE Tube
425 PIPE Device for smoking tobacco
426 PIPE-LINE Line of joined pipes
427 PIPISTRELLE Variety of bat
428 PIPIT Variety of bird
429 PIRANHA Variety of fish
430 PIRATE One who practises robbery at sea
431 PIROUETTE Spinning on tiptoe while dancing
432 PISCATION Fishing
433 PISCATOR Fisherman

434 PISCES Twelth sign of the zodiac; the fishes
435 PISMIRE Ant
436 PISTIL Female organ of a flower

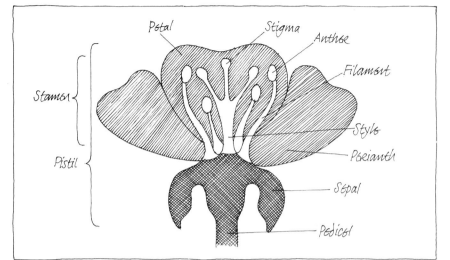

437 PISTOL Handgun
438 PITCH Slope of a roof
439 PITCHER Earthenware jug
440 PITCHFORK Long-handled tool for pitching hay
441 PITH HELMET Lightweight tropical hat
442 PITTA Variety of bird
443 PIXIE Small supernatural being
444 PIZZLE Animal's penis
445 PLACENTARY Placental mammal
446 PLAFOND Ceiling
447 PLAGIARISM A purloined artistic idea
448 PLAICE Variety of fish
449 PLAID Tartan
450 PLAIN Unpatterned
451 PLAIN An expanse of flat land
452 PLAIT Braid of intertwisted hair
453 PLAN-CHEST Chest for storing large flat papers
454 PLANE Tool for smoothing wood
455 PLANET World orbiting around the sun
456 PLANK Long thick slab of timber
457 PLANKING Quantity of fitted planks
458 PLANT Vegetable organism
459 PLANTAIN Variety of banana-like fruit
460 PLANTAIN EATER Variety of bird
461 PLANTIGRADE Creature that walks upon the soles of its feet
462 PLAQUE Inscribed wall tablet
463 PLASH Splash
464 PLASTER Smooth wall and ceiling coating
465 PLASTER Adhesive medical dressing
466 PLASTER CAST Immobilizing case enclosing broken limb
467 PLASTERWORK Work done with plaster
468 PLASTIC Versatile synthetic substance
469 PLASTRON Broad cloth front of uniform
470 PLAT Braid of intertwisted hair
471 PLATE Flat shallow round dish
472 PLATE Heraldic device
473 PLATEAU Flat area of elevated land

474 PLATEN Area of press that presses paper against inked surface
475 PLATFORM Raised floor area

476 PLATINUM Element; atomic number 78
477 PLATTER Plate for food
478 PLATY Variety of fish
479 PLAY Dramatic entertainment
480 PLAY Pleasurable amusement
481 PLAY-ACTOR Male dramatic entertainer
482 PLAY-ACTRESS Female dramatic entertainer
483 PLAYER Actor
484 PLAYFELLOW Child who plays with another
485 PLAYHOUSE Theatre
486 PLAYING Performing upon a musical instrument
487 PLAYING CARD Card used in various games
488 PLAYMATE Playfellow
489 PLAYTHING Toy
490 PLEAT Fold in cloth
491 PLEBEIAN Member of the common people
492 PLECTRUM Device for plucking strings
493 PLESIOSAUR Variety of extinct marine reptile
494 PLEURONECT Flat-fish
495 PLEXURE Plait
496 PLIERS Grasping tool; pincers
497 PLIMSOLL Rubber-soled canvas shoe
498 PLIMSOLL MARK Load-line mark on ship's side

499 PLINTH Base for a statue
500 PLOUGH Agricultural soil-breaking device
501 PLOUGH Constellation of Ursa Major
502 PLOUGH-BEAM Central beam of a plough
503 PLOUGH-BOY Boy who leads plough-horse
504 PLOUGH-IRON Ploughshare
505 PLOUGH-MAN Man who drives a plough
506 PLOUGH-TREE Plough handle
507 PLOUGHER One who ploughs
508 PLOUGHING Cutting the earth with a plough
509 PLOUGHSHARE Blade of a plough
510 PLOVER Variety of bird
511 PLUG Device to connect electrical apparatus to current
512 PLUG HAT Bowler hat
513 PLUM Variety of fruit
514 PLUM-PUDDING Type of boiled pudding eaten at Christmas
515 PLUMAGE Bird's feathers
516 PLUME Feathers worn as an ornament
517 PLUMOSE Feathered
518 PLUMP Stout
519 PLUNGE Sudden dive into water
520 PLUNGER Suction cup device for unblocking pipes
521 PLUNGER-PUMP Force-pump
522 PLUS Mathematical addition symbol (+)
523 PLUS FOURS Style of knee-length trousers
524 PLUTO Symbol for the planet furthest from the sun
525 PLUTONIUM Element; atomic number 94
526 PLYWOOD Type of laminated wood
527 PNEUMONOPHOROUS With lungs
528 POCHARD Variety of duck
529 POCKET Pouch forming part of garment
530 POCKET-HANDKERCHIEF Handkerchief carried in the pocket
531 POCKET-KNIFE Folding knife carried in the pocket
532 POD Seed-vessel of pea
533 POD-PEPPER Variety of vegetable
534 PODIUM Low wall, supporting pillars
535 PODOTHECA Bird's leg-covering
536 POGO-STICK Spring-loaded jumping-stick
537 POINT Full stop
538 POINT Small headland
539 POINT Sharp tip
540 POINT-DUTY Directing traffic
541 POINTE Tiptoe ballet position
542 POINTED Tipped with a point

Plimsoll Mark

LR = Lloyds Register
TF = Tropical Fresh Water
F = Fresh Water
T = Tropics (Sea Water)
S = Summer
W = Winter
WNA = Winter North Atlantic

543 POINTER That which points
544 POINTER Breed of dog
545 POINTING Mortar between masonry
546 POINTING Indicating with the finger
547 POISON Deadly substance
548 POKE Small sack
549 POKE Projecting rim or poke-bonnet
550 POKE-BONNET Style of woman's bonnet
551 POLAND Flag of East European country
552 POLAR BEAR Variety of animal
553 POLE Long rounded piece of wood
554 POLE Each end of a magnet
555 POLECAT Variety of animal
556 POLICE OFFICER Law officer
557 POLICEMAN Police officer
558 POLKA-DOT Pattern of small dots
559 POLL Back of horse's head
560 POLLACK Variety of fish
561 POLLEX Thumb
562 POLLINATOR Creature that distributes pollen
563 POLLUTION Dirty contaminating matter
564 POLONAISE Style of dress
565 POLONIUM Element; atomic number 84
566 POLYCEPHALIC Many-headed
567 POLYGON Many-sided figure
568 POLYGRAM Figure of many intersecting lines

Regular Polygons

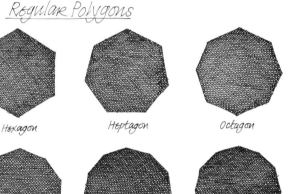

Pentagon Hexagon Heptagon Octagon

Nonagon Decagon Hendecagon Dodecagon

569 POLYPHEMUS Variety of moth
570 POMEGRANATE Variety of fruit
571 POMELO Variety of fruit; grapefruit
572 POMERANIAN Breed of dog
573 POMEYS Heraldic device
574 POMMEL Knob of sword-hilt
575 POMMETTY CROSS Type of heraldic cross
576 POMPION Pumpkin
577 POMPOLEON Grapefruit
578 POMPON Round ornamental tuft
579 POND Pool of water
580 PONIARD Dagger
581 PONT-LEVIS Drawbridge
582 PONTIFF Pope
583 PONY Small horse
584 PONY-TAIL Drawn back hanging hair-style
585 POOCH Dog

586 POODLE Breed of dog
587 POOL Small body of still water
588 POOL Swimming pool
589 POP-ART Mid-twentieth-century art style
590 POPE Head of the Roman Catholic church
591 POPE Variety of fish
592 POPINJAY Parrot
593 POPLAR Variety of tree
594 POPPY Variety of plant
595 PORBEAGLE Variety of shark
596 PORCH Roofed area in front of a doorway
597 PORCUPINE Variety of animal
598 PORK Pig
599 PORKET Piglet
600 PORKLING Piglet
601 PORPOISE Variety of aquatic mammal
602 PORRINGER Type of small bowl
603 PORT Harbour
604 PORT Left side of a ship
605 PORT-CRAYON Pencil holder
606 PORT-HOLE Circular window in ship
607 PORTABLE Able to be carried
608 PORTAL Large door
609 PORTCULLIS Defensive grating
610 PORTEFEUILLE Container for drawings; portfolio

611 PORTFOLIO Container for drawings
612 PORTICO Porch with columns
613 PORTLY Stout
614 PORTRAIT Picture of a person
615 PORTRAYAL Portrait
616 PORTUGAL Flag of South-west European country
617 POSEIDON Ancient Greek god of the sea
618 POSITION Place
619 POSITIVE Electrical symbol for positive
620 POSITIVE Photographic print made from a negative
621 POSSESSION Something owned
622 POSSUM Variety of animal
623 POST Upright wooden pillar
624 POST-BOX Box for dispatching letters
625 POST-HORN Type of musical instrument

626 POSTILION Rider of near horse of carriage team
627 POST MERIDIEM After midday
628 POSY Bunch of flowers; nosegay
629 POT Cooking vessel
630 POT-BELLY Protruding belly
631 POT-HOLE Hole in road surface
632 POT-LIT Lid of a pot
633 POTASSIUM Chemical symbol (K)
634 POTASSIUM Element; atomic number 19
635 POTATO Variety of vegetable
636 POTATO-BEETLE Variety of insect; Colorado beetle
637 POTENT CROSS Type of heraldic cross
638 POTION Poisonous liquid
639 POTTINGER Type of dish; porringer
640 POTTO Variety of animal
641 POUCH Small bag
642 POUFFE Low seating cushion
643 POULDRON Armour protecting the shoulder
644 POULTRY Domestic fowls
645 POUND Symbol for measure of weight
646 POUND Symbol for British monetary unit
647 POUND Enclosure; pen
648 POUNDER Pestle
649 POWDER Fine dry grains of matter
650 POWDER-FLASK Gunpowder container
651 POWDER-HORN Gunpowder container
652 POWER-PLANT Factory for producing energy
653 POWER-HOUSE Power-plant
654 POWER-STATION Power-plant
655 POWERBOAT Vessel propelled by an engine
656 PRACTISING Exercising to gain skill
657 PRAENOMEN First name
658 PRAIRIE-SCHOONER Covered wagon
659 PRAIRIE-DOG Variety of animal
660 PRAM Baby-carriage
661 PRANCE Springing forward
662 PRANTINCOLE Variety of bird
663 PRASEODYMIUM Element; atomic number 59
664 PRAWN Variety of crustacean
665 PRAYING Engaged in prayer
666 PRAYER Communication with God
667 PRE-NAME First name
668 PRECIPICE Cliff
669 PREDATOR Creature that preys on others
670 PREFIX Word placed before another
671 PREGNANT Expecting a child
672 PREHENSILE Able to grasp
673 PREHISTORIC Before written history
674 PRELATE High-ranking clergyman
675 PREPARED Ready to be consumed
676 PREPUCE Foreskin
677 PRESA Musical notation mark
678 PRESIDENT Flag of the President of the United States
679 PRESS Printing machine
680 PRICE TAG Ticket indicating price
681 PRICKET Type of tall candlestick
682 PRIEST Clergyman
683 PRIMARY COLOURS Red, blue and yellow
684 PRIMATE Patriarch
685 PRIMATE Highest order of mammals
686 PRIME NUMBER Number divisible by itself
687 PRIMING Base coat of paint
688 PRIMROSE Variety of plant
689 PRINCE Son of a sovereign

690 PRINCESS Daughter of a sovereign
691 PRINIA Variety of bird
692 PRINT Image formed by printing
693 PRINT Positive photographic image on paper
694 PRINT Pattern on a fabric
695 PRINTING Impression left by inked surface
696 PRINTING-PRESS Machine for producing printed images
697 PRISM Solid geometrical figure
698 PRISON Building for confining criminals
699 PRISON-BARS Bars of a prison
700 PRISONER Person confined to prison
701 PRIVATE Lowest ranking soldier
702 PRIZE Trophy gained by merit
703 PRIZE-FIGHT Professional boxing match
704 PRIZE-FIGHTER Professional boxer
705 PRIZE-RING Professional boxing ring
706 PROBOSCIS Elephant's trunk
707 PROBOSCIS MONKEY Variety of animal
708 PRODUCE Crops, fruit, vegetables etc.
709 PRODUCTION That which is produced
710 PROFESSIONAL Sportsman who competes for money
711 PROFILE Side view of a face
712 PROG Stiletto
713 PROGENY Children
714 PROJECTOR Apparatus for throwing a picture on to a screen
715 PROLETARIAN Member of the working class
716 PROMENADE Area for walking
717 PROMETHEA MOTH Variety of moth
718 PROMETHIUM Element; atomic number 61
719 PROMINENCE Hill
720 PROMONTORY Headland
721 PROMPT-BOX Box where prompter sits
722 PROMPT-SIDE Side of the stage on the actor's left (UK) or right (US)
723 PRONE Lying face down
724 PRONG Each point of a fork
725 PRONGHORN Variety of antelope
726 PROOF Preliminary printed impression
727 PROPELLER Screw of an aircraft
728 PROPULSION Powered passage through the water
729 PRORE Prow
730 PROSCENIUM Arch framing stage
731 PROSE Language other than poetry
732 PROSTRATE Laying face downwards
733 PROTACTINIUM Element; atomic number 91
734 PROTAGONIST Person in contest
735 PROTECTOR Device for protecting
736 PROTESTANT Non Roman Catholic or Orthodox Christian
737 PROTRACTOR Instrument for measuring angles
738 PROVISIONS Supply of food
739 PROW Ship's bow
740 PRUNE Dried plum
741 PRUNING-KNIFE Knife used for pruning plants
742 PRUSSIAN Inhabitant of Prussia
743 PSALTERY Type of musical instrument
744 PSAMMODROMUS Variety of lizard
745 PSEUDELEPHANT Mastodon
746 PSI Twenty-third letter of the Greek alphabet
747 PSITTACINE Parrot
748 PSYKTER Type of Greek vessel
749 PTAH Ancient Egyptian creator of the universe

750 PTARMIGAN Variety of bird
751 PTERANODON Variety of extinct flying reptile
752 PUBIS Bone of the pelvis
753 PUBLICATION Published book
754 PUCE Brownish purple colour
755 PUDDING Boiled sweet foodstuff
756 PUDDLE Shallow pool of water
757 PUERTO RICO Flag of Caribbean island
758 PUFF-BALL Variety of fungus
759 PUFFER Variety of fish
760 PUFFIN Variety of bird
761 PUG Breed of dog
762 PUGGAREE Veil tied around sun helmet
763 PUGILISM Boxing
764 PUGILIST Boxer
765 PUGNACIOUS Combative
766 PUKU Variety of antelope; kob
767 PULLEY Hoisting mechanism
768 PULL Single printed proof
769 PULL Drag
770 PULLOVER Loose woollen upper garment
771 PULP Fleshy part of fruit
772 PULSE Seed of leguminous plant
773 PUMA Variety of animal; cougar
774 PUMP Apparatus for raising liquids
775 PUMP-HANDLE Lever of a pump
776 PUMPKIN Variety of fruit
777 PUNCH Striking with the fist
778 PUNCH Puppet character
779 PUNCH-BALL Ball for punching practice
780 PUNCHINELLO Puppet character; Punch
781 PUNCHEON Large cask
782 PUNCHER Person delivering punch
783 PUNCTUATION Written marks indicating pauses etc.
784 PUNISHMENT Penalty inflicted
785 PUNT Type of flat-bottomed vessel
786 PUPA Chrysalis
787 PUPIL Opening in the eye's iris
788 PUPPET Small figure moved by hand
789 PUPPETEER Puppet operator
790 PURPLE Colour between red and blue
791 PURSE Small bag
792 PUSHING Propelling in front of one
793 PUSH-BIKE Self-propelled bicycle
794 PUSH-CYCLE Push-bike
795 PUSH-PIN Drawing-pin
796 PUSHER One who pushes
797 PUSS-MOTH Variety of moth
798 PUTTEE Wrap-around leggings
799 PUTTER Putting-iron
800 PUTTING-IRON Type of golf club
801 PUTTO Naked figure of young boy
802 PYGMY Member of African race of small stature
803 PYGMY POSSUM Variety of animal
804 PYJAMAS Loose-fitting sleeping suit
805 PYLON Structure for carrying overhead cables
806 PYRAMID Large ancient Egyptian stone tomb
807 PYRAMIDION Pointed apex of an obelisk
808 PYRENE Fruit stone
809 PYRENEAN MOUNTAIN DOG Breed of dog
810 PYTHON Variety of large snake

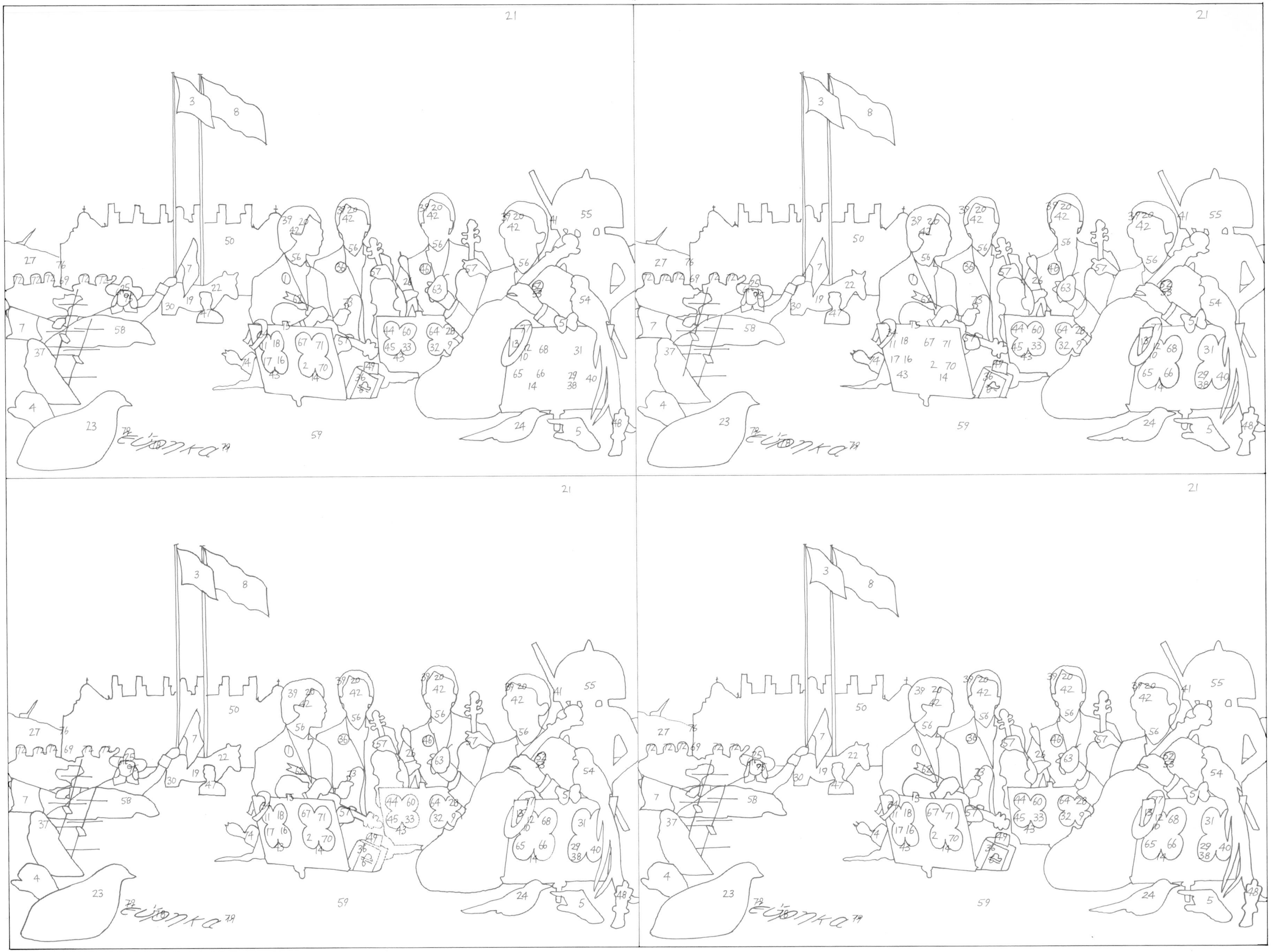

Q

1 Q Seventeenth letter of the alphabet
2 Q Braille alphabet
3 Q International signal flag
4 Q Manual alphabet – Anglo/Australian system
5 Q Manual alphabet – American system
6 Q Morse code alphabet
7 Q Semaphore alphabet
8 QATAR Flag of independent South-west Asian country
9 QOPH Nineteenth letter of the Hebrew alphabet
10 QUADRANGLE Rectangle
11 QUADRANT A quarter of a circle
12 QUADRATE Square
13 QUADRATURE Astronomical symbol
14 QUADRIFOIL Foil with four lobes; quatrefoil

27 QUARRY Open mine from which stone is extracted
28 QUART Two pints
29 QUARTER One-fourth
30 QUARTER Limb and surrounding area of a quadruped
31 QUARTER Twenty-eight pounds weight
32 QUARTER Twenty-five cents
33 QUARTER Each of the four points of the compass
34 QUARTER Half of a horseshoe
35 QUARTER-NOTE Musical note; crotchet
36 QUARTER-BINDING Style of bookbinding
37 QUARTER-DECK Raised deck at stern of ship
38 QUARTERN A quarter
39 QUARTERNION A quartet
40 QUARTERNION The number four
41 QUARTERSTAFF Stout pole used as a weapon
42 QUARTET Group of four musicians
43 QUATREFOIL Foil with four lobes
44 QUATTUORDECILLION Ten to the 84th power – British numerical system
45 QUATTUORDECILLION Ten to the 45th power – American numerical system
46 QUAVER Musical note; eighth note
47 QUEEN Female sovereign

Queen

62 QUILL Feather-pen
63 QUINCE Variety of fruit
64 QUINCUNX Arrangement of five dots
65 QUINDECILLION Ten to the 90th power – British numerical system
66 QUINDECILLION Ten to the 48th power – American numerical system
67 QUINQUANGLE Pentagon
68 QUINTAL 112 pounds weight; hundredweight
69 QUINTET Group of five musicians

Chessmen

Pawn   Rook or Castle   Knight   Bishop   Queen   King

15 QUADRILATERAL Four-sided
16 QUADRILLION Ten to the twenty-fourth power – British numerical system
17 QUADRILLION Ten to the fifteenth power – American numerical system
18 QUADRISECTION Division into four equal parts
19 QUADRUPED Animal with four legs
20 QUADRUPLET One of four born at the same time
21 QUADRUPLICATION Four-fold copy
22 QUAGGA Variety of extinct zebra-like animal
23 QUAIL Variety of game bird
24 QUAIL-THRUSH Variety of bird
25 QUAKER Member of the Society of Friends
26 QUARREL Square-headed crossbow bolt

48 QUEEN Most powerful chess-piece
49 QUEEN Court playing-card
50 QUEEN ANNE Style of architecture
51 QUEEN PURPLE TIP Variety of butterfly
52 QUERY Question mark
53 QUESTION MARK Punctuation mark indicating question
54 QUETZAL Variety of bird
55 QUETZALCOATL Ancient Aztec god
56 QUICK Alive
57 QUICK Flesh below finger-nail
58 QUICKHATCH Variety of animal; wolverine
59 QUICKSAND Wet sand into which objects sink
60 QUICKSILVER Mercury; chemical symbol (Hg)
61 QUIFF Curl of hair on the forehead

70 QUINTILLION Ten to the 30th power – British numerical system
71 QUINTILLION Ten to the 18th power – American numerical system
72 QUINTUPLET One of five born at the same time
73 QUIRT Type of riding whip
74 QUIVER Container for arrows
75 QUIZZING-GLASS Monocle
76 QUOIN Outer corner of a wall
77 QUOIT Ring used in throwing game
78 QUOTATION Repetition of another's words (in this case Archimedes' words)
79 QUOTATION MARKS Punctuation marks indicating quoted words

R

1 R Eighteenth letter of the alphabet
2 R Braille alphabet
3 R International signal flag
4 R Manual alphabet – American system
5 R Morse code alphabet
6 R Semaphore alphabet
7 RA Ancient Egyptian god of the sun
8 RABAB Type of musical instrument
9 RABATO Style of collar
10 RABBIT Variety of animal
11 RACE Speed contest
12 RACER Competitor in a race
13 RACERUNNER Variety of lizard
14 RACKET Strung bat used in tennis
15 RACKET-TAIL Variety of bird; motmot
16 RACKETT Type of musical instrument
17 RACOON Variety of animal
18 RACOON DOG Variety of racoon-like animal
19 RADIATOR Device for cooling car engine (this one belongs to a Rolls Royce)
20 RADIO Wireless receiver
21 RADIOSONDE Weather balloon and transmitter
22 RADIUM Element; atomic number 88
23 RADIUS Bone of the forearm
24 RADIUS Spoke of a wheel
25 RADIUS From centre to circumference of a circle
26 RADON Element; atomic number 86
27 RAFTER Support for a roof

36 RAIN QUAIL Variety of bird
37 RAINBOW Coloured arc in the sky
38 RAKE Slope of a ship's stern
39 RAM Male sheep
40 RAM Variety of fish
41 RAM'S-HORN The horn of a ram
42 RAM-ROD Rod for loading a gun
43 RAMIFEROUS With branches
44 RAMMER Ram-rod
45 RAMPANT Heraldic device
46 RAMPIKE Erect broken tree
47 RANDOM Left to chance
48 RAPIER Type of sword
49 RAPTOR Bird of prey
50 RAQUET Broad stringed bat
51 RAQUET-TAILED KINGFISHER Variety of bird
52 RASORBA Variety of fish
53 RASPBERRY Variety of fruit
54 RASSE Variety of animal
55 RAT Variety of animal
56 RAT-KANGAROO Variety of animal
57 RATEL Variety of animal; honey badger
58 RATLINE Rope steps to the rigging of a ship
59 RATTLE Noise-making tip of rattlesnake's tail
60 RATTLER Rattlesnake
61 RATTLESNAKE Variety of venomous snake
62 RAVEN Variety of bird
63 RAY Shaft of light
64 RAY Variety of fish
65 RAYONNANT STYLE Style of gothic architecture; decorated gothic
66 RAYONNY Heraldic device
67 RAZOR FISH Variety of fish
68 RE Ancient Egyptian sun god; Ra
69 READING Studying a book
70 READABLE Legible
71 READER Person engaged in reading
72 REAPHOOK Type of agricultural tool; sickle
73 REAR Behind
74 REAR Stand on hind legs
75 REBECK Type of musical instrument
76 REBUS Words represented by letters and pictures

Rebus

28 RAGGED Tattered
29 RAGULY Heraldic device
30 RAIA Variety of flat-fish; ray
31 RAIL Metal bar
32 RAIL Variety of bird
33 RAILING Fence made of rails
34 RAIMENT Clothing
35 RAIN Meteorological symbol

77 RECAMIER Type of daybed
78 RECEIVER Radio
79 RECEPTACLE Container
80 RECERCELE Type of heraldic cross
81 RECESS Area set back into something
82 RECLINE Lie down
83 RECORDER Type of musical instrument
84 RECTANGLE Oblong or square

85 RECTO Right-hand page of a book
86 RECUMBENT Lying down
87 RED A primary colour
88 RED ADMIRAL Variety of butterfly
89 RED BUG Variety of insect
90 RED CRESENT Islamic counterpart to the Red Cross
91 RED CROSS International medical care organization
92 RED DEER Variety of animal
93 RED FOX Variety of animal
94 RED KITE Variety of bird of prey
95 RED RIVER HOG Variety of animal
96 RED SQUIRREL Variety of animal
97 RED SEA BREAM Variety of fish
98 RED-RUMPED SWALLOW Variety of bird
99 REDBREAST Variety of bird; robin
100 REDCAP Variety of bird; goldfinch
101 REDHEAD Person with red hair
102 REDPOLL Variety of bird
103 REDSHANK Variety of bird
104 REDSTART Variety of bird
105 REDUPLICATION Repetition
106 REDWING Variety of bird
107 REED-BUNTING Variety of bird
108 REEDBUCK Variety of antelope
109 REEDLING Variety of bird; bearded titmouse
110 REEF Rocks just beneath sea
111 REEF KNOT Type of knot
112 REEFED Rolled up (of sails)
113 REFLECTION Image thrown back from a shiny surface
114 REFLECTOR That which reflects
115 REGALIA Royal insignia
116 REGARDING Looking
117 REGARDANT Heraldic device
118 REGARDER One who looks
119 REGULAR Symmetrical
120 REIN Strap for controlling horse
121 REIN Reindeer
122 REINDEER Variety of animal
123 REITERATION Repetition
124 RELAXED Resting
125 RELIC Thing surviving from the past
126 RELIEF Carving that projects from a surface
127 RELIGIEUSE Nun
128 RELIGIOUS Devout
129 REMAINS Ruins
130 REMAINS Corpse
131 REMEX Bird's wing feather
132 REMUS One of the legendary founders of Rome
133 RENIFORM Kidney-shaped
134 REMORA Variety of fish
135 RENT Tear
136 REPAIR Work to return to good condition
137 REPEATER Gun that fires many shots without reloading
138 REPETITION The doing of something more than once
139 REPLICA Copy
140 REPOSE Rest
141 REPRESENTATION Depiction
142 REPTANT Crawling
143 REPTILE Crawling creature
144 REPUBLIC Country with an elected government

145 REQUIESCENCE Repose
146 RERE-BRACE Armour protecting upper arm
147 RESARCELEE Type of heraldic cross
148 RESEMBLANCE Likeness
149 RESH Twentieth letter of the Hebrew alphabet
150 RESIDENCE Large house
151 RESPIRATOR Gas-mask
152 RESTING Relaxing
153 RESTORATION Repair
154 RESUPINE Lying-down
155 RETAINER Thing for retaining something; container
156 RETORT Type of vessel
157 RETRIEVER Breed of dog
158 RETROGRADE Backwards
159 REVERSED Backwards
160 REVOLVER Pistol with rotating ammunition chamber
161 RHEA Variety of large flightless bird

Séjant   Passant   Couchant   Salient

Réguardant   Dormant   Rampant   Séjant Erect

162 RHENIUM Element; atomic number 75
163 RHESUS MONKEY Variety of animal
164 RHINOCEROS Variety of animal
165 RHO Seventeenth letter of the Greek alphabet
166 RHODE ISLAND RED Variety of domestic fowl
167 RHODESIAN RIDGEBACK Breed of dog
168 RHODIUM Element; atomic number 45
169 RHOMBOID Type of geometric figure
170 RHINOCEROS-BEETLE Variety of insect
171 RIATA Lariat; lasso
172 RIB Bone of the chest
173 RIB Leaf vein
174 RIB-CAGE The ribs
175 RIBAND Ribbon
176 RIBBON Length of narrow fabric
177 RICKSHAW Hand-drawn two-wheeled carriage
178 RIDDLE Puzzle
179 RIDER Driver of a horse
180 RIDGE Long raised strip
181 RIDGE-POLE Timber supporting rafters
182 RIDING Driving a horse
183 RIFLE Type of gun
184 RIFLEMAN Variety of bird
185 RIFLESCOPE Telescopic rifle sight
186 RIFT Crack
187 RIG Clothing
188 RIG Masts and sails of a ship
189 RIG-OUT Clothes
190 RIGGER Long-haired paintbrush

191 RIGGING Ship's ropes controlling sails
192 RIGHT Opposite side to left
193 RIGHT ANGLE Angle of 90 degrees
194 RIGHT-LINE Straight line
195 RIGHT WHALE Variety of aquatic mammal
196 RIGID Stiff
197 RIM Outside edge of a wheel
198 RIM Brim of a vessel
199 RINCEAU Style of architectural ornamentation
200 RING Small circular ornament for the finger
201 RING-BILLED GULL Variety of sea-bird
202 RING-FINGER Third finger of the left hand
203 RING-TAILED RACOON Variety of animal
204 RINGTAIL Variety of animal; cacomistle
205 RIP Tear
206 RISER Vertical part of step
207 RISING SUN Ancient Egyptian amulet style
208 RITTER Mounted knight
209 RIVE Tear
210 RIVER-FISH River-dwelling fish
211 RIVET Bolt-like metal fastening
212 ROACH Variety of fish
213 ROAD-RUNNER Variety of bird; chaparral cock
214 ROAN Type of animal colouring
215 ROAN-ANTELOPE Variety of antelope
216 ROBBER CRAB Variety of crustacean
217 ROBE Loose-flowing outer garment
218 ROBIN Variety of European bird
219 ROBIN Variety of American bird
220 ROBIN MOTH Variety of moth
221 ROBOT Human-like machine
222 ROCK Hard mineral mass
223 ROCK BASS Variety of fish
224 ROCK BUNTING Variety of bird
225 ROCK COOK Variety of fish
226 ROCKFOWL Variety of bird
227 ROCK HYRAX Variety of animal
228 ROCK RABBIT Rock hyrax
229 ROCK SPARROW Variety of bird
230 ROCK THRUSH Variety of bird
231 ROCK DOVE Variety of bird
232 ROCK-HOPPER Variety of penguin
233 ROCKET Rocket-powered missile
234 ROCKLING Variety of fish
235 ROD Round slender stick
236 RODENT Animal with incisors and no canine teeth
237 ROE-DEER Variety of animal

238 ROEBUCK Male roe-deer
239 ROLL Flat object formed into a cylinder
240 ROLLER Variety of bird
241 ROLLER-SKATE Skate fitted with wheels
242 ROLLING-PIN Implement for rolling out pastry
243 ROMAN Normal upright letter
244 ROMAN Numerals based on capital letters
245 ROMAN CATHOLIC Member of the Roman Catholic church
246 ROMANIA Flag of Eastern European country
247 ROMANIST Roman Catholic
248 ROMULUS One of the legendary founders of Rome
249 ROOF Covering on top of a building
250 ROOF-TREE Ridgepole
251 ROOFED TERRAPIN Variety of amphibian
252 ROOFTOP Top of a roof
253 ROOK Variety of bird
254 ROOK Castle chess-piece
255 ROOSTER Adult male domestic fowl; cock
256 ROOT Mathematical symbol for root
257 ROPE Stout twisted cord
258 ROSARY Prayer-beads
259 ROSE Variety of flower
260 ROSE Deep pink colour
261 ROSE Decorative sound-hole of stringed instrument
262 ROSE-WINDOW Tracery-filled circular window
263 ROSEBUD Bud of the rose
264 ROSELLA Variety of bird
265 ROSETTE Rose-shaped award
266 ROSTAL COLUMN Ancient Roman column celebrating naval victories
267 ROTTWEILER Breed of dog
268 ROTULA Knee or elbow

RUNES

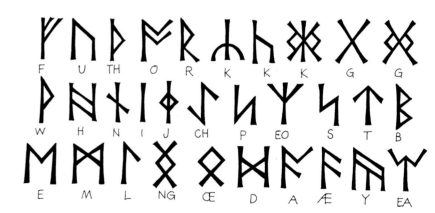

269 ROTUNDA Domed circular building
270 ROUGH Uneven
271 ROUNCY Riding horse
272 ROUND Circular
273 ROUND Type of paintbrush
274 ROUND Bullet
275 ROUNDEL Circular motif
276 ROUNDEL Heraldic device
277 ROWING Propelling a boat with oars
278 ROW-BOAT Boat propelled by oars
279 ROWEL Disk of spur

280 ROWER Person who rows
281 ROWLOCK Retaining fork for an oar
282 ROYAL Status of a king or queen
283 ROYAL ANTELOPE Variety of small antelope
284 ROYAL BLUE Deep blue colour
285 ROYAL FLYCATCHER Variety of bird
286 ROYALTY Royal person
287 RUBBLE Rough fragments of stone
288 RUBIDIUM Element; atomic number 37
289 RUBY-THROATED HUMMINGBIRD Variety of bird
290 RUCK Crease
291 RUCKSACK Backpack
292 RUDDER Steering vane of a ship
293 RUDDOCK Robin
294 RUDE Rough
295 RUFF Style of frilly collar
296 RUFFE Variety of fish
297 RUFOUS Reddish-brown colour
298 RUFOUS BUSH ROBIN Variety of bird
299 RUFOUS MOTMOT Variety of bird
300 RUFOUS RAT KANGAROO Variety of animal
301 RUG Small carpet
302 RUGBY Type of football
303 RUGGED Rough
304 RUGOSE Wrinkled
305 RUIN Partly destroyed building
306 RUIN LIZARD Variety of lizard
307 RULER Measuring instrument
308 RULER One who governs; sovereign
309 RUMINANT Animal with several stomachs
310 RUMP Buttocks
311 RUMPLED Creased; wrinkled
312 RUN Move fast on foot
313 RUNE Ancient written character
314 RUNG Step of a ladder
315 RUNNER Person who runs
316 RUNNER-UP One who takes second place
317 RUSA Variety of animal
318 RUSHER Person hurrying at speed
319 RUSHING To hurry at speed
320 RUSSET Reddish-brown colour
321 RUSSIA Flag of the Soviet Union
322 RUT Groove worn in the ground
323 RUTHENIUM Element; atomic number 44
324 RWANDA Flag of East African republic

S

1 S Nineteenth letter of the alphabet
2 S Braille alphabet
3 S International signal flag
4 S Manual alphabet – American system
5 S Morse code alphabet
6 S Semaphore alphabet
7 SABLE Variety of animal
8 SABLE Heraldic name for black
9 SABLE ANTELOPE Variety of antelope
10 SABOT Clog
11 SABRE Type of cavalry sword
12 SABRE-TOOTHED CAT Variety of extinct animal; smilodon
13 SABREFIN Variety of fish
14 SABRETACHE Satchel carried by cavalry officer
15 SABREUR Swordsman armed with a sabre
16 SACK Large cloth bag
17 SACKING Coarse fabric from which sacks are made
18 SACRED IBIS Variety of bird
19 SACRUM Part of the pelvis
20 SAD-IRON Flat-iron
21 SADDLE Seat for fastening to a horse

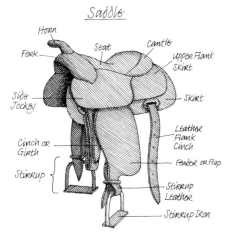

Saddle

22 SADDLE BLANKET Cloth placed beneath a saddle
23 SADDLE HORN Knot at front of a saddle
24 SADDLEBAG Bag attached to a saddle
25 SADDLECLOTH Saddle blanket
26 SADDLED Fitted with a saddle
27 SADHE Eighteenth letter of the Hebrew alphabet
28 SAFE Lockable steel cupboard

29 SAFETY-BELT Restraining belt fitted to a car
30 SAFETY-PIN Closable fastening device
31 SAFFRON Variety of flowering plant
32 SAFFRON Bright orange/yellow colour
33 SAGITTARIUS Ninth sign of the zodiac; the archer
34 SAGUARO Variety of cactus
35 SAIGA Variety of animal
36 SAIL Cloth used to catch the wind on a sailing ship
37 SAIL-BOAT Boat propelled by sail
38 SAILER Sail-boat
39 SAILING Propelled by sail
40 SAILOR Mariner
41 SAILPLANE Glider
42 SAILYARD Spar on which sails are set
43 SAINT Holy person (Saint Sebastian shown here)
44 SAINT ANDREW'S CROSS Flag of Scotland
45 SAINT ANTHONY'S CROSS Style of cross with only three arms
46 SAINT BERNARD Breed of dog
47 SAINT CHRISTOPHER-NEVIS Flag of Caribbean island group
48 SAINT HELENA Flag of South Atlantic island
49 SAINT LUCIA Flag of Caribbean island
50 SAINT SEBASTIAN Early Christian saint
51 SAINT VINCENT Flag of Caribbean island
52 SAITHE Variety of fish; coal fish
53 SALAMANDER Variety of amphibian
54 SALAMI Type of large sausage
55 SALESMAN Person employed to sell goods
56 SALIENTIAN Frog or toad
57 SALIVA Spittle
58 SALIVATION Secreting saliva
59 SALLET Style of helmet
60 SALMON Variety of fish
61 SALOMONICA Style of twisted column
62 SALT Seasoning for food
63 SALTBOX Style of house
64 SALTIRE Heraldic X-shaped cross
65 SALTSHAKER Sprinkler for salt
66 SALUKI Breed of dog
67 SALUTE Raising the hand to the cap
68 SALVER Large flat tray
69 SAMARA Sycamore seed
70 SAMARIUM Element; atomic number 62
71 SAMBAR Variety of animal
72 SAMEKH Fifteenth letter of the Hebrew alphabet
73 SAMOA Flag of Pacific island group (Western Samoa)
74 SAMOA Flag of Pacific island group (American Samoa)
75 SAMOVAR Russian tea-urn
76 SAMPAN Type of oriental boat
77 SAN MARINO Flag of Southern European republic
78 SAND Loose granular mineral powder
79 SAND-BIRD Variety of bird; sandpiper
80 SANDFISH Variety of fish
81 SAND-LIZARD Variety of lizard
82 SAND-RUNNER Sandpiper
83 SAND-SNIPE Sandpiper
84 SAND-STORM Meteorological symbol for sand-storm
85 SANDAL Style of open shoe

86 SANDERLING Variety of bird
87 SANDGLASS Time-keeping device; hour-glass
88 SANDPIPER Variety of bird
89 SANDWICH Snack made from filled slices of bread
90 SANGUINE Reddish colour
91 SANSERIF Letterform without serifs
92 SANSKRIT Ancient Hindu language
93 SANTA CLAUS Father Christmas
94 SAO TOME AND PRINCIPE Flag of West African republic
95 SAPPHIRE Type of gemstone
96 SARANGI Type of musical instrument
97 SARCELLY Type of heraldic cross
98 SAREE Type of Indian woman's garment
99 SARONG Type of East Indian wrap-around garment
100 SASH Decorative waist-band
101 SASSABY Variety of antelope; hartebeeste
102 SATAN The Devil
103 SATCHEL Small bag
104 SATELLITE A moon
105 SATELLITE Machine orbiting in space
106 SATSUMA Variety of fruit
107 SATURDAY Astrological symbol for Saturday
108 SATURN Sixth planet of the sun
109 SATURN Astrological symbol for Saturn
110 SATYR Ancient Greek supernatural being
111 SAUCE BOAT Vessel for serving sauce
112 SAUCEPAN Long-handled cooking-pot
113 SAUCER Small shallow dish to retain cup
114 SAUCISSON Sausage
115 SAUDI ARABIA Flag of South-west Asian kingdom
116 SAUPE Variety of fish
117 SAURIAN Dinosaur
118 SAURY Variety of fish; skipper
119 SAUSAGE Minced meat stuffed in a skin
120 SAVONAROLA CHAIR Style of chair; scissors chair
121 SAW Cutting tool
122 SAWDUST Dust formed from sawn wood
123 SAXHORN Type of musical instrument
124 SAXOPHONE Type of musical instrument
125 SCABBARD Sword sheath
126 SCAD Variety of fish
127 SCALE Rung of a ladder
128 SCALE Ladder
129 SCALE Staircase
130 SCALE Series of musical notes
131 SCALE Measured gradations on an instrument
132 SCALENE Triangle with unequal sides and angles
133 SCALES Flakes on a snake's skin
134 SCALES Weighing machine
135 SCALLOP Type of sea-shell
136 SCALP Hairy skin on top of the head
137 SCALPEL Surgeon's cutting tool
138 SCALY ANTEATER Variety of animal; pangolin
139 SCANDINAVIA Norway, Sweden, Finland and Denmark
140 SCANDIUM Element; atomic number 21
141 SCANTY Insufficient; brief
142 SCAPE Scene

143 SCAPE Shaft of a column
144 SCAPE Stalk
145 SCAPULA Shoulder-blade
146 SCAPUS Shaft of a feather
147 SCAR Mark left by a healed wound
148 SCAR Cliff
149 SCARAB Variety of beetle; dung-beetle
150 SCARABAEUS Scarab
151 SCARCE SWALLOWTAIL Variety of butterfly
152 SCARECROW Figure to frighten birds
153 SCARF Fabric worn around neck
154 SCARLET Brilliant red
155 SCARLET IBIS Variety of bird
156 SCARP Cliff
157 SCENE Episode of a play
158 SCENERY Stage-setting
159 SCENERY Landscape

160 SCENE-SHIFTER Stage-hand who moves scenery
161 SCEPTRE Ceremonial rod
162 SCHLEGEL'S PIT VIPER Variety of snake
163 SCHNEIDER Variety of fish
164 SCHNORKEL Underwater breathing tube
165 SCHOONER Type of sailing vessel
166 SCHWENKEL Style of flag
167 SCIMITAR Type of oriental sword
168 SCIMITAR-BABBLER Variety of bird
169 SCIMITAR-BILL Variety of bird
170 SCION Young shoot
171 SCISSORS Cutting tool
172 SCISSORS CHAIR Type of chair; savonarola chair
173 SCIURINE Squirrel
174 SCOOP Type of shovel for lifting loose substances
175 SCORE Incised groove
176 SCORE Musical notation
177 SCORE Twenty
178 SCORPIO Eighth sign of the zodiac; the scorpion
179 SCORPION Variety of arachnid

180 SCOTLAND Flag of Western European country
181 SCOTTISH TERRIER Breed of dog
182 SCRAP Fragment
183 SCREAMER Variety of bird
184 SCREEN Front window of car; windscreen
185 SCREW Small fastening device
186 SCREWDRIVER Tool for turning screws
187 SCRIBBLE Meaningless lines
188 SCRIMSHAW Ornamental object made from sea-ivory
189 SCRIPT Flowing writing
190 SCRIPTION Handwriting
191 SCROLL Ornament in the shape of a roll of material
192 SCROTUM Pouch of flesh containing testicles
193 SCRUFF Nape of the neck

Apothecaries' Symbols

ounce • one ounce • half an ounce • one and a half ounces

two ounces • fluid ounce • dram • fluid dram

scruple • pound

194 SCRUPLE Apothecaries' weight symbol
195 SCUBA Acronym for SELF CONTAINED UNDERWATER BREATHING APPARATUS
196 SCULPTURE Three-dimensional work of art
197 SCUTIFORM Shield-shaped
198 SCUTTLE Container for coal
199 SCYE Where the sleeve is inserted into a garment
200 SCYTHE Tool for reaping or mowing
201 SCYTHEBILL Variety of bird
202 SEA Large expanse of salt water
203 SEA STAR Starfish
204 SEA-BIRD Fish-eating bird that lives around the coast
205 SEA-BOARD Coastline
206 SEA-CALF Seal
207 SEA-COAST Sea-shore
208 SEA-DOG Sailor
209 SEA-FISH Fish found in the sea
210 SEA-FRONT Coastline
211 SEA-GOING Vessel that sails on the sea
212 SEA-HORSE Variety of fish
213 SEA-IVORY Ivory obtained from sea creatures
214 SEA-LAWYER Shark

215 SEA-LINE Horizon of the sea
216 SEA-LION Variety of aquatic mammal
217 SEA-MAID Mermaid
218 SEA-PIECE Painting representing the sea; seascape
219 SEA-PURSE Egg sack of the skate
220 SEA-SHELL Shell of marine creature
221 SEA-SHORE Coastline
222 SEA-URCHIN Variety of sea creature; echinus
223 SEA-VIEW Seascape
224 SEAFARER Sailor
225 SEAL Variety of aquatic mammal
226 SEAL-CALF Young seal
227 SEAL-POINT Breed of Siamese cat
228 SEAM Sewn joint
229 SEAM Place where planks join
230 SEAMAN Sailor
231 SEAPLANE Plane equipped to land on the sea
232 SEARCE Sieve
233 SEARCHLIGHT Lamp with powerful beam
234 SEASCAPE Picture featuring the sea
235 SEASIDE Land bordering the sea
236 SEASTRAND Shore
237 SEAT Chair
238 SEAT Buttocks
239 SEAT Portion of a saddle for sitting upon
240 SEAT-BELT Safety-belt in a car
241 SEATED Sitting
242 SEAT-STICK Walking-stick with a folding seat
243 SECATEUR Gardener's cutting tool

244 SECOND Sixtieth part of a minute
245 SECOND Position between first and third
246 SECOND-HAND Clock hand indicating seconds
247 SECOND-HAND Goods that are not new
248 SECONDARY COLOUR Green, orange and purple
249 SECONDARY FEATHER Feathers of bird's wing other than primaries and coverts
250 SECRETAIRE Type of writing desk
251 SECRETARY Secretaire
252 SECRETARY-BIRD Variety of bird
253 SECRETUM Private seal
254 SECTION Portion
255 SECTION-MARK Printer's sign to indicate footnote
256 SECTOR Portion of a circle
257 SEDAN CHAIR Antique form of transport
258 SEDENT Sitting
259 SEED Fertilized ovule of a plant
260 SEGMENT Fragment
261 SEGMENTAL ARCH Style of arch
262 SEGNO Musical symbol to mark a repeat
263 SEJANT Heraldic device
264 SELACHIAN Shark
265 SELENIUM Element; atomic number 34
266 SELEVIN'S MOUSE Variety of animal
267 SELF-PORTRAIT Portrait of the artist by himself
268 SELL Sadle
269 SEMAPHORE System of signalling using flags

270 SEMBLANT A likeness
271 SEME Dotted
272 SEMEIOLOGY Sign language
273 SEMINUDE Half-naked
274 SEMIBREVE Type of musical note; whole note
275 SEMICIRCLE Half circle
276 SEMICIRQUE Semicircle
277 SEMICOLON Type of punction mark (;)
278 SEMICOLON Morse code for semicolon
279 SEMIDEMISEMIQUAVER Type of musical note; sixty-fourth note
280 SEMI-LUNE Crescent
281 SEMINIFEROUS Seed bearing
282 SEMIQUAVER Type of musical note; sixteenth note
283 SEMITONE Musical interval
284 SENARY DIVISION Division into six portions
285 SENDING Dispatching a message
286 SENDER Dispatcher of a message
287 SENEGAL Flag of West African republic
288 SENSORY Sense organ
289 SENTINEL Guard; sentry
290 SENTRY Sentinel
291 SENTRY-BOX Shelter for a sentry
292 SEPAL Segment of a calyx
293 SEPIA Dark-brown colour
294 SEPTANGLE Seven-sided geometrical figure
295 SEPTFOIL Foil with seven lobes
296 SEPTIME Seventh position in fencing
297 SEPTUM Partition between the nostrils
298 SEQUACIOUS Following in regular order
299 SEQUENCE Series; things in order
300 SERAPH Type of superior angel
301 SERGEANT Non-commissioned officer above a corporal
302 SERGEANT-MAJOR Variety of fish
303 SERIES Sequence
304 SERIF Short stroke terminating letters
305 SERIN Variety of bird
306 SEROTINE Variety of bat
307 SERPENT Snake
308 SERPENT Type of musical instrument
309 SERPENT-EATER Variety of bird; secretary bird
310 SERPENTIFORM Serpentine
311 SERPENTINE In the form of a snake
312 SERRATION Saw-like edge
313 SERVAL Variety of animal
314 SERVER Salver
315 SET Stage scene
316 SET Disappear from sight
317 SET Complete collection
318 SET-SQUARE Right-angled drawing instrument
319 SETBACK Step-like recession in skyscraper façade
320 SETH Ancient Egyptian god
321 SETTEE Long upholstered seat
322 SETTER Breed of dog
323 SETTLE Style of long wooden seat
324 SETTLED Fixed in position
325 SEVEN Prime number between six and eight
326 SEVEN Roman numeral for seven
327 SEVENTEEN Seven more than ten
328 SEVENTEEN Roman numeral for seventeen
329 SEVENTH In order between sixth and eighth

330 SEVENTH Seventh part of a whole
331 SEVENTY Seven times ten
332 SEVENTY Roman numeral for seventy
333 SEVERED Separated
334 SEWELLEL Variety of animal
335 SEWING Join made by stitches
336 SEX Genitals
337 SEXDIGITAL Six-fingered
338 SEXDIGITIST Person with six fingers
339 SEXFOIL Foil with six lobes
340 SEXPARTITE Divided into six parts
341 SEYCHELLES Flag of Indian Ocean island group
342 SHACK Wooden cabin
343 SHACKLE Fetters
344 SHACKLED Fettered
345 SHADDOCK Grapefruit
346 SHADE Ghost
347 SHADE Covering for a lamp
348 SHADE Parasol
349 SHADE Shadow
350 SHADING Depiction of form
351 SHADOW Dark area of obstructed light
352 SHADOW Ghost
353 SHAFT Arrow
354 SHAFT Handle of a spear
355 SHAFT Ray of light
356 SHAFT Main body of a column
357 SHAFT Long central part of an anchor
358 SHAG Variety of bird
359 SHAITAN The Devil
360 SHAKO Style of military hat
361 SHAMROCK Symbol based on a variety of trefoil
362 SHANK Shin
363 SHANK Lower leg of a horse
364 SHANK Shaft of an anchor
365 SHANK Each half of a pair of scissors
366 SHANK Stem of a wine glass
367 SHANK Stem of a plant
368 SHANNY Variety of fish
369 SHANTY Shack
370 SHAPE Outward form
371 SHARD Fragment of pottery
372 SHARD Wingcase of an insect
373 SHARK Variety of fish
374 SHARP Pointed
375 SHARP Musical notation symbol
376 SHARPBILL Variety of bird
377 SHARPENER Device for sharpening
378 SHAVING-BRUSH Brush for applying shaving lather
379 SHEAF Bundle of wheat
380 SHEARS Scissors
381 SHEATH Scabbard
382 SHEATHBILL Variety of bird
383 SHEBANG Shed
384 SHED Small wooden building; hut
385 SHED Parting in the hair
386 SHEDDING Casting of light
387 SHEDDING Losing of blood
388 SHEEP Variety of domestic animal
389 SHEEP-DOG Dog used to tend sheep
390 SHEEPSHANK Type of knot
391 SHEER Steep
392 SHEER Curve of a ship's deck
393 SHEET Leaf of paper

394 SHEET Pane of glass
395 SHEET Rope controlling a sail
396 SHEET BEND Type of knot
397 SHELDGOOSE Variety of bird
398 SHELF Horizontal board fixed in a cupboard
399 SHELL Hard outer coat of certain creatures
400 SHELL Explosive projectile
401 SHELTER Shack
402 SHELTIE Breed of dog; Shetland sheepdog
403 SHEPHERD DOG Sheepdog
404 SHEPHERD'S CHECK Type of pattern
405 SHETLAND SHEEPDOG Breed of dog
406 SHIELD Escutcheon
407 SHIELDBUG Variety of insect
408 SHIKRA Variety of bird
409 SHILLING Symbol for a shilling
410 SHIN Front part of lower human leg
411 SHIN Twenty-second letter of the Hebrew alphabet
412 SHIN-BONE Tibia
413 SHINGLE Coarse gravel
414 SHINY Bright
415 SHINZO Type of Japanese statue
416 SHIP Square-rigged sailing vessel
417 SHIP-RAT Variety of rodent
418 SHIP-RIGGED Rigged like a ship
419 SHIPMAN Sailor
420 SHIPWRECK Destruction of a ship
421 SHIRE HORSE Breed of horse
422 SHIRT Man's loose upper garment
423 SHIRT-SLEEVE Sleeve of a shirt
424 SHIRTFRONT Front of a shirt
425 SHOD Wearing shoes
426 SHOE Covering for the foot
427 SHOE TREE Device to preserve the shape of a shoe
428 SHOE-BEAK Variety of bird; shoe-bill
429 SHOE-BILL Variety of bird
430 SHOE-BIRD Shoe-bill
431 SHOE-HORN Device to aid putting on shoes
432 SHOE-LACE Shoe fastening
433 SHOESTRING Shoe-lace
434 SHOOT New growth on a plant
435 SHOOTER Gun
436 SHOOTING BRAKE Station wagon
437 SHOOTING-IRON Gun
438 SHOOTING-STAR Meteorite
439 SHOOTING-STICK Walking-stick incorporating folding seat
440 SHOP Building where goods are sold
441 SHOP-BOARD Shop-counter
442 SHOP-COUNTER Shelf between shopper and shopkeeper
443 SHOPKEEPER Owner of a shop
444 SHOPMAN Male shopkeeper
445 SHORE Where the sea meets the land
446 SHORE-LINE Coastline
447 SHORT-HAIR Breed of cat with short hair
448 SHORTS Short trousers
449 SHOT Hit by a missile
450 SHOT-STAR Meteorite
451 SHOULDER Where the arm joins the body
452 SHOULDER BOARD Epaulette
453 SHOULDER-BLADE Scapula
454 SHOULDER-BONE Shoulder-blade
455 SHOULDER-JOINT Joint where the arm joins the body

Semaphore Alphabet

A&1 B&2 C&3 D&4 E&5 F&6 G&7 H&8
I&9 J&0 K L M N O
P Q R S T U
V W X Y Z ERROR END OF WORD NUMERALS FOLLOW

456 SHOULDERED Military drill position
457 SHOUTING Calling out loudly
458 SHOUTER Person who shouts
459 SHOVEL Digging tool
460 SHOVEL-BILL Variety of duck. Spoonbill
461 SHOVELARD Spoonbill
462 SHOVELLER Spoonbill
463 SHOW Theatrical entertainment
464 SHOW-CASE Glass case for displaying articles
465 SHOWER Meteorological symbol for shower
466 SHOWER Meteorological symbol for rain shower
467 SHOWER Meteorological symbol for hail shower
468 SHOWROOM Room where goods are displayed for sale
469 SHRED Fragment
470 SHREW Variety of small animal
471 SHREWMOUSE Shrew
472 SHRIKE Variety of bird
473 SHRIMP Variety of crustacean
474 SHRIMP FISH Variety of fish
475 SHROUD Rope from side of ship to masthead
476 SHUT Closed
477 SHUT-EYE Sleep
478 SHUTTLE Vehicle for repeated journeys
479 SHUTTLECOCK Feathered projectile used in badminton
480 SIAMANG Variety of ape
481 SIAMESE CAT Breed of cat
482 SIAMESE FIGHTING FISH Variety of fish
483 SICE Six at dice
484 SICKLE Reaping tool
485 SICKLEFIN KILLI Variety of fish; sabrefin
486 SIDE Left or right of external surface
487 SIDE DRUM Small drum
488 SIDE HORSE Gymnastic horse
489 SIDE JOCKEY Side part of a saddle
490 SIDE-ARM Pistol
491 SIDEFACE Profile
492 SIDELIGHT Parking light of a car
493 SIDESADDLE Style of ladies' saddle
494 SIDEVIEW View seen from the side
495 SIDEWALL Side surface of tyre
496 SIDEWHEEL Paddle wheel mounted at the side of a vessel
497 SIDEWHEELER Vessel propelled by side-wheels
498 SIDEBURNS Whiskers at the side of the face
499 SIENNA Rich light-brown colour
500 SIERRA LEONE Flag of West African republic
501 SIEVE Apparatus for separating large particles from small
502 SIFAKA Variety of animal
503 SIGHT Aiming device on a gun
504 SIGHT Area enclosed by a picture frame
505 SIGHT HOLE End of telescope held to the eye
506 SIGIL Signet
507 SIGMA Eighteenth letter of the Greek alphabet
508 SIGN Gesture conveying meaning
509 SIGN Zodiacal symbol
510 SIGN-MANUAL Hand language of deaf mutes
511 SIGNPOST Direction indicator

512 SIGNAL Method of communication over distance
513 SIGNAL Device for conveying information to trains
514 SIGNALIST Signaller
515 SIGNALLER Person who signals
516 SIGNALLING Making a signal
517 SIGNALMAN Signaller
518 SIGNATURE Personal mark
519 SIGNET Small personal seal
520 SIGNET RING Ring with personal seal
521 SIKA Variety of deer
522 SIKH Flag of the Sikh religion
523 SILHOUETTE Portrait profile in solid black and white
524 SILICON Element; atomic number 14
525 SILK-HAT Top-hat made from silk
526 SILVER Chemical symbol (Ag)
527 SILVER Element; atomic number 47
528 SIMIAN Ape
529 SIN Twenty-first letter of the Hebrew alphabet
530 SINCIPUT Front of the head
531 SINGAPORE Flag of South-east Asian republic
532 SINGLE KNOT Type of knot
533 SINGLET Sleeveless undervest
534 SINISTER Heraldic term for left
535 SINK Kitchen basin
536 SINKING Failing to float
537 SIPHON Bottle for discharging aerated water
538 SISKIN Varety of bird
539 SISTER-HOOK S-shaped hook
540 SITAR Type of musical instrument
541 SITATUNGA Variety of antelope
542 SITTER Seated person
543 SITTING Resting upon the buttocks
544 SIVA A principal Hindu god
545 SIX Prime number between five and seven
546 SIX Roman numeral for six
547 SIX Face of a dice displaying six spots
548 SIX-GUN Revolver with six shots
549 SIX-SHOOTER Six-gun
550 SIXFOIL Foil with six lobes; sexfoil
551 SIXSCORE One hundred and twenty
552 SIXTE Sixth fencing position
553 SIXTEEN Six more than ten
554 SIXTEEN Roman numeral for sixteen
555 SIXTEENTH NOTE Semiquaver
556 SIXTH Position between fifth and seventh
557 SIXTH Sixth part of a whole
558 SIXTY Six times ten
559 SIXTY Roman numeral for sixty
560 SIXTY-FOURTH NOTE Semidemisemiquaver
561 SIZE Indication of fitting
562 SKATE Variety of fish
563 SKATE Steel blade fitted to shoe
564 SKELETON The complete bones of the body
565 SKETCH Rough drawing
566 SKETCHBOOK Book containing sketches
567 SKEWBALD Horse irregularly marked with colours
568 SKI Device for sliding over snow
569 SKI BOOT Boot for attaching to skis
570 SKI MASK Face-mask worn by skiers
571 SKI RUN Trail for skiing
572 SKI-BOB Steerable vehicle for skiing

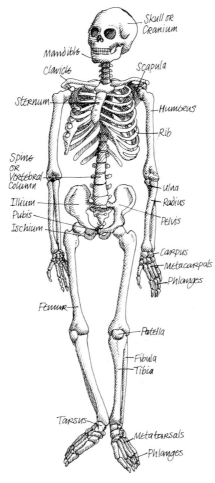

The Skeleton

Skull OR Cranium
Mandible
Clavicle
Scapula
Sternum
Humerus
Rib
Spine OR Vertebral Column
Ulna
Radius
Pelvis
Ilium
Pubis
Ischium
Carpus
Metacarpals
Phalanges
Femur
Patella
Fibula
Tibia
Tarsus
Metatarsals
Phalanges

573 SKI-JUMPER Person ski-jumping
574 SKI-JUMPING Sport involving leaping from a ramp on skis
575 SKI-LIFT Conveyer for transporting skiers up mountains
576 SKI-WEAR Clothes worn for skiing
577 SKIER Person skiing
578 SKIING Travelling on skis
579 SKILLET Long-handled cooking vessel
580 SKILLING Shed
581 SKIMOBILE Snowmobile
582 SKIN Covering of the body
583 SKIN Vibrating surface of a drum
584 SKIN-DIVER Underwater swimmer
585 SKIN-DIVING Underwater swimming
586 SKINLESS Without skin
587 SKI POLE Poles held while skiing
588 SKIPPER Variety of fish
589 SKIRT Part of a saddle
590 SKITTLE Pin aimed at in bowling
591 SKULL Bone of the head
592 SKULL-CAP Small cap worn on the back of the head
593 SKUNK Variety of animal

594 SKUNK BOTIA Variety of fish
595 SKY Upper part of Earth's atmosphere
596 SKY-BLUE Colour of the clear sky
597 SKYLINE Horizon
598 SKYSCRAPER Very tall building
599 SKYE TERRIER Breed of dog
600 SKYLARK Variety of bird
601 SKYLIGHT Overhead window
602 SKYSAIL Type of sail set above royal
603 SLALOM Downhill skiing between obstacle poles
604 SLANGS Fetters; manacles
605 SLANTINDICULAR Slanting
606 SLANTING Sloping
607 SLANTWISE Slanting
608 SLASH Cut
609 SLAT Narrow strip of wood
610 SLED Small sledge
611 SLEDGE Vehicle on runners
612 SLEEPER Person sleeping
613 SLEEPING Naturally unconscious
614 SLEET Meteorological symbol for sleet
615 SLEEVE Part of a garment that covers the arm
616 SLEEVELESS Without sleeves
617 SLICE Broad thin portion
618 SLIDE Photographic transparency
619 SLIDE PROJECTOR Apparatus for projecting an image from a slide
620 SLING Support for an injured arm
621 SLING-SHOT Catapult
622 SLIP-KNOT Type of knot
623 SLIPPER Soft indoor shoe
624 SLIT Narrow clean cut
625 SLOPE Incline
626 SLOT Slit; groove
627 SLOTH Variety of animal
628 SLUG Shell-less mollusc
629 SLUG Bullet
630 SLUMBERER Sleeper
631 SLUMBERING Sleeping
632 SLUNG Suspended
633 SLUR Smudge
634 SMALL-ARM Pistol
635 SMEAR Smudge
636 SMEE Variety of bird; smew
637 SMELT Variety of fish
638 SMEW Variety of bird
639 SMILE Facial expression of pleasure
640 SMILODON Variety of extinct animal; sabretooth cat
641 SMOKE Vapour from a fire
642 SMOKE-STACK Funnel
643 SMOKER Tobacco smoker
644 SMOKING Inhaling tobacco smoke
645 SMOOTH Even surfaced
646 SMOOTHING-IRON Tool for pressing fabric
647 SMOOTHING-PLANE Tool for smoothing wood
648 SMOUCH Smudge
649 SMUDGE Blur; smear
650 SMUT Dirty mark
651 SMUTCH Smudge
652 SNAIL Variety of mollusc
653 SNAKE Variety of reptile; serpent
654 SNAKE-BIRD Variety of bird; anhinga
655 SNAKEHEAD Variety of fish

656 SNAPPED Broken in pieces
657 SNAPPER Variety of fish
658 SNAPSHOT Photograph
659 SNARE DRUM Type of musical instrument
660 SNARES Vibrating wires beneath snare drum
661 SNATH Scythe handle
662 SNEAKER Style of canvas shoe
663 SNIPPERS Scissors
664 SNOOD Decorative hairnet
665 SNOOZE Light sleep
666 SNOUT Animal's nose; muzzle
667 SNOW Flakes of frozen water vapour
668 SNOW Meteorological symbol for snow
669 SNOW-BUNTING Variety of bird
670 SNOWFALL Fall of snow
671 SNOWFIELD Area covered with fallen snow
672 SNOWFLAKE Particle of frozen water vapour
673 SNOW-LEOPARD Variety of animal. Ounce
674 SNOW-PANTHER Snow-leopard
675 SNOWSCAPE Painting featuring snow covered landscape
676 SNOWSHOE Strung frame for walking on snow
677 SNOWBIRD Variety of bird; snow-bunting
678 SNOWDROP Variety of plant
679 SNOWMAN Figure built from snow
680 SNOWMOBILE Motorized vehicle for travelling on snow
681 SNOWMOBILER Driver of a snowmobile
682 SNOWMOBILING Travelling by snowmobile
683 SNOWY-OWL Variety of bird
684 SNOWY SHEATHBILL Variety of bird
685 SOAP Lathering cleaning agent
686 SOAP-SUDS Lather from soap
687 SOBOLIFEROUS With shoots
688 SOCK Short stocking
689 SOCKET Hollow of the eyes
690 SOCKEYE Variety of fish; salmon
691 SOD Turf
692 SODA-WATER Effervescent water
693 SODIUM Chemical symbol (Na)
694 SODIUM Element; atomic number 11
695 SOFA Long upholstered seat
696 SOFFIT Underside of an arch; intrados
697 SOIFFE Variety of fish
698 SOIL Earth
699 SOILED Dirty
700 SOILURE Stain
701 SOLAR PANEL Apparatus for extracting power from sunlight
702 SOLARIUM Sundial
703 SOLDADO Variety of fish; squirrel fish
704 SOLDIER Man trained to fight on land
705 SOLDIERFISH Variety of fish; squirrel fish
706 SOLE Under-surface of shoe
707 SOLID Neither gas nor liquid
708 SOLIDUS Oblique stroke of fraction or shilling symbol
709 SOLIPED Animal with uncloven hoof
710 SOLITAIRE Type of game for one player
711 SOLITAIRE Variety of extinct dodo-like bird
712 SOLLERET Armour protecting the foot
713 SOLOMON ISLANDS Flag of South-west Pacific island group
714 SOLOMON'S SEAL Type of six-pointed star
715 SOMA Body of an organism
716 SOMALIA Flag of North-east African country

717 SOMBRERO Style of wide-brimmed hat
718 SOMEBODY Unspecified person
719 SOMEONE Somebody
720 SOMETHING Unspecified thing
721 SOMNOLENT Sleeping
722 SONG-BIRD Bird that sings
723 SOPORIFIC Somnolent
724 SOUSAPHONE Type of musical instrument
725 SOUTH Cardinal point of the compass opposite to north
726 SOUTH AFRICA Flag of Southern African country
727 SOUTH-EAST Direction between south and east
728 SOUTH-SOUTH-EAST Direction between south and south-east
729 SOUTH-SOUTH-WEST Direction between south and south-west
730 SOUTH-WEST Direction between south and west
731 SOUTHERN CROSS Constellation of the southern hemisphere
732 SOUTHWESTER Style of waterproof hat
733 SOVIET UNION Flag of East European and Asian country
734 SOW Female pig
735 SPACE Gap between words
736 SPACE Void between stars and planets
737 SPACE-SHUTTLE Vehicle for frequent journeys into space
738 SPACE-STATION Orbiting habitation in space
739 SPACE-SUIT Protective suit worn by people in space
740 SPACECRAFT Vehicle for travelling in space
741 SPACEMAN Person equipped to live in space
742 SPACESHIP Spacecraft
743 SPADE Digging tool
744 SPADE Suit of playing cards
745 SPADEFOOT TOAD Variety of toad
746 SPAIN Flag of Western European country
747 SPALL Shoulder
748 SPAN Extent of stretched hand
749 SPAN Distance between pillars of an arch
750 SPAN Area across the wings of an aircraft
751 SPANDREL Rectangle enclosing arch
752 SPANIARD Native of Spain
753 SPANIEL Breed of dog
754 SPANISH FLY Varety of insect
755 SPANISH MINNOWCARP Variety of fish
756 SPANKER Type of sail
757 SPANNER Tool for turning bolts
758 SPAR Yard
759 SPARROW Variety of bird
760 SPATULETAIL Variety of hummingbird
761 SPEAKER Loudspeaker
762 SPEAKING-TRUMPET Megaphone
763 SPEAR Pointed weapon with long handle
764 SPEAR-HEAD Metal tip of spear
765 SPECIES Type; variety
766 SPECK Blemish
767 SPECTACLE Performance
768 SPECTACLED BEAR Variety of animal
769 SPECTACLED OWL Variety of bird
770 SPECTACLES Glasses
771 SPECTRE Ghost
772 SPECTRUM Graduated series of colours
773 SPECTRUM Ghost

774 SPELLING Correct order of letters in a word
775 SPERM WHALE Varety of large marine mammal
776 SPHERE Globe
777 SPHINX Type of mythological creature
778 SPHINX-MOTH Variety of moth
779 SPIDER Variety of arachnid
780 SPIDER CRAB Variety of crustacean
781 SPIDER MONKEY Variety of animal
782 SPIDER-WEB Cobweb
783 SPIGOT Faucet; tap
784 SPILE Spigot
785 SPILLAGE Spilt liquid
786 SPILT Fallen from a vessel
787 SPILTH Spillage
788 SPINDLE Heraldic device; fusil
789 SPINDLE SHELL Variety of shell
790 SPINE Backbone
791 SPINE Pointed growth on fish's back
792 SPINE Back of a book
793 SPINIFEROUS With spines
794 SPINNAKER Type of sail
795 SPINNER Spider
796 SPINODE Cusp of foil
797 SPINY With spines
798 SPINY ANTEATER Variety of animal; echidna
799 SPIRACLE Whale's blow-hole
800 SPIRAL Coil
801 SPIRE Steeple
802 SPIRE Stalk

SPIRES

Broach Spire   Lead Spire   Storied Spire   Flèche

803 SPIRE Prong of an antler
804 SPIRE Complete convolution of a spiral
805 SPIRIFORM Spiral in shape
806 SPIRIT Ghost
807 SPIRIT-LEVEL Instrument for determining horizontal
808 SPIT Land jutting out to sea
809 SPIT Saliva
810 SPITTLE Saliva
811 SPITTOON Cuspidor
812 SPLASH Sudden displacement of liquid
813 SPLINE Slat
814 SPLINT Wood tied to broken limb
815 SPLIT Lengthways tear
816 SPLODGE Irregular stain

817 SPLOTCH Splodge
818 SPOILER Vane to direct airflow on car
819 SPOKE Bar joining rim to hub of wheel
820 SPOKESHAVE Tool for shaping wood
821 SPONGE Fibrous skeleton of marine animal
822 SPONSON Triangular plate joining paddle-wheel to vessel
823 SPOOK Ghost
824 SPOOL Cylinder of wound yarn
825 SPOON Eating utensil
826 SPOONBILL Variety of bird
827 SPOONBILL-DUCK Variety of duck; shoveller
828 SPOONERISM Transposition of sounds in adjacent words
829 SPORIFEROUS With spores
830 SPORT Competitive physical activity
831 SPORTER Sportsman or woman
832 SPORTSMAN Male engaged in sport
833 SPORTSWOMAN Female engaged in sport
834 SPOT Small round mark
835 SPOTLIGHT Lamp with a strong narrow beam
836 SPOTBILL DUCK Variety of duck
837 SPOTTED Patterned with spots
838 SPOTTED OWL Variety of bird
839 SPOTTED SAWTOOTH Variety of butterfly
840 SPOTTY Covered with spots
841 SPOUT Pouring tube of vessel
842 SPOUT Plume of water sent up by whale
843 SPOUT-HOLE Spiracle
844 SPOUTER Spouting whale
845 SPOUTING Discharging water
846 SPRAY Fine particles of blown liquid
847 SPRAY Shoot
848 SPREAD-EAGLE Heraldic device
849 SPRIG Shoot; spray
850 SPRING Coil of resilient metal
851 SPRINGBOK Variety of antelope
852 SPRINGER Springbok
853 SPRINGER SPANIEL Breed of dog
854 SPRINGHARE Variety of animal
855 SPRINTER Athlete who runs short distances
856 SPRIT Boom
857 SPRITE Ghost
858 SPROCKET Tooth on a sprocket-wheel
859 SPROCKET-WHEEL Toothed wheel
860 SPROUT Shoot
861 SPUME Froth; foam
862 SPUR Spiked wheel fitted to heel
863 SPUR Strut; small buttress
864 SPUR-DOG Variety of fish
865 SPUR-LEATHER Strap for attaching spur to foot
866 SPUR-ROWEL Spiked wheel of spur
867 SPURGE HAWKMOTH Variety of moth
868 SPURT Plume of water
869 SPURTLE Spurt
870 SPUTNIK Artificial orbiting satellite
871 SPY-GLASS Telescope
872 SQUAB Sofa
873 SQUALL Storm
874 SQUALOID Shark
875 SQUALUS Shark
876 SQUAMATE With scales
877 SQUAMIFEROUS With scales
878 SQUAMOSE With scales
879 SQUARE Rectangle with equal sides

880 SQUARE Set-square
881 SQUARE-KNOT Type of knot
882 SQUARE-RIGGED With rectangular sails hung from yards
883 SQUARE-RIGGER Square-rigged vessel
884 SQUARE-SAIL Rectangular sail
885 SQUID Variety of sea creature; cuttle-fish
886 SQUIGGLE Twisting line
887 SQUINCH Arch set across corner
888 SQUINT Inability of eyes to look in same direction
889 SQUIRREL Variety of animal
890 SQUIRREL-FISH Variety of fish
891 SQUIRREL-MONKEY Variety of animal
892 SQUIRT Eject a plume of water
893 SQUIRTER That which squirts
894 SRI LANKA Flag of Southern Asian island republic
895 STACK Funnel
896 STAFF Shaft
897 STAFF Rod supporting legs of a chair
898 STAFF Lines on which music is written
899 STAG Male deer
900 STAG-BEETLE Variety of insect
901 STAGE Platform for theatrical performances
902 STAGE Section of a rocket
903 STAGE-PLAYER Actor or actress
904 STAGEHAND Person who works behind the scenes in a theatre
905 STAGER Actor or actress
906 STAGESET Theatrical scenery
907 STAIN Blemish
908 STAINED GLASS Decorative coloured glass
909 STAIR One of a series of steps
910 STAIR-HEAD Top of a flight of stairs
911 STAIRCASE Flight of stairs
912 STAIRWAY Staircase
913 STALACTITE Hanging spike of rock
914 STALAGMITE Rising spike of rock
915 STALK Stem of a plant
916 STALK Chimney
917 STALK Stem of a wine glass
918 STAMEN Male organ of flower
919 STAMINATE With stamens
920 STAMINIFEROUS With stamens
921 STAMP Postage stamp
922 STANCHION Upright support
923 STAND Plinth; support
924 STANDING Supported by legs
925 STANDARD Banner (British Royal standard shown here)
926 STANDARD-LAMP Lamp supported by pole
927 STANDER Person standing
928 STANDING-LADDER Step-ladder
929 STANDING-RIGGING Fixed ship's rigging
930 STANDING ROPES Standing-rigging
931 STAPLE Curved fixing device
932 STAPLER Machine for inserting staples
933 STAR Distant sun
934 STAR Symbol for a star
935 STAR OF BETHLEHEM Variety of plant
936 STAR OF DAVID Interwoven six-pointed star
937 STAR SPANGLED BANNER Flag of the United States
938 STARFISH Variety of marine creature
939 STARBOARD Nautical term for right
940 STARK-NAKED Unclothed

941 STARLING Variety of bird
942 STARS AND BARS Flag of the Confederate States of America
943 STARS AND STRIPES Flag of the United States
944 STARTER Person about to start
945 STARTING-BLOCK Sprinter's block for the feet
946 STATIC Not moving
947 STATION-WAGON Car with a rear door; shooting brake
948 STATIONARY Not moving
949 STATIVE Stationary
950 STATUE Three-dimensional work of art
951 STATUETTE Small statue
952 STAVE Plank of a barrel
953 STAVE Strip of wood
954 STAVE Staff upon which music is written
955 STAY Rope supporting mast
956 STAY Prop
957 STAYSAIL Sail extended by a stay
958 STEAM Water vapour
959 STEAMBOAT Boat powered by steam
960 STEAM-ENGINE Locomotive powered by steam
961 STEAMSHIP Steam-boat
962 STEAMER DUCK Variety of duck
963 STEED Horse
964 STEEL Type of hard metal
965 STEEPLE Spire
966 STEEPLE CUP Style of ornamental cup
967 STEERING-WHEEL Control wheel of a car
968 STEEVE Slope of a bowsprit
969 STEGANOPOD Snake-bird
970 STEGOSAURUS Variety of dinosaur
971 STEIN Type of drinking vessel
972 STEINBOK Variety of antelope
973 STELA Sculpted slab
974 STELLATE Star-shaped
975 STELLIFORM Star-shaped
976 STEM Shank of a musical note
977 STEM Shank of a wine glass
978 STEM Bow of a ship
979 STEM Stalk of a plant
980 STENCIL Template for applying paint
981 STENTOROPHONIC-HORN Megaphone
982 STEP Stair
983 STEPLADDER Folding ladder
984 STEPS Step-ladder
985 STEREOGRAPH Slide with stereoscopic image
986 STEREOSCOPE Instrument for viewing stereographic images
987 STERN Back end of a vessel
988 STERNEBRA Part of the sternum
989 STERNUM Breast-bone
990 STETHOSCOPE Instrument for listening to bodily sounds
991 STETSON Style of hat
992 STEVEDORE KNOT Type of knot
993 STICK Rod for beating a drum
994 STICK-INSECT Variety of insect
995 STICKER Spear
996 STICKER Adhesive label
997 STICKLEBACK Variety of fish
998 STIFF Rigid
999 STIFFLE Hind knee of a dog

1000 STIGMA Part of the head of a flower
1001 STILETTO Narrow-bladed knife
1002 STILETTO-HEEL Thin heel on woman's shoe
1003 STILL Stationary
1004 STILL LIFE Painting of inanimate objects
1005 STILT Pole for walking on
1006 STILT Variety of bird
1007 STING Sharp organ of some creatures
1008 STINKBUG Variety of insect
1009 STIPE Stalk of fungus
1010 STIPPLE Drawing using dots as shading
1011 STIRRUP Foot support hung from a saddle
1012 STIRRUP-IRON Metal part of a stirrup
1013 STIRRUP-LEATHER Leather part of a stirrup
1014 STITCH Loop made through a surface with a threaded needle
1015 STICHERY Stitching
1016 STITCHING Series of stitches
1017 STOAT Variety of animal
1018 STOCK Goods for sale
1019 STOCK Crossbar of an anchor
1020 STOCK Handle of a pistol
1021 STOCK Livestock
1022 STOCKING Tight covering for the leg
1023 STOMACH Abdomen
1024 STONE Hard mineral
1025 STONE Gem
1026 STONE Fourteen pounds weight
1027 STONECHAT Variety of bird
1028 STOOL Low backless seat
1029 STOP Indentation in dog's face
1030 STOP Cease moving (the signal indicates 'stop')
1031 STOPWATCH Watch than can be stopped and started
1032 STORE Shop
1033 STOREKEEPER Person in charge of a store
1034 STOREY Floor of a building
1035 STORK Variety of bird
1036 STORM Tempest
1037 STORM-CLOUD Type of cloud accompanying storm
1038 STOVE Heating apparatus
1039 STOVE-PIPE Style of hat
1040 STRABISMUS Squint
1041 STRADDLE Plant one leg each side
1042 STRAIGHT Not curved or bent
1043 STRAND Single thread
1044 STRAND Shore
1045 STRAP Strip of leather used as a fastening
1046 STRAW Drinking tube
1047 STRAWBERRY Variety of fruit
1048 STREAMER Type of long flag
1049 STREAMLINED Aerodynamically efficient shape
1050 STREBER Variety of fish
1051 STRETCHER Brick laid lengthways
1052 STRETCHER Rod separating chair legs
1053 STRETCHING-COURSE Line of bricks laid lengthways
1054 STRETCHING-BOND Brickwork made up of stretchers
1055 STRIG Groove
1056 STRIG Stalk
1057 STRING Thin cord
1058 STRING Stretched wire of a musical instrument

1059 STRINGED Fitted with strings
1060 STRIPE Narrow band of colour
1061 STRIPED Patterned with stripes
1062 STRIPED OWL Variety of bird
1063 STRIPED SKUNK Variety of animal
1064 STRIPPED Without clothes
1065 STRIPPER Striptease artiste
1066 STRIPTEASE Removing clothes as entertainment
1067 STROKE Bolt of lightning
1068 STROKE Arm movement in swimming
1069 STRONTIUM Element; atomic number 38
1070 STRUCTURE Building
1071 STRUNG Fitted with strings
1072 STRUT Support
1073 STUB Worn-down pencil
1074 STUD Pin with flattened head
1075 STUDDED Fitted with studs
1076 STUDDING SAIL Type of extra sail
1077 STUDY Sketch
1078 STUFF Matter
1079 STUFFED Filled with stuffing
1080 STUFFING Filling
1081 STUMP Stub
1082 STUMPS Upright rods used in the game of cricket
1083 STURGEON Variety of fish
1084 STURIONIAN Sturgeon
1085 STYLE Gnomon
1086 STYLE Fashion
1087 STYLE Support of stigma
1088 STYLET Stiletto
1089 STYLOGRAPH Type of pen
1090 STYLOMMATOPHOROUS Like a snail
1091 STYLUS Gnomon
1092 SUBAERIAL In the open air
1093 SUBDIVISION Part formed by dividing whole
1094 SUBDOMINANT Fourth tone of musical scale
1095 SUBJECT Thing painted
1096 SUBMARINE Underwater vessel
1097 SUBMAXILLA Jawbone
1098 SUBMEDIANT Sixth tone of musical scale
1099 SUBMERGED Beneath the water
1100 SUBMERSED Submerged
1101 SUBMERSIBLE Submarine
1102 SUBSCRIPT Signature
1103 SUBSCRIPTION Signature
1104 SUBSTANCE Matter
1105 SUBTERRANEAN Underground
1106 SUBTERRESTRIAL Underground
1107 SUCCESSION Series
1108 SUCKLE Feed young with milk
1109 SUDAN Flag of Northern African republic
1110 SUDS Soap lather
1111 SUIT Spades, clubs, hearts and diamonds
1112 SUIT Set of matching garments
1113 SUITCASE Container for clothes
1114 SULPHUR Element; atomic number 16
1115 SULPHUR TUFT Variety of fungus
1116 SULTAN TIT Variety of bird
1117 SUM Simple arithmetical calculation
1118 SUMATRA BARB Variety of fish
1119 SUMEN Sow's udder
1120 SUMMIT Peak of a mountain
1121 SUN Luminous body at centre of the solar system
1122 SUN Astrological symbol for the sun

1123 SUN DISC Type of ancient Egyptian ammulet
1124 SUN PARAKEET Variety of bird
1125 SUNTAN Darkening of the skin due to exposure to sun
1126 SUNBATHER Person acquiring suntan
1127 SUNBATHING Acquiring a suntan
1128 SUNDIAL Device for telling the time by the sun
1129 SUNFISH Variety of fish
1130 SUNGLASSES Spectacles with darkened lenses
1131 SUNHAT Style of large hat
1132 SUNHELMET Style of sunhat
1133 SUN-UP Rising sun
1134 SUNBEAM Shaft of sunlight
1135 SUNBIRD Variety of bird
1136 SUNBURNT Suntanned
1137 SUNDAE Icecream with fruit and syrup
1138 SUNDAY Astrological symbol for Sunday
1139 SUNDERED Broken
1140 SUNDOWN Sunset
1141 SUNFLOWER Variety of flowering plant
1142 SUNI Variety of antelope
1143 SUNLIGHT Bright daylight; light from the sun
1144 SUNLIT Lit by the sun
1145 SUNNY Lit by the sun
1146 SUNRISE First appearance of the sun
1147 SUNROOF Opening roof in a car; moonroof
1148 SUNSET The end of the day
1149 SUNSHADE Parasol
1150 SUNSHINE Sunlight
1151 SUPERFICIES Outer surface of the body
1152 SUPERNATANT Swimming on the surface
1153 SUPERNATURAL Beyond the laws of nature
1154 SUPERPOWERS United States and Soviet Union
1155 SUPERSONIC Capable of travelling faster than sound
1156 SUPERSTRUCTURE Part of a ship above the deck
1157 SUPERTERRANEAN Above ground
1158 SUPERTONIC Second tone in musical scale
1159 SUPINE Lying down on the back
1160 SUPPORT Prop
1161 SUPPORT Base
1162 SUPPORTER Figures on either side of coat of arms
1163 SUPRAMARINE Above the sea
1164 SUPRANATURAL Supernatural
1165 SURBASE Upper part of the base of a column
1166 SURF Waves breaking on shore
1167 SURF-BOARD Device for riding waves
1168 SURFACE Outside of something
1169 SURFACE Top of a body of water
1170 SURFACE-SHIP Ship that travels on the surface
1171 SURFER Person using a surf-board
1172 SURFING Using a surf-board
1173 SURGEON-FISH Variety of fish
1174 SURGEON'S KNOT Type of knot
1175 SURICATE Variety of animal
1176 SURINAM Flag of South American republic
1177 SURNAME Last name
1178 SURREALIST Fantastic artist (Salvador Dali)
1179 SURRENDER Flag of submission
1180 SURVIVOR Person remaining alive after calamity
1181 SUSPENDED Hung up

1182 SUSPENDER BELT Belt to hold up stockings; garter belt
1183 SUSPENDERS Straps to hold up trousers; braces

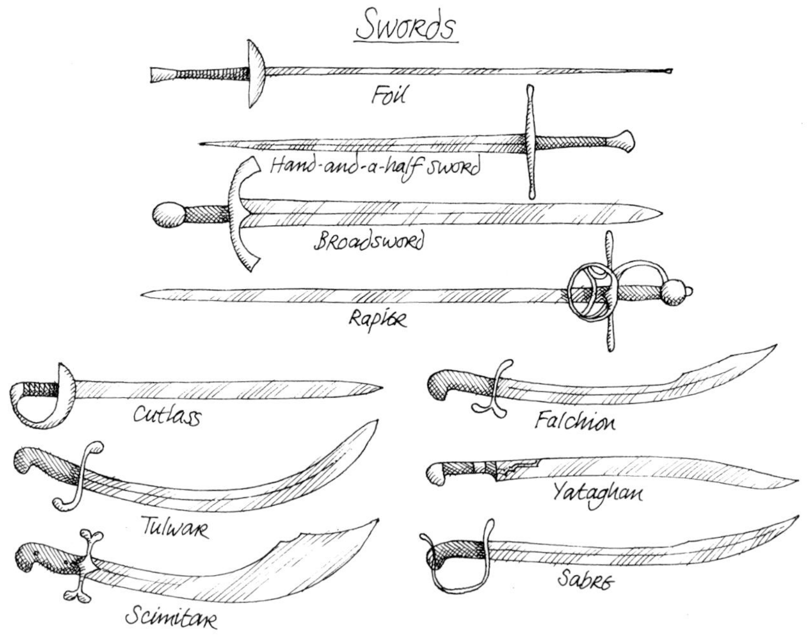

Swords

Foil

Hand-and-a-half sword

Broadsword

Rapier

Cutlass

Falchion

Tulwar

Yataghan

Scimitar

Sabre

1184 SUSPENDERS Straps to hold up stockings
1185 SUSTENANCE Food
1186 SUSTENTATION Sustenance
1187 SUTURE Stitched seam
1188 SWAG Ornament representing sagging cloth; festoon
1189 SWALLOW Variety of bird
1190 SWALLOW-TAILED FLYCATCHER Variety of bird
1191 SWALLOWTAIL Variety of butterfly
1192 SWALLOWTAIL Type of banner
1193 SWAMPHEN Variety of bird
1194 SWAN Variety of bird
1195 SWAN-PAN Abacus
1196 SWASH Fancy letterform
1197 SWASTIKA Type of hooked cross
1198 SWAZILAND Flag of Southern African country
1199 SWEAT-BAND Head-band to absorb perspiration
1200 SWEATER Woollen upper garment
1201 SWEDEN Flag of Scandinavian country
1202 SWEET LIPS Variety of fish
1203 SWELL Waves
1204 SWEPT-BACK Type of wing design
1205 SWIFT Variety of bird
1206 SWIM FIN Swimming aid attached to foot; flipper
1207 SWIM-SUIT Bathing costume
1208 SWIMMER Person engaged in swimming
1209 SWIMMERET Propulsion fins of shrimp
1210 SWIMMING Propelling oneself through water
1211 SWINE Pig
1212 SWINHOE'S PHEASANT Variety of bird
1213 SWITCH On/off control

1214 SWITCH Electrical symbol for switch
1215 SWITZERLAND Flag of Western European country
1216 SWORD Long bladed weapon

1217 SWORD KNOT Ornamental knot attached to sword
1218 SWORD-ARM Arm that holds a sword
1219 SWORD-BELT Belt from which sword is hung
1220 SWORD-BLADE Blade of a sword
1221 SWORD-TAIL Variety of fish
1222 SWORDER Swordsman
1223 SWORDFISH Variety of fish
1224 SWORDPLAY Fencing
1225 SWORDPLAYER Fencer
1226 SWORDSMAN Fencer
1227 SYCAMORE Variety of tree (leaf and seed shown here)
1228 SYLLABLE One part of the sound of a word
1229 SYMBOL Sign representing something else
1230 SYMMETRICAL Both sides exactly alike
1231 SYNDACTYL Webbed foot
1232 SYRIA Flag of South-west Asian republic
1233 SYRINGE Tube with piston for injecting liquid
1234 SYRINX Pan-pipes

1 T Twentieth letter of the alphabet
2 T Braille alphabet
3 T International signal flag
4 T Manual alphabet – American system
5 T Morse code alphabet
6 T Semaphore alphabet
7 T-SQUARE Draughtsman's T-shaped ruler
8 T-SHIRT Collarless short-sleeved cotton shirt
9 TABARD Style of sleeveless tunic
10 TABERDAR Wearer of a tabard
11 TABLA Pair of small Indian drums
12 TABLE Flat-topped piece of furniture
13 TABLETOP Flat top of a table
14 TABLE-BOARD Tabletop
15 TABLECLOTH Fabric covering for a table
16 TABLE-LAMP Lamp for use on top of a table
17 TABLE-LINEN Fabric used on a table
18 TABLE-STONE Standing stone; dolmen
19 TABLEWARE Crockery
20 TABOR Type of small drum
21 TABORER Tabor player
22 TABORET Type of stool
23 TACHE Clasp; buckle
24 TACKLE Lifting gear
25 TACKLE Harness
26 TADPOLE Immature form of a frog
27 TAG Hanging ticket
28 TAHR Variety of animal
29 TAIL Long projection from rear of an animal
30 TAIL Hanging part at rear of coat
31 TAIL LAMP Rear light of a vehicle
32 TAIL PLANE Tail surfaces of an aircraft
33 TAIL-COAT Style of coat with tails
34 TAIL-LIGHT Rear light of vehicle
35 TAILOR-BIRD Variety of bird
36 TAIWAN Flag of East Asian republic
37 TAKAHE Variety of bird
38 TAKIN Variety of animal
39 TALARIA Winged sandals
40 TAM O'SHANTER Style of bonnet
41 TAMANDUA Variety of animal; anteater
42 TAMBOUR Type of musical instrument; bass drum
43 TAMBOURA Type of Indian musical instrument
44 TAMBOURINE Type of musical instrument; small drum
45 TAME Domesticated
46 TAMPION Plug for the barrel of a gun
47 TAN Golden brown colour
48 TANGERINE Variety of fruit
49 TANGRAM Chinese paper puzzle
50 TANK Armoured fighting vehicle
51 TANKARD Type of drinking vessel
52 TANTALUM Element; atomic number 73

53 TANZANIA Flag of East African republic
54 TAP Faucet
55 TAPE Long flat strip of material
56 TAPE DECK Deck of a tape recorder
57 TAPE RECORDER Machine for recording sound on to magnetic tape
58 TAPE MEASURE Flexible fabric ruler
59 TAPER Small thin candle
60 TAPER Tadpole
61 TAPER Become narrower
62 TAPIR Variety of animal
63 TARBOOSH Style of hat; fez
64 TARGET Object at which shots are aimed
65 TARPON Variety of fish
66 TARSIER Variety of animal
67 TARSUS Hind knee of an animal
68 TART Open pie
69 TARTAN Type of check pattern
70 TASMANIAN TIGER Variety of animal; thylacine
71 TASMANIAN WOLF Thylacine
72 TASSE Skirt of a suit of armour
73 TASSEL Ornamental bunch of hanging threads
74 TATTOO Indelible design on the skin
75 TAU Nineteenth letter of the Greek alphabet
76 TAU CROSS T-shaped cross
77 TAURUS Second sign of the zodiac; the bull
78 TAUT Stretched tight
79 TAW Twenty-third and last letter of Hebrew alphabet
80 TAWNY OWL Variety of bird
81 TEA-COSY Insulating cover for a teapot
82 TEACUP Cup for drinking tea out of
83 TEA-KETTLE Vessel for boiling water to make tea

Tangram

84 TEAPOT Vessel for making tea in
85 TEA-TRAY Tray on which tea is served
86 TEAR Rip
87 TEAT Nipple
88 TECHNETIUM Element; atomic number 43
89 TEDDY BEAR Toy in the form of a bear
90 TEEPEE American Indian dwelling
91 TEETH Biting projections of the mouth
92 TELEPHONE Communication instrument
93 TELESCOPE Instrument for viewing distant objects
94 TELEVISION Receiver for televised pictures
95 TELLURIAN Inhabitant of the Earth
96 TELLURIUM Element; atomic number 52
97 TEMPLE Ancient place of worship

Styles of Temple

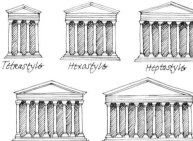

Tetrastyle   Hexastyle   Heptastyle

Octastyle   Decastyle

98 TEMPLE Side of the forehead
99 TEN One more than nine
100 TEN Roman numeral for ten
101 TEN-POUNDER Variety of fish
102 TENCH Variety of fish
103 TENEBROUS Gloomy; dark
104 TENNIS-BALL Ball used in the game of tennis
105 TENNIS-RACKET Bat used in the game of tennis
106 TENON-SAW Type of cutting tool
107 TENOR-DRUM Type of musical instrument
108 TENREC Variety of animal
109 TENSE Taut
110 TENT Portable shelter
111 TERBIUM Element; atomic number 65
112 TERM Type of statue
113 TERMITE Variety of insect
114 TERN Variety of bird
115 TERRA FIRMA Dry land
116 TERRA-COTTA Brownish-red pottery
117 TERRAIN Tract of land
118 TERRAPIN Variety of amphibian; freshwater turtle
119 TERRESTRIAL Of the earth
120 TERRET Ring on a collar
121 TERRIER Breed of dog
122 TERTIARY Third order of colours; browns etc.
123 TESTACEOUS With a shell
124 TESTER Armour protecting horse's head
125 TESTICLES Sperm-secreting gland
126 TETH Ninth letter of the Hebrew alphabet
127 TETHER Rope securing animal
128 TETRAGON Square
129 TETRAGRAM Four-lettered word

130 TETRAHEDRON Geometric solid with four equal sides
131 TETRAPOD Four-footed animal
132 TETRASTYLE Classical architectural style with four columns
133 TEXTILE Fabric
134 THAILAND Flag of South-east Asian country
135 THALASSIAN Sea-turtle
136 THALLIUM Element; atomic number 81
137 THATCH Straw used as a roofing material
138 THENAR Palm of the hand
139 THEORBIST Theorbo player
140 THEORBO Type of musical instrument; lute
141 THERMOS-FLASK Vacuum-flask
142 THETA Eighth letter of the Greek alphabet
143 THIGH Upper part of the leg
144 THIGH-PIECE Armour protecting the thigh
145 THIMBLE Protective cover for the finger while sewing
146 THING Indeterminate object
147 THINKER Person engaged in thought
148 THINKING Pondering
149 THIRTEEN Three more than ten
150 THIRTEEN Roman numeral for thirteen
151 THIRTY Three times ten
152 THIRTY Roman numeral for thirty
153 THIRTY-SECOND NOTE Type of musical note; demisemiquaver
154 THISTLE Variety of plant
155 THONG Leather strap
156 THORAX Chest region of body
157 THORAX Middle region of insect's body
158 THORIUM Element; atomic number 90
159 THOTH Ancient Egyptian ibis-headed god of learning
160 THOUSAND Ten to the third power
161 THOUSAND Roman numeral for a thousand
162 THREE Prime number between two and four
163 THREE-QUARTER BINDING Style of bookbinding
164 THREESCORE Sixty
165 THRESHER Variety of shark
166 THREESOME Group of three
167 THROAT Front part of the neck
168 THRUM Strum
169 THULIUM Element; atomic number 69
170 THUMB Inner digit of the hand
171 THUMB-NAIL Horny growth at the end of the thumb
172 THUNDERSTORM Meteorological symbol for thunderstorm
173 THURSDAY Astrological symbol for Thursday
174 THYLACINE Variety of animal; Tasmanian tiger
175 TIARA Pope's triple crown
176 TICK Mark indicating correctness
177 TICKET Price-tag
178 TIE Fabric strip worn around the neck
179 TIE-KNOT Knot made in a tie
180 TIED Tethered
181 TIERED Ranked one above the other
182 TIERCED Heraldic device
183 TIGE Shaft of a column
184 TIGE Stalk
185 TIGER Variety of animal
186 TIGHTS Close-fitting lower garment
187 TILT Joust
188 TILT Inclined

189 TILTER Jouster
190 TILTING-HELM Helmet worn by jousters
191 TIMBAL Type of musical instrument; kettle drum
192 TIMBER Trees
193 TIMBREL Tambourine
194 TIME Hour of the day
195 TIMEPIECE Clock
196 TIMPANI Type of musical instrument; kettle drum
197 TIN Chemical symbol (Sn)
198 TIN Element; atomic number 50
199 TINAMOU Variety of bird
200 TINCTURE Colour used in heraldry
201 TINE Prong of a fork
202 TIP Point; end
203 TIPPLER Drinker
204 TIPTOE Standing on the toes
205 TISSUE Bodily matter
206 TITANIUM Element; atomic number 22
207 TJERKESKA Style of garment worn by Cossaks
208 TOAD Variety of amphibian
209 TOADSTOOL Non-edible fungus
210 TOAST Grilled bread
211 TOAST-RACK Rack for toast
212 TOBY-JUG Style of vessel
213 TOE Digit of the foot
214 TOECAP Cap at toe of shoe
215 TOENAIL Horny growth at the end of toe
216 TOGA Style of ancient Roman garment
217 TOGO Flag of West African republic
218 TOIL Work
219 TOILER Worker
220 TOM-TOM Type of drum
221 TOMAHAWK Type of hatchet
222 TOMATO Variety of vegetable
223 TOMBSTONE Grave marker
224 TOME Large book
225 TONGA Flag of South-west Pacific island
226 TONGUE Muscular organ of the mouth
227 TONGUE Leather flap in a shoe
228 TONSURE Style of partially shaved head
229 TOOL Working utensil
230 TOOTH Hard biting projection of the mouth
231 TOOTH Projection of a cog
232 TOOTHBRUSH Cleaning brush for the teeth
233 TOOTH-WHEEL Cog-wheel
234 TOP Highest point
235 TOP-BOOT Style of tall boot
236 TOP-COAT Overcoat
237 TOP-HAT Style of tall hat
238 TOPE Variety of fish
239 TOPI Variety of animal
240 TOPIARY Trees cut into ornamental shapes
241 TOPKNOT Variety of fish
242 TOPLESS Naked on the upper body
243 TOPSHELL Variety of shell
244 TORCH Burning brand
245 TORCHBEARER Carrier of a torch
246 TORCHLIGHT Light shed by a torch
247 TORII Japanese ceremonial gateway
248 TORPEDO Self-propelled underwater bomb
249 TORPEDO Variety of fish; electric ray
250 TORQUE Twisted metal bracelet
251 TORSE Twisted fabric band around helmet
252 TORSK Variety of fish
253 TORSO Upper part of body

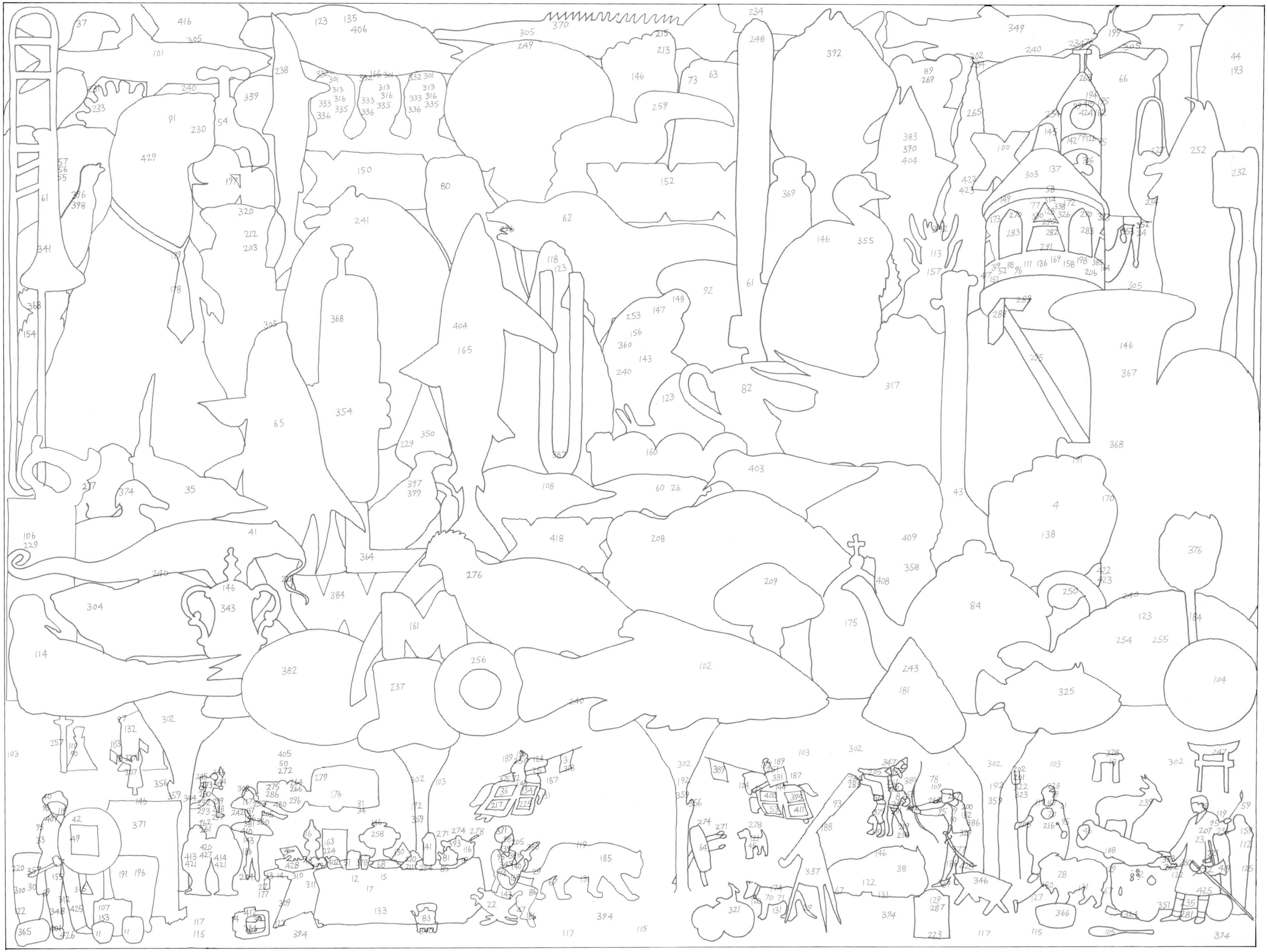

Some Trees

Lombardy Poplar

Walnut

Ash

Cedar of Lebanon

Horse Chestnut or Buckeye

English Elm

Pedunculate Oak

Sycamore

Yew

372 TUCK Type of sword; rapier
373 TUESDAY Astrological symbol for Tuesday
374 TUFTED DUCK Variety of duck
375 TUILLE Skirt of a suit of armour
376 TULIP Variety of flowering plant
377 TULWAR Type of curved Indian sword
378 TUMBLER Straight-sided glass
379 TUMBLER Acrobat
380 TUMBLING Acrobatics
381 TUMMY Abdomen; belly
382 TUN Cask
383 TUNA Variety of fish
384 TUNGSTEN Chemical symbol (W)
385 TUNGSTEN Element; atomic number 74
386 TUNIC Sleeveless surcoat
387 TUNING FORK Vibrating tuning instrument
388 TUNING PEG Peg for altering the tension of musical strings
389 TUNISIA Flag of North African republic
390 TUNNY Variety of fish; tuna
391 TURBAN Eastern head-covering
392 TURBOT Variety of fish
393 TUREEN Deep vessel for soup
394 TURF Land covered with grass
395 TURKEY Flag of South-west Asian country
396 TURKEY Variety of domestic fowl
397 TURKEY-BUZZARD Variety of bird
398 TURKEY-COCK Male turkey
399 TURKEY-VULTURE Turkey-buzzard
400 TURKS AND CAICOS ISLANDS Flag of Caribbean island group
401 TURN-UP Cuff at the bottom of trousers
402 TURNIP Variety of vegetable
403 TURNSTONE Variety of bird
404 TURQUOISE Bluish-green colour
405 TURRET Revolving gun compartment of a tank
406 TURTLE Variety of marine tortoise
407 TURTLENECK High rolled collar of sweater
408 TUSK Long pointed elephant's tooth
409 TUSKER Elephant
410 TUTU Short frilled ballet skirt
411 TUVALU Flag of Central Pacific island group
412 TV Television set
413 TWEEDLEDEE Twin brother of Tweedledum (to be found in *Alice Through the Looking Glass*)
414 TWEEDLEDUM Twin brother of Tweedledee
415 TWELVE Two more than ten
416 TWELVE Roman numeral for twelve
417 TWENTY Twice ten
418 TWENTY Roman numeral for twenty
419 TWIBILL Type of double-headed battle-axe
420 TWINS Two children born at the same time
421 TWIN-BROTHER Male twin
422 TWIST Wind; turn
423 TWISTED Wound; turned
424 TWO Prime number between one and three
425 TWO-LEGGED With two legs
426 TWO-TONE In two colours
427 TWOSOME Pair
428 TYPEWRITER Machine for writing text
429 TYRANNOSAURUS Variety of dinosaur
430 TYRE Inflatable rubber band on wheel of vehicle

1 U Twenty-first letter of the alphabet
2 U Braille alphabet
3 U International signal flag
4 U Manual alphabet – American system
5 U Morse code alphabet
6 U Semaphore alphabet
7 UAKARI Variety of animal
8 UFO Acronym for UNIDENTIFIED FLYING OBJECT
9 UGANDA Flag of East African republic
10 UGANDA GRASS HARE Variety of animal
11 UGGLESOME Ugly
12 UGLY Unpleasant to look at
13 UINTATHERIUM Variety of extinct animal
14 UKULELE Type of musical instrument
15 ULI FIGURE Type of wooden statue from the South Pacific
16 ULTRAMARINE Deep blue colour
17 UMBER Brown colour
18 UMBILICAL Tube joining foetus to placenta
19 UMBO Raised boss in centre of a shield
20 UMBRELLA Folding device for protection against rain
21 UMBRELLA BIRD Variety of bird
22 UMBRERE Visor
23 UMBRIL Visor
24 UMLAUT Symbol placed over letter indicating change of vowel
25 UNADORNED Plain
26 UNATTRACTIVE Ugly
27 UNBEARDED Without a beard
28 UNBEAUTIFUL Ugly
29 UNBONNETED Bareheaded
30 UNBUTTONED Unfastened; undone
31 UNCIAL Style of letterform

Uncials

ABCDEFGHIJ
KLMNOPQR
STUVWXYZ

32 UNCLAD Naked
33 UNCLE SAM Poetic personification of America
34 UNCLOTHED Naked
35 UNCLOUDED Clear
36 UNCOLOURED Plain; without colour
37 UNCOMELY Ugly
38 UNCONSCIOUS Having lost consciousness; asleep
39 UNCOVERED Bare
40 UNDECILLION Ten to the 36th power – American numerical system
41 UNDECILLION Ten to the 66th power – British numerical system
42 UNDER-BODY Undersides of an animal
43 UNDER-JAW Lower jaw
44 UNDER-LID Lower lid of the eye
45 UNDER-SOIL Soil beneath the surface
46 UNDERARM Armpit
47 UNDERBELLY Lower part of the belly
48 UNDERBRUSH Undergrowth
49 UNDERCARRIAGE Landing wheels of an aircraft
50 UNDERCLOTHES Garments worn next to the skin
51 UNDERCLOTHING Underclothes
52 UNDERDRAWERS Garment worn on lower body next to the skin
53 UNDERDRESS Underclothes
54 UNDERGARMENT Article of underclothes
55 UNDERGROWTH Low growing plants and shrubs
56 UNDERLINED Marked with a line drawn beneath
57 UNDERLIP Lower lip
58 UNDERNEATH Below
59 UNDERPANTS Lower body garment worn next to the skin
60 UNDERPART Under-body
61 UNDERSCORED Underlined
62 UNDERSHIRT Underwear for upper body; undervest
63 UNDERSHORTS Underpants
64 UNDERSIDE Beneath
65 UNDERSURFACE Underside
66 UNDERTHINGS Underwear
67 UNDERTURF Under-soil
68 UNDERVEST Undershirt

69 UNDERWEAR Underclothes
70 UNDIES Underclothes
71 UNDONE Unfastened
72 UNDRAPED Naked
73 UNDRESSED Naked
74 UNDY Heraldic device
75 UNEARTHED Dug up
76 UNEMBELLISHED Plain
77 UNFASTENED Not fastened
78 UNFURLED Unrolled
79 UNGARMENTED Naked
80 UNGULATE Hoofed animal
81 UNICOLOURED Of one colour
82 UNICORN Variety of fabulous beast
83 UNICORN-BIRD Variety of bird; horned screamer
84 UNICORN-FISH Variety of whale; narwhal
85 UNICYCLE One wheeled self-propelled vehicle
86 UNIFORM Distinctive garments worn by all members of a regiment etc.
87 UNION JACK Flag of the United Kingdom

England
Scotland
Ireland
The United Kingdom

88 UNION OF SOVIET SOCIALIST REPUBLICS Flag of European and Asian country
89 UNION FLAG Union Jack
90 UNITED ARAB EMIRATES Flag of South-west Asian group of emirates
91 UNITED KINGDOM Flag of West European country
92 UNITED NATIONS Flag of United Nations Organization
93 UNITED STATES OF AMERICA Flag of North American republic
94 UNLACED With laces undone
95 UNLOVELY Ugly
96 UNMENTIONABLES Euphemism for underwear
97 UNPLEASANT Disagreeable
98 UNPLEASING Disagreeable
99 UNROBED Naked
100 UNSHEATHED Drawn from its sheath
101 UNSHOD Without shoes
102 UNSIGHTLY Ugly

103 UNSMILING Straightfaced; without a smile
104 UNSTRUNG Without strings
105 UP Direction opposite from down
106 UP-ENDED Stood on end; upside-down
107 UPLAND GOOSE Variety of bird
108 UPPER Leather forming upper surface of shoe
109 UPPER CASE Capital letter
110 UPPER VOLTA Flag of West African country
111 UPPER-LEATHER Upper of shoe
112 UPPER-LIP Top lip
113 UPRIGHT Erect
114 UPSIDE-DOWN Inverted
115 UPSIDE-DOWN CATFISH Variety of fish
116 UPSILON Twentieth letter of the Greek alphabet
117 UPTURNED Upside-down
118 UPWARDS Direction opposite to downwards; up
119 URAEUS Ancient Egyptian headdress in the form of an asp
120 URANIA MOTH Variety of moth
121 URANIUM Element; atomic number 92
122 URANUS Astrological symbol for Uranus
123 URCHIN Hedgehog
124 URDEE CROSS Type of heraldic cross
125 URDY Heraldic device
126 URINAL Receptacle for urine
127 URINANT Heraldic device
128 URN Large vase
129 URSA MAJOR Constellation of the Great Bear; the Plough; the Big Dipper
130 URSA MINOR Constellation of the Little Bear; the Little Dipper
131 URUGUAY Flag of South American republic
132 USHABTI FIGURE Ancient Egyptian funerary statuette
133 UTENSIL Tool

Stars = The fifty states
Stripes = The thirteen original colonies
The United States of America

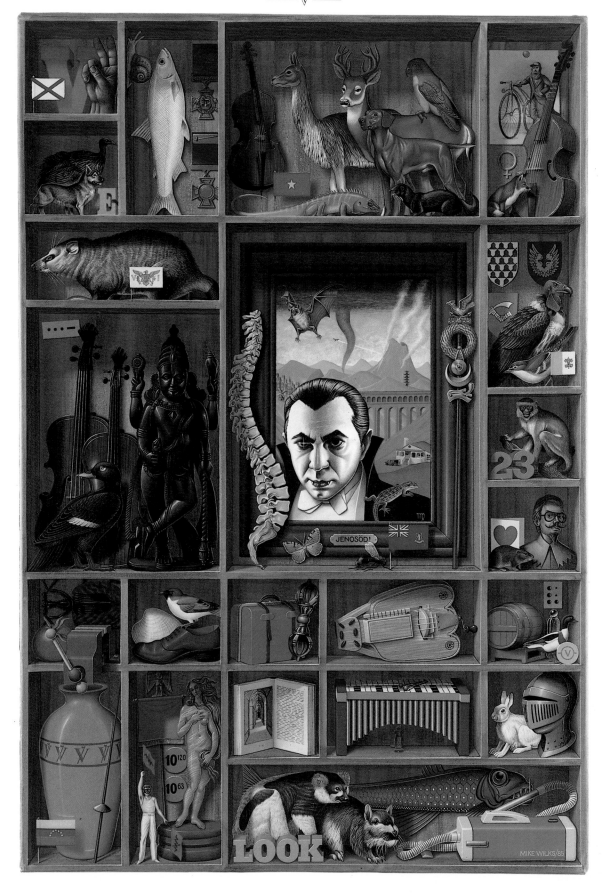

1 V Twenty-second letter of the alphabet
2 V Braille alphabet
3 V International signal flag
4 V Manual alphabet – American system
5 V Morse code alphabet
6 V Semaphore alphabet
7 V-MOTH Variety of moth
8 V-SIGN Victory salute
9 VACUUM-CLEANER Suction cleaning apparatus
10 VAIR Heraldic device
11 VAJRA Tibetan Buddhist ritual object
12 VALE Valley
13 VALENTINE Amorous greeting card
14 VALISE Travelling bag
15 VALLEY Narrow depressed area of land
16 VALLHUND Breed of dog
17 VAMBRACE Heraldic device
18 VAMP Front of upper on a shoe
19 VAMPIRE Supernatural being that sucks blood
20 VAMPIRE-BAT Variety of blood-sucking bat
21 VAMPLATE Hand-guard on a jousting lance
22 VAN Enclosed goods vehicle
23 VAN Sail of a windmill
24 VANADIUM Element; atomic number 23
25 VANDYKE Style of collar
26 VANDYKE Style of beard
27 VANE Sail of a windmill
28 VANGA Variety of bird
29 VANISHING POINT Point in picture where perspective lines merge
30 VAPOUR Gaseous emissions from a volcano
31 VAPOUR-TRAIL Trail of vapour left behind an aircraft
32 VARELLA Pagoda
33 VARI Variety of animal; ruffed Lemur
34 VARIABLE LIZARD Variety of colour-changing lizard
35 VARIABLE RESISTOR Electrical symbol for variable resistor
36 VARYING-HARE Variety of animal
37 VASE Ornamental vessel
38 VAT Cask
39 VATICAN CITY Flag of European city-state
40 VAULT Arched roof
41 VEGETABLE Edible cultivated plant
42 VEHICLE Wheeled conveyance
43 VEIN Marking on marble
44 VEIN Framework on an insect's wing
45 VEINING Pattern of veins
46 VELOCIPEDE Early form of bicycle
47 VELOCIPEDIST Rider of a velocipede
48 VELVET ANT Variety of insect
49 VELVET SCOTER Variety of duck

50 VENATION Veining
51 VENDACE Variety of fish
52 VENEZUELA Flag of South American republic
53 VENT Hole through which vapour escapes
54 VENTAIL Part of a helmet below the visor
55 VENTRAL-FIN Fin on the underside
56 VENUS Ancient Roman goddess of love and beauty
57 VENUS Astrological symbol for the planet Venus
58 VENUS SHELL Variety of shell
59 VERANDAH Covered platform outside a house
60 VERB Word that states an action
61 VERMEIL Bright red colour; vermilion
62 VERMILION Bright red colour
63 VERNAL HANGING PARROT Variety of parrot
64 VERSANT Mountain side
65 VERSICLE Symbol marking a part in singing a psalm
66 VERSO Left-hand page of a book
67 VERSO Reverse of a medal
68 VERT Heraldic term for green
69 VERTEBRA Joint of the spine
70 VERTEBRAL-COLUMN Spine
71 VERTEBRATE Creature with a backbone
72 VERTEX Top of the head
73 VERTEX Summit of a hill
74 VERTEX Point of an arch
75 VERTICAL Upright; perpendicular
76 VERVET Variety of monkey
77 VESSEL Container
78 VEST Waistcoat
79 VEST Undershirt; singlet
80 VESTURE Clothing
81 VEXILLOID Primitive form of banner
82 VEXILLOLOGICAL Pertaining to flags and banners
83 VEXILLUM Banner carried by Roman troops
84 VIADUCT Elevated roadway
85 VIAL Small bottle
86 VIAND Food
87 VIBRAHARP Vibraphone
88 VIBRAPHONE Type of musical instrument
89 VICE Device for gripping objects
90 VICTORIA CROSS British gallantry medal
91 VICTUALS Food
92 VICUNA Variety of llama-like animal
93 VIELLE Type of musical instrument; hurdy-gurdy
94 VIETNAM Flag of South-east Asian country
95 VIEW Scenery
96 VIGINTILLION Ten to the 63rd power – American numerical system
97 VIGINTILLION Ten to the 120th power – British numerical system
98 VIGNETTE Picture with an indefinite edge
99 VILLA Country house set in grounds
100 VILLAGE Small group of houses
101 VIOLA DA GAMBA Type of musical instrument
102 VIOL Type of musical instrument; viola da gamba
103 VIOLA Type of musical instrument
104 VIOLET Purplish-blue colour
105 VIOLIN Type of musical instrument
106 VIOLIN BEETLE Variety of insect
107 VIOLONCELLO Type of musical instrument; cello

The Violin Family

Peg or Pin
VIOLIN
Nut
VIOLA
f-hole
Scroll
Finger-board
DOUBLE BASS
Chin Rest
Neck
VIOLINCELLO OR CELLO
Belly
Bouts
Bridge
Tail-piece

108 VIPER-FISH Variety of fish
109 VIREO Variety of bird
110 VIRGIN ISLANDS Flag of Caribbean island group; British Virgin Islands
111 VIRGIN ISLANDS Flag of Caribbean island group; territory of the Virgin Islands of the United States
112 VIRGINIAN DEER Variety of deer
113 VIRGINIAN OPOSSUM Variety of animal
114 VIRGO Sixth sign of the zodiac; the virgin
115 VIRGULE Oblique line used as punctuation
116 VISAGE Face
117 VISCACHA Variety of animal
118 VISHNU A principal Hindu god
119 VISIBLE Able to be seen
120 VISON Variety of animal; American mink
121 VISOR Movable face-covering of a helmet
122 VISOR Peak of a cap
123 VISTA View
124 VIVID Brilliant
125 VIVIPAROUS LIZARD Variety of lizard
126 VIXEN Female fox
127 VIZARD Visor

128 VIZARD-MASK Mask covering upper face
129 VIZSLA Breed of dog
130 VOITURE Vehicle
131 VOL Heraldic device
132 VOLAPUK Type of international language (it says 'AMEN!')
133 VOLATILE Flying creature
134 VOLCAN Volcano
135 VOLCANO Mountain built by molten rock
136 VOLE Variety of animal
137 VOLIATION Flying
138 VOLTMETER Electrical symbol for voltmeter
139 VOLUME Book
140 VOLUTION Whorl of a spiral shell
141 VORAGO Chasm
142 VORTEX Whirlwind
143 VOUSSOIR Part of an arch or vault
144 VOWEL The letters A E I O U
145 VRAISEMBLANCE Picture
146 VULPANSER Variety of duck; sheldrake
147 VULPINE Like a fox
148 VULTURE Variety of bird
149 VULTURINE GUINEA FOWL Variety of bird

1 W Twenty-third letter of the alphabet
2 W Braille alphabet
3 W International signal flag
4 W Morse code alphabet
5 W Semaphore alphabet
6 WADER Wading bird
7 WAGTAIL Variety of bird
8 WAIST Part of the body between ribs and hips
9 WAISTCOAT Type of sleeveless garment; vest
10 WAKE Disturbed water
11 WAKED Not asleep; awake
12 WAKEFUL Alert
13 WAKENED Awake
14 WALE Gunwale of vessel
15 WALE Finishing at top of a basket
16 WALES Flag of West European country
17 WALKING-STICK Cane used to aid walking
18 WALL Upright structure enclosing an area
19 WALL LIZARD Variety of lizard
20 WALLABY Variety of animal; small kangaroo
21 WALLER'S GAZELLE Variety of antelope
22 WALRUS Variety of marine mammal
23 WAND Magical stick
24 WANDERER Variety of butterfly; monarch
25 WANING Decreasing in size
26 WAPITI Variety of animal; elk
27 WAR-PAINT American Indian wartime face-paint
28 WARBLER Variety of bird
29 WARBONNET American Indian ceremonial headdress
30 WAREHOUSE Large storage building
31 WARES Goods
32 WARLOCK Male witch; wizard
33 WARM FRONT Meteorological symbol for warm front
34 WARM-BLOODED Creature able to regulate own body temperature
35 WARMING-PAN Apparatus for warming bed
36 WARP Rope attached to harpoon
37 WARP Twist; buckle
38 WARRIOR Fighting-man
39 WART Hard growth on the skin
40 WARTHOG Variety of animal
41 WASH To clean with water
42 WASH Wave caused by moving vessel
43 WASH-TUB Container for washing water
44 WASHBOARD Corrugated board for scrubbing clothes against
45 WASHER Person washing
46 WASHERWOMAN Laundry-maid
47 WASHING Cleaning with soap and water
48 WASHING Washed clothes
49 WASHWOMAN Washerwoman

50 WASP Variety of insect
51 WASP BEETLE Variety of insect
52 WATCH Instrument for indicating the time
53 WATCH Observe
54 WATCH-GLASS Glass protecting the face of a watch
55 WATCHBAND Strap securing watch to wrist
56 WATCHER Person who watches
57 WATCHING Observing
58 WATER Transparent colourless liquid
59 WATER Chemical symbol for water (H_2O)
60 WATER BUFFALO Variety of animal
61 WATERFRONT Land adjacent to a body of water
62 WATER-HORSE Variety of animal; hippopotamus
63 WATER-LINE Painted line on a boat to where the water rises
64 WATER-MELON Variety of fruit
65 WATER-MILL Mill powered by water
66 WATER-SKIER Sportsman skiing on water
67 WATER-SKIING Skiing on the surface of the water
68 WATER-STREAM River
69 WATER-TOWER Storage container for water
70 WATER-WAY River
71 WATER-WHEEL Mill-wheel driven by water
72 WATERBOK Variety of antelope
73 WATERCOURSE Waterway
74 WATERCRAFT Boat
75 WATERFALL Water falling from a height; cascade
76 WATERING-CAN Vessel used to water plants
77 WATERMAN Boatman
78 WATERSIDE Edge of a river
79 WATTLE Fence of woven wood
80 WATTLE Fleshy growth
81 WATTLE-EYE Variety of bird
82 WAVE Undulation on the surface of water
83 WAW Sixth letter of the Hebrew alphabet
84 WAX Substance that melts at low temperature
85 WAX Increase in size
86 WAX-CANDLE Candle made from wax
87 WAX-LIGHT Wax-candle
88 WAXWING Variety of bird
89 WEAPON Instrument for attack or defence
90 WEARING To have on the body
91 WEASEL Variety of animal
92 WEATHER FISH Variety of fish
93 WEATHER WORKS Book by Mike Wilks
94 WEAVER'S HITCH Type of knot; sheet bend
95 WEAVER'S KNOT Weaver's hitch
96 WEAVER-BIRD Variety of bird
97 WEB Cobweb
98 WEB-FOOT Foot with membrane between the toes
99 WEDDING-RING Gold ring indicating married state
100 WEDGE V-shaped piece of wood
101 WEDNESDAY Astrological symbol for Wednesday
102 WEED Garment
103 WEEVER Variety of fish
104 WEIGHT Heavy object used in weight-lifting
105 WEIGHTLIFTER Athlete specializing in lifting heavy objects
106 WEIGHTLIFTING Sport of lifting heavy objects

107 WEIMARANER Breed of dog
108 WELKIN Sky
109 WELL Shaft sunk to underground water
110 WELL Healthy
111 WELL-BEAM Beam over well
112 WELL-BUCKET Bucket to collect water from bottom of well
113 WELL-CURB Masonry structure surrounding well
114 WELL-HEAD Structure at the top of a well
115 WELLINGTON BOOT Style of tall boot
116 WELSH CORGI Breed of dog
117 WELT Leather strip attaching sole to upper of shoe
118 WEN Runic character
119 WENTLETRAP Variety of shell
120 WEREWOLF Supernatural being who changes into a wolf
121 WESTERNER Person of European descent
122 WET Soaked with liquid
123 WET SUIT Skin-diver's rubber garment
124 WHALE Variety of large marine mammal
125 WHALE-HEADED STORK Variety of bird
126 WHARF Berth for loading and unloading ships
127 WHEATEAR Variety of bird
128 WHEEL Circular revolving device
129 WHINCHAT Variety of bird
130 WHIP Lash attached to handle
131 WHIP Arm of a windmill
132 WHIP-HANDLE Handle of a whip
133 WHIP-LASH Lash of a whip
134 WHIP-SNAKE Variety of snake
135 WHIP-STOCK Whip-handle
136 WHIPPER Person wielding a whip
137 WHIPPET Breed of dog
138 WHIPSTAFF Whip-handle
139 WHIRLIGIG Variety of beetle
140 WHIRLPOOL Circular eddy in water
141 WHISK Device for beating eggs
142 WHISKERED AGAMA Variety of lizard
143 WHISKERED BAT Variety of bat
144 WHISKERLESS Clean-shaven
145 WHISKERS Beard
146 WHISTLE Wind instrument for producing single note
147 WHISTLER Variety of bird
148 WHITE Reflected light without colour
149 WHITE White-skinned
150 WHITE-IBIS Variety of bird
151 WHITE PELICAN Variety of bird
152 WHITE RHINOCEROS Variety of animal
153 WHITE STORK Variety of bird
154 WHITE WATER Fast-moving water coloured white by foam
155 WHITE WINE Wine made from white grapes
156 WHITE-BEARDED WILDEBEESTE Variety of animal; wildebeeste
157 WHITE-BELLIED PARROT Variety of bird
158 WHITE-BREASTED BUZZARD Variety of bird of prey; white-tailed hawk
159 WHITE-EYE Variety of bird
160 WHITE-TAILED DEER Variety of animal
161 WHITE-TAILED HAWK Variety of bird of prey
162 WHITE-TAILED KITE Variety of bird of prey
163 WHITE-THROAT Variety of bird
164 WHITE-THROATED GUENON Variety of monkey

165 WHOLE NOTE Musical note; semibreve
166 WHOOPING CRANE Variety of bird
167 WHORL Single coil of a spiral
168 WHYDAH Variety of bird
169 WICK Thread through the centre of a candle
170 WICKER Thin flexible twig
171 WICKERWORK Object made from wicker
172 WICKYUP Conical American Indian dwelling
173 WIDDERSHINS Anti-clockwise
174 WIDE-AWAKE Alert
175 WIDOW'S PEAK Point of hair on forehead
176 WIELDER Person who handles something
177 WIELDING Handling
178 WIG False hair
179 WIG-BLOCK Block for wig when not being worn
180 WIGHT Human being

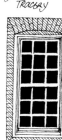
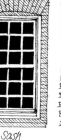

Windows

Lancet   Plate Tracery   Ogee Curvilinear Tracery   Perpendicular Tracery

Oriel   Rose   Sash   French

Venetian   Bay

181 WIGWAM Domed American Indian dwelling
182 WILD Not domesticated; untamed
183 WILD BOAR Variety of animal
184 WILD CAT Variety of animal
185 WILDEBEESTE Variety of animal

186 WILDFOWL Undomesticated bird hunted for food
187 WILDLIFE Undomesticated animals
188 WILKS Bespectacled artist
189 WIMPLE Linen head-covering
190 WIMPLE FISH Variety of fish
191 WINCH Device for raising objects; hoist
192 WIND-CONE Fabric cone to indicate wind direction
193 WIND-SLEEVE Wind-cone
194 WIND-SOCK Wind-cone
195 WINDLASS Winch
196 WINDMILL Mill powered by the wind
197 WINDMILL Variety of butterfly
198 WINDOW Opening in wall to admit light
199 WINDOW-BOX Flower-tub on window-sill
200 WINDOW-PANE Glass sheet in window
201 WINDOW-SILL Narrow shelf beneath window
202 WINDSAIL Sail of a windmill
203 WINE Alcoholic drink made from grapes
204 WINE-GLASS Drinking-vessel for wine
205 WING Limb used by bird or insect to fly

206 WING-CASE Hard covering over insect's wing
207 WING-COVERT Small feathers of bird's wing
208 WING-TIP End of a wing
209 WING NUT Nut able to be tightened by hand
210 WINK To close one eye as a signal
211 WINKER Person winking
212 WINKING Performing a wink
213 WIRE Thin metal thread
214 WISENT Variety of animal; European bison
215 WISHBONE Forked breastbone of a bird; furcula
216 WITCH Sorceress
217 WITCH-HAT Style of hat worn by witches
218 WITHERS Shoulder blades of an animal
219 WITHERSHINS Anti-clockwise
220 WIZARD Sorcerer
221 WOK Chinese cooking vessel
222 WOLF Variety of animal
223 WOLVERINE Variety of animal; glutton
224 WOMAN Female person
225 WOMBAT Variety of animal
226 WONE Dwelling; abode
227 WOOD Timber
228 WOOD Large area of tree-covered land
229 WOOD-DUCK Variety of duck
230 WOOD-PIGEON Variety of bird
231 WOODCOCK Variety of bird
232 WOODCREEPER Variety of bird
233 WOODEN-LEG Crude artificial leg
234 WOODPECKER Variety of bird
235 WOODWORK Object crafted from wood
236 WORD Unit of language
237 WORK Purposeful activity
238 WORKER Person engaged in work
239 WORKING Undertaking work
240 WORKMAN Man engaged in work
241 WORKWOMAN Woman engaged in work
242 WORLD The Earth
243 WORLDLING Inhabitant of the world
244 WORM Long invertebrate creature
245 WORM Dragon
246 WORM-HOLE Hole made by a worm
247 WORRY BEADS Beads for playing with
248 WOUND Injury; rent in the skin
249 WOUNDER Inflicter of wound
250 WOUNDING Inflicting a wound
251 WOVEN Made by weaving
252 WRECK Ruined ship or boat
253 WRECKAGE Remains of wreck
254 WREN Variety of bird
255 WRENCH Tool for turning nuts; spanner
256 WRINGER Machine for forcing water from clothes
257 WRINKLE Crease in the skin
258 WRIST Joint between hand and forearm
259 WRISTWATCH Timepiece worn on the wrist
260 WRISTLET Bracelet
261 WRITER Person writing
262 WRITHE To twist into coils
263 WRITING Inscribing words with a pen
264 WRITING Lettering
265 WROUGHT Fashioned; formed
266 WRY Bent; twisted
267 WRYBILL Variety of bird
268 WYVERN Type of mythical beast; dragon

Mike Wilks 1985

1 X Twenty-fourth letter of the alphabet
2 X Braille alphabet
3 X International signal flag
4 X Manual alphabet – Anglo/Australian system
5 X Manual alphabet – American system
6 X Morse code alphabet
7 X Semaphore alphabet
8 X-HEIGHT Height of lower case characters a c
   e m n o r s u v w x z
9 X-RAY Internal photograph of body
10 X-RAY FISH Variety of fish
11 XANTHIC Yellow
12 XANTHOCHROID Yellow-haired pale-skinned
   person
13 XANTHOUS With yellow hair and pale skin
14 XEBEC Type of Levantine sailing vessel

15 XENACANTHUS Variety of extinct fish
16 XENON Element; atomic number 54
17 XENOPS Variety of bird
18 XI Fourteenth letter of the Greek alphabet
19 XILONEN Ancient Mexican corn goddess
20 XIPE TOTEC Ancient Mexican god of spring
21 XIPHIAS Variety of fish; swordfish
22 XMAS Christmas
23 XYLOGRAPH Wood engraving
24 XYLOGRAPHER Wood engraver
25 XYLOGRAPHIST Wood engraver; xylographer
26 XYLOGRAPHY Art of wood engraving
27 XYLOPHAGAN Variety of wood-eating beetle
28 XYLOPHILIAN Variety of wood inhabiting
   beetle
29 XYLOPHONE Type of musical instrument
30 XYLOPHONIST Xylophone player
 * This is a red herring

Ascenders

a b e f g k m p] X-Height

Descenders

Xylography (Wood Engraving) Tools

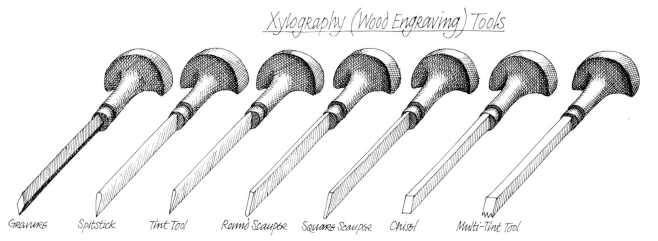

Gravure   Spitstick   Tint Tool   Round Scauper   Square Scauper   Chisel   Multi-Tint Tool

Y

1 Y Twenty-fifth letter of the alphabet
2 Y Braille alphabet
3 Y International signal flag
4 Y Manual alphabet – American system
5 Y Morse code alphabet
6 Y Semaphore alphabet
7 YACHT Small sailing vessel
8 YACHTSMAN Sailor of a yacht
9 YAD Jewish ritual object
10 YAK Variety of animal
11 YAKUT Breed of horse
12 YAM Variety of vegetable
13 YANG Symbol for the masculine active principal in Chinese cosmology
14 YANTRA Motif used as a meditation aid
15 YAPOCK Variety of animal
16 YARD Spar supporting sail
17 YARD Measure of thirty-six inches
18 YARD-ARM Outer extremity of a yard
19 YARD-OF-ALE GLASS Type of drinking vessel
20 YARD-WAND Yardstick
21 YARDSTICK Ruler thirty-six inches long
22 YARMULKE Skullcap
23 YARN Thread
24 YASHMAK Veil worn by Muslim women
25 YATAGHAN Type of sword
26 YAWL Type of sailing yacht
27 YCLAD Clothed

28 YEAR Date when picture was painted
29 YELLOW Primary colour
30 YELLOW-BELLIED SUNBIRD Variety of bird
31 YELLOW CARDINAL Variety of bird
32 YELLOWLEGS Variety of bird
33 YELLOW WAGTAIL Variety of bird
34 YELLOW-BACKED ANGELFISH Variety of fish
35 YELLOW-BACKED DAMSELFISH Variety of fish
36 YELLOW-BACKED DUIKER Variety of antelope
37 YELLOW-BAKED SUNBIRD Variety of bird
38 YELLOW-BELLIED SAPSUCKER Variety of bird
39 YELLOW-CHEEKED PARROT Variety of bird
40 YELLOWFIN TUNA Variety of fish
41 YELLOW-FRONTED BARBET Variety of bird
42 YELLOW-FRONTED CHAT Variety of bird
43 YELLOWHAMMER Variety of bird
44 YELLOW-HEADED PARROT Variety of bird
45 YELLOW JACKET Variety of insect; wasp
46 YELLOW-LEGGED BUTTONQUAIL Variety of bird
47 YELLOW OCHRE Brownish-yellow colour
48 YELLOW PANSY Variety of butterfly
49 YELLOW-PATE Yellowhammer
50 YELLOW-TAIL Variety of moth
51 YELLOW-WATTLED LAPWING Variety of bird
52 YEMEN Flag of South-west Asian country (Republic of Yemen)

Parts of an Egg

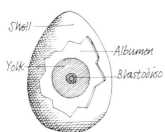

53 YEMEN Flag of South-west Asian country (Yemen Arab Republic)
54 YEW Variety of tree
55 YIN Symbol for the feminine passive principal in Chinese cosmology
56 YO-YO Toy that can be made to rise and fall
57 YOD Tenth letter of the Hebrew alphabet
58 YOGA Hindu system of exercise
59 YOGI Person who practises yoga
60 YOKE Bar used to carry loads
61 YOLK Yellow part of an egg
62 YORKSHIRE TERRIER Breed of dog
63 YOUNG Juvenile
64 YOUNGLING Young person
65 YOUNG MAN Young male person
66 YOUNGSTER Young person
67 YOUNKER Young man
68 YOURT Mongol dwelling
69 YOUTH Young person
70 YPSILIFORM Y-shaped
71 YTTERBIUM Element, atomic number 70
72 YTTRIUM Element; atomic number 39
73 YUGOSLAVIA Flag of Eastern European country
74 YUEH-CH'IN Type of musical instrument

Yin–Yang Symbol

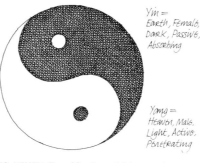

Yin =
Earth, Female,
Dark, Passive,
Absorbing

Yang =
Heaven, Male,
Light, Active,
Penetrating

Yawl

Ketch

Z

1 Z Twenty-sixth letter of the alphabet
2 Z Braille alphabet
3 Z International signal flag
4 Z Morse code alphabet
5 ZAG One leg of a zigzag
6 ZAGAIE Type of Zulu spear. Assagai
7 ZAHRTE Variety of fish
8 ZAIRE Flag of Central African republic
9 ZAMANDREA'S LAMPREY Variety of fish
10 ZAMBIA Flag of East African republic
11 ZANDER Variety of fish
12 ZAYIN Seventh letter of the Hebrew alphabet
13 ZEBRA Variety of animal
14 ZEBRA BARB Variety of fish
15 ZEBRA DANIO Variety of fish
16 ZEBRA DUIKER Variety of antelope
17 ZEBRA LOACH Variety of fish
18 ZEBRA NYASA CICHLID Variety of fish
19 ZEBRA-FISH Variety of fish. Zebra danio
20 ZEBRA-OPOSSUM Variety of animal; thylacine
21 ZEBRA-WOLF Thylacine
22 ZEBU Variety of animal
23 ZENICK Variety of animal; suricate
24 ZENITH Highest point of the sun
25 ZEPPELIN Rigid airship
26 ZERDA Variety of animal; fennec

27 ZERO Nought
28 ZETA Sixth letter of the Greek alphabet
29 ZEUS Chief god of the Ancient Greeks
30 ZIBET Variety of animal; civet
31 ZIEGE Variety of fish
32 ZIG One leg of a zigzag
33 ZIGGURAT Type of terraced pyramid
34 ZIGZAG Line with regular sharp changes of
   direction
35 ZIMBABWE Flag of southern African republic
36 ZINC Element; atomic number 30
37 ZINGEL Variety of fish
38 ZINNIA Variety of flowering plant
39 ZIP Type of clothes fastener
40 ZIRCONIUM Element; atomic number 40
41 ZITHER Type of musical instrument
42 ZODIAC Twelve signs of the heavens
43 ZOETROPE Device for producing moving
   pictures

Zones of the Earth

44 ZONE One of five climatic regions of the earth
45 ZOOM-LENS Lens with variable focal length
46 ZOOPHAGOUS Carnivorous
47 ZOOPHYTE Plant-like animal (coral shown
   here)
48 ZOPE Variety of fish
49 ZOPILOTE Variety of bird; turkey buzzard
50 ZORI Japanese thonged sandal
51 ZORIL Variety of animal
52 ZORILLA Variety of animal; zoril
53 ZOUAVE Type of French soldier recruited from
   Algeria
54 ZUCCHETTO Skullcap worn by Roman
   Catholic clergymen
55 ZUCCHINI Variety of vegetable; courgette
56 ZULU Member of southern African tribe
57 ZYGOMA Cheek-bone

Zodiac Symbols

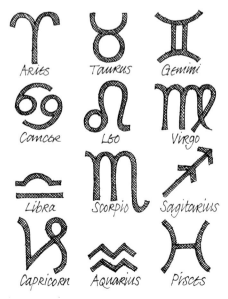

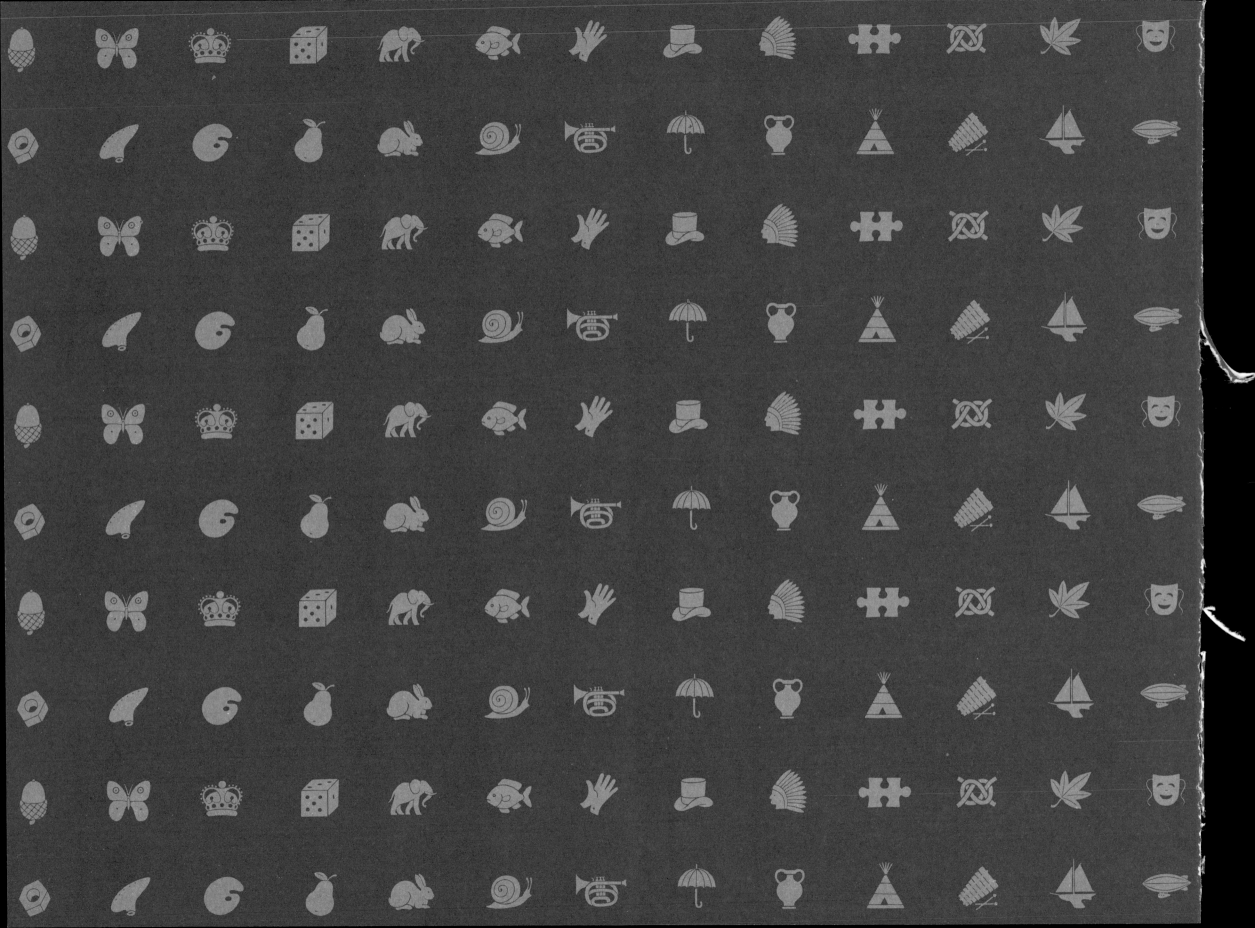